HEADTEACHER STRESS, COPING AND HEALTH

To Carol and John.

Headteacher Stress, Coping and Health

ALISTAIR OSTELL
BSc, DPhil, CPsychol, AFBPsS
Management Centre
University of Bradford

SUSAN OAKLAND
BA (Hons), PhD
Management Centre
University of Bradford

Avebury

Aldershot • Brookfield USA • Hong Kong • Singapore • Sydney

Published by
Avebury
Ashgate Publishing Limited
Gower House
Croft Road
Aldershot
Hants GU11 3HR
England

Ashgate Publishing Company
Old Post Road
Brookfield
Vermont 05036
USA

British Library Cataloguing in Publication Data

Ostell, Alistair
  Headteacher Stress, Coping and Health
  I. Title II. Oakland, Susan
  371.1
ISBN 1 85972 164 8

Library of Congress Catalog Card Number: 95-81138

Printed and bound by Athenaeum Press, Ltd.,
Gateshead, Tyne & Wear.

Contents

Figures and tables

Acknowledgements

Thanks are due to a number of people who helped to make this book possible. We are indebted to the headteachers who took time from their hectic working schedule to participate in the interview and complete the questionnaire used in this study. Thanks are also due to Educational Psychologists Bob Baynham and Barry Chisholm, and Francis Marslen-Wilson and June Sanderson for their encouragement and helpful advice and comments in the initial stages of the study.

We are grateful to the Economic and Social Science Research Council who funded the research (Award No. F00428722056).

Very special thanks are extended to Barbara Ward who has demonstrated exceptional patience, skill and capacity for hard work in preparing this book.

Preface

During the last decade there have been unprecedented changes in the education system within the UK, changes which have affected all involved including pupils and teaching staff, ancillary staff, parents, Boards of Governors, school advisers, inspectors, educational psychologists and so on. The intended purposes of these changes were to improve the quality of the education offered to pupils of all ages and at the same time, to make the whole system more cost-effective. At times it seemed to some observers, however, that the impact of these changes upon the headteachers and teachers responsible for implementing change at the 'coal face', were overlooked or ignored.

A number of reasons prompted the writing of this book. First, at a time when there is still constant media and public interest in these changes in education and their effects, the book provides an important medium for disseminating the findings of an in-depth study of headteacher stress, coping behaviour and health. Second, this book is only one of relatively few texts concerned with stress in headteachers. To date, most research projects, articles and books have focused on teachers as opposed to headteachers and thus, have largely ignored important issues and problems which represent key responsibilities for many heads. Third, although the book is concerned with the experience and consequences of stress in headship, it should prove useful to a wide range of readers other than headteachers. For instance, deputy heads, teachers, educational psychologists and educationalists responsible for advising, supporting and training headteachers should find the text useful, not only for better understanding the potential stressors of headship, but also as a guide for coping with those stressors. Moreover, the value of the book is not confined to practitioners in education. Students and researchers working in any facet of the stress, coping and health area should find the book a useful source of research literature and of ideas for future research designs and data analyses. Indeed, the questionnaire and semi-structured interview schedule used in this study would require only minor modifications to make it appropriate for studying stress, coping and health in virtually any sample group. Above all, however, the book was written to draw attention to the real difficulties facing many headteachers as they attempt to cope with their rapidly changing roles in the workplace and to raise awareness of the implications this can have for their psychological well-being and physical health.

1 A perspective on stress, coping and health

1.1 Introduction and overview

This book is concerned with the subject of stress. It examines the stress of headteachers as they cope with the changing problems of their current jobs and the consequences of this stress for their psychological and physical health.

Stress is a topic which has attracted considerable public interest in recent years largely because of media reporting about the consequences of large-scale catastrophes (e.g., earthquakes, wars), major disasters (e.g., Bradford Football Stadium fire, sinking of the Zeebrugge ferry) and various traumatic experiences of individuals (e.g., being a hostage, physical assaults such as rape and mugging). Yet stress is not simply a consequence of extraordinary and traumatic events but is very much a part of everyday life and results, typically, from much less dramatic incidents than catastrophes or disasters (Ostell, 1995b). A common feature of life which often proves difficult for people to handle is change, particularly unpredicted and undesired change (Sarason, Johnson and Siegel, 1978). Over the past three decades people living in the United Kingdom, as in many other countries, have witnessed considerable economic, social, cultural and political change. Much of this change was heralded by the election of a Conservative Government in 1979. Socialist doctrines of state ownership of or support for industry were soon replaced by emphases on business and industry surviving by virtue of their competitiveness within a market economy, the privatization of public utilities and the principles of the market economy being introduced into areas of the public sector.

These changes have had massive ramifications for social groups and individuals. The decline of major industries such as mining and steel resulted in large scale redundancies and the disruption of whole communities. Most of those industries which survived did so by virtue of increasing their competitiveness. In common

1

parlance they became 'leaner and fitter' which meant fewer people doing more work in shorter periods of time and more cost-effective ways. The demands upon those in work often escalated considerably and to retain their jobs, or find new jobs, many people had to re-train and become multi-skilled. Changes of this kind were not restricted to the private sector but also took place within the public sector as the government attempted to reduce public spending and promote what it saw as greater efficiencies in local government, the National Health Service and the education system.

The 1980's also witnessed the emergence of new technologies and industries such as software and information systems. These industries, together with the growth of the financial services sector, opened up new job opportunities but ones that frequently required specialist skills which were in short supply. Those fortunate enough to qualify for such jobs were often rewarded extremely well but criticism of aspects of the educational system grew for its failure, as many within business and industry saw it, to supply young people to the labour market who possessed the relevant skills or competencies needed by these developing industries. The education system was due for a huge 'shake-up'. The future for people in work seemed secure, however, until the recessions of the late 1980's and early 1990's arrived. The result was high interest rates, bankruptcies and company closures leading to further redundancies, shrinkage and re-structuring of the building industry due in part to a collapse of the housing market, and house repossessions because of the inability of people to pay high mortgage rates. These political, economic and social changes faced many people with problems at work, in the home and socially which represented the kind of disruptions to everyday life that are difficult to cope with. Some have found it possible to rise to these challenges, others have not and there is growing evidence that the latter have suffered significantly in terms of their psychological and physical health, victims of stress (Cooper, Cooper and Eaker, 1988a; Totman, 1990).

The field of stress is concerned with identifying the kinds of situations and problems (whether work, domestic, social or personal in nature) that people find difficult to handle, the processes by which people become psychologically upset as they attempt to cope with these problems and the consequences for them and their relationships with others of the failure to cope adequately. The enormous volume of available evidence points to stress having damaging consequences for many aspects of a person's life. Mental and emotional consequences include such effects as trouble concentrating and making decisions, narrowed focus of attention, difficulty stopping thinking about disturbing events, anger, anxiety, guilt and depression, lowered belief in the ability to cope and self-condemnation (Cox, 1978; Levi, 1994; Williams, Watts, Macleod and Mathews, 1988). Behavioural consequences of stress have been shown to include drug taking (Dobson, 1982), excessive eating (McKenna, 1972), smoking (Hawkins, White and Morris, 1983), drinking (Sloan and Cooper, 1986), argumentative and quarrelsome behaviour (Averill, 1982) and inability to sleep (Quick and Quick, 1984). Further, there appears little doubt that stress plays an important role in such health disorders as coronary heart disease (Cooper and Marshall, 1976), hypertension (Melhuish, 1978), alimentary conditions such as ulcers and dyspepsia (Quick and Quick, 1984) and general impairment of immunological functioning (Fletcher, 1989) both by contributing to their aetiology and in producing an unfavourable prognosis. Within organizations the consequences of employee stress include poor interpersonal relations, absenteeism and a high rate of staff turnover (Cooper, 1988).

It is important that stress research does not simply focus upon identifying the kinds of situations which are typically stressful for people and the kinds of stress reactions, whether psychological or physical, that people characteristically experience in response to these situations. If we are to gain a better understanding of the nature of stress it is crucial that we identify precisely the processes individuals use to make sense of and cope with particular situations which they find 'stressful', and relate specific processes to specific outcomes (thoughts, feelings, actions, health consequences, etc.) resulting from these processes.

Thus this research into headteacher stress is concerned with three main issues:

- investigating the specific ways in which individual headteachers react to and attempt to cope with 'stressful' situations at work;

- exploring the factors which best predict a 'successful' outcome to a problem situation and those which best predict an 'unsuccessful' outcome;

- determining the outcomes for headteachers with respect to psychological well-being and physical health of their efforts to cope with problem situations.

Overview of the book

Because the terms 'stress' and 'coping' have been the subject of serious debate and dispute for at least three decades (Dewe, Cox & Ferguson, 1993; Fleming, Baum and Singer, 1984; Ostell, 1988), this first chapter provides a perspective on stress and coping with regard to how they are to be conceptualized in this study and their relationship to health. First, the concept of stress will be discussed and defined as transactional in nature. Next, the concepts of cognitive appraisal and coping which form the basis of a transactional definition of stress will be discussed in relation to their role in the aetiology of stress reactions and ultimately, health outcomes. Finally, a model of stress, appraisal, coping and health will be presented to illustrate the key psychological processes involved when a person appraises and reacts to a potentially stressful situation and to highlight important areas worthy of research attention.

Chapters 2 and 3 contain a critical review of the stress and coping literature and provide a rationale for the focus, major objectives and reasons for the design of this research. Chapter 4 begins by reviewing research in education to highlight the fact that usually, teachers rather than headteachers are the focus of studies on stress. Next the unprecedented changes in schools brought about by the 1988 Education Reform Act are outlined in terms of the implications for schools in general, but headteachers in particular. Then, the design of the questionnaire and semi-structured interview schedule used in this study are detailed and discussed in relation to reliability and validity.

Chapters 5 and 6 cover the quantitative and qualitative data analyses and draw attention to the most salient results. The main variables which were found to be related to successful and unsuccessful outcomes for problem situations are discussed in chapter 7, whilst chapter 8 is primarily concerned with the variables which were found to be the main influences on the psychological health and physical symptoms of the headteachers. The main findings of this research are summarized in chapter 9 and recommendations made for ways in which headteachers can be helped to cope better with their current roles. The final chapter acknowledges certain limitations of the study, but also highlights the advantages of adopting a methodology which uses both quantitative and qualitative data. Suggestions are given for future research which attempts to explore the complex relationship between stress, coping behaviour and health.

1.2   Perspectives on stress

It is almost traditional, as Vingerhoets and Marcelissen (1988) note, for articles on stress to begin by pointing to the lack of agreement when defining stress. The elusiveness of the stress definition is not surprising, however, given that scientific interest in stress has developed from many disciplines including anthropology, endocrinology, ergonomics, pharmacology, physiology, psychology, medicine and sociology. However, from this array of disciplines research has flourished in two basic traditions: one from a biological perspective based on physiology and endocrinology and the other based on a psychosocial tradition (Cox, 1978; Ostell, 1995b for brief reviews). It is work, however, that has integrated these two traditions which provides the perspective on stress in this study.

Biological perspective

Stress research from the biological viewpoint has long been influenced and guided by definitions that focus on the different components to the stress process. Here, stress is described in terms of either a stimulus, that is, a condition that generates disturbance or reactive change of some sort, or as a response or reaction to disturbances. Though medical interest in stress can be traced back to antiquity, the modern roots of the biological tradition began with Cannon's (1936) work on emotional stress. He viewed stress and the individual's 'emergency response' to stress as adaptive processes which prepared the individual to cope with threatening stimuli. According to Cannon, recognition of threat or danger resulted in adrenal gland activity and sympathetic arousal that increased heart rate, respiration and skeletal muscle tone, while reducing blood flow to the skin and internal organs. This heightened state of arousal thus facilitated the individual's 'fight' response to the threatening situation.

The stimulus-response view of stress also received impetus from the work of Hans Selye (see for example Selye, 1936, 1956, 1976). Selye found that a common triad of physiological effects, namely - shrinkage of the thymus gland, enlargement of the adrenal gland and ulceration in the gastro intestinal tract - accompanied the administration of noxious agents to laboratory animals, irrespective of whether those agents were injections of hormone extracts, application of irritants or exposure to heat. In other words, the animals appeared to respond physiologically to all forms of stress in the same way. From this, Selye went on to propose and document an elaborate theory of stress centred around his General Adaptation Syndrome. The stimulus-response views of stress have a certain inevitability about them by suggesting that if people are faced with particular kinds of (noxious) stimuli then a fixed and universal pattern of physiological responses occurs intended to mobilize people so that they can defend themselves against those stimuli.

Not until the work of Mason and his colleagues (Mason, 1974; Mason, Maher, Hartley, Mougey, Perlow and Jones, 1976) did it become apparent that significant individual differences existed at the physiological level between how individuals responded to stress. Research showed, for example, that anxiety-type reactions to uncertainty or ambiguity were associated with increases in norepinephrine, epinephrine and cortisol, whereas only increases in norepinephrine and cortisol were associated with anger-type reactions. Moreover, Mason argued that since all of these responses were integrated by the central nervous system, they must be mediated by the psychological recognition of danger. Mason's work therefore represented an integration of the biological and psychosocial perspectives on stress, even though he drew no explicit links to the psychosocial literature (Fleming et al., 1984).

Psychosocial perspective

To accommodate the individual differences in responding to stress, theorists and researchers introduced cognition as both a mediating and moderating variable (Ostell, 1995b; Parkes, 1994). This psychosocial perspective on stress has generated a stream of research that is usually independent of physiological studies (Fleming et al., 1984) even though initially, cognition was introduced as a physiological process and described in terms of the operation of the recticular activating system of the brain (Stensrud and Stensrud, 1983).

From the psychosocial view, the concept of stress is defined as relational in nature involving some kind of relationship or interaction between the individual and the environment (Lazarus, 1966). At the extreme, this view suggests that nothing is stressful unless the individual defines it as such. Thus, no situations or events are universally stressful; rather, it is the way in which the individual appraises and reacts to a situation which results in a state of psychological stress (Lazarus and Launier, 1978).

An early research example of this conception of stress was provided by the classic work of Lazarus and his colleagues (Speisman, Lazarus, Mordkoff and Davison, 1964). In this study volunteers were shown anxiety-threat inducing films and given different viewing instructions. Some instructions encouraged threatening appraisals. Other instructions such as 'These people are actors and are not really being harmed' encouraged non-threatening appraisals. Various psycho-physiological responses (e.g., heart rate and galvanic skin response) were recorded during the experiment and results indicated that the magnitude of these responses depended on the viewing instructions. In other words, stress responses were related to the appraisal of the events in the films. It is this relational or transactional perspective of stress which forms the basis of the conceptualization of stress in this research.

Transactional perspective

In recent years, many writers have conceded that the concept of stress is most useful when it is defined as relational in nature, involving some sort of relationship or transaction between the individual and the environment (Cox, 1978, 1987; Cox & Ferguson, 1994; Folkman, Lazarus, Gruen & DeLongis, 1986a; Latack and Havlovic, 1992; Ostell, 1988, 1991). For example, Folkman et al.,. define stress as 'a relationship between the person and the environment, that is appraised by the person as taxing or exceeding his or her resources and as endangering well-being' (1986, p.572). Cox suggests that 'occupational stress exists in the person's recognition of their inability to cope with demands relating to work' (1987, p.6). Similarly, Ostell defines psychological stress as

> a state of affairs which arises when a person perceives a situation as being a problem which has significant costs for that person and reacts in such a way as to tax or exceed that person's coping resources.

> (Ostell, 1991, p.12, added emphasis)

In terms of this study, Ostell's definition is particularly appealing for three reasons. First, it emphasizes that people are not disturbed by situations per se but by the ways in which they think about and react to situations. Second, the definition highlights the transactional, bidirectional nature of stress whereby a person is both influenced by and has to react to a situation in a dynamic, reciprocal way. Third, the definition uses the concepts of a problem and perceived costs associated with problem situations and these are particularly valuable for understanding why certain situations prove stressful for people. Since this research is primarily concerned with how individuals react to problem situations which people find stressful, this last point warrants further elaboration.

Problems, costs and stress reactions

Recently, a number of authors have integrated ideas from problem solving theory and a transactional view to develop models for understanding why people become distressed by problems and in what ways they can be helped to cope (Cox, 1987; Meichenbaum, 1985; Ostell, 1988, 1991). For example, Ostell (1988) begins with the generic definition of a problem 'as the existence of a gap or discrepancy between an actual state of affairs and a desired state of affairs' (Kepner and Tregoe, 1965). Thus, problem situations arise when there is a disparity between what a person desires should happen and what in reality is happening (D'Zurilla and Goldfried, 1971; Ostell, 1991). Put another way, people only view situations as 'problematic' if they compare their desires, beliefs, goals, values etc., against an existing state of affairs and perceive a disparity with no immediately obvious way of removing the disparity (Ostell, 1988).

Hence, the concept of a problem is an interactional/transactional one: situations are not inherently problematic, but only become so when they are discrepant with a person's values, goals, desires and so on. Likewise, the transactional view of stress emphasizes that situations are not inherently stressful but rather, people are distressed by the ways they appraise and respond to situations.

To illustrate how the idea of a problem is useful in understanding people's stress reactions, Ostell (1988) discusses six types of 'costs' associated with problem situations. Actual or potential costs can be related to:

1. **Self-esteem** - e.g., failing to pass an examination;

2. **Own physical well-being/safety** - e.g., physical injury or danger;

3. **Well-being/safety of other people** - e.g., events endanger a loved one;

4. **Disapproval of other people** - e.g., failing to fulfil other people's expectations;

5. **Utilitarian goals** - e.g., failing to achieve a much desired promotion;

6. **Beliefs/values** - e.g., when an individual perceives that other people are behaving in ways which s/he feels are morally wrong.

7

These costs are crucial to understanding why certain situations prove stressful for people because appraisal of a problem situation always involves an evaluation of significant costs and, the perception of any one or more of these generally leads to the arousal of negative, distressing emotions (Folkman et al., 1986a; Ostell, 1988; 1991). In sum, a transactional definition of stress which includes the concept of a problem and associated costs is preferred for this study which is primarily concerned with determining and understanding the ways in which people react to stressful situations. Nonetheless, the real basis of this (or any) transactional definition is Lazarus's (1966) theory of cognitive appraisal. It is argued that if an individual appraises a situation as having significant costs, this leads to the arousal of negative, distressing cognitions, emotions and behaviours which, depending upon how the individual then reacts to the situation, can result in the person taxing or exceeding their coping resources and can, over a period of time, lead to a deterioration in the person's physical health and psychological well-being (Lazarus and Launier, 1978; Ostell, 1988). Hence, this cognitive theory of psychological stress ultimately identifies two processes - cognitive appraisal and coping - as critical mediators of the stressful person-environment relationship and indicators of adaptational status, i.e., health.

1.3 Cognitive appraisal, coping behaviour and health

Cognitive appraisal

The process of cognitive appraisal can be defined as an evaluative process that imbues a situation with meaning (Holroyd and Lazarus, 1982). It is the process through which an individual evaluates whether a particular situation poses significant costs, and if so, in what ways. The initial stages of this process are illustrated in Figure 1.1.

Primary appraisal

In the context of a given situation, the individual makes a primary appraisal of the actual or potential costs of the situation in terms of his or her well-being. Thus, primary appraisal is focused on the question 'Is this a problem?'. Discussion has already shown how these appraisals are typically concerned with 'costs' (real or perceived) to the individual's own physical safety, utilitarian costs, threats to self-esteem, personal goals, beliefs and/or values and/or the well-being of significant others (Folkman, Lazarus, Dunkel-Schetter, De Longis and Gruen, 1986b; Ostell, 1988).

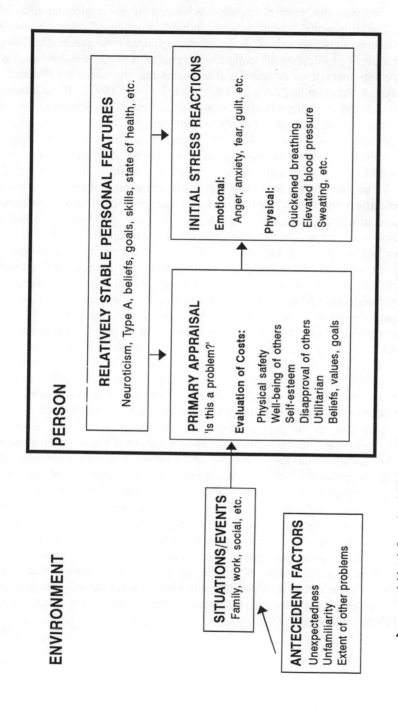

Figure 1.1   Primary appraisal & initial stress reactions

9

Figure 1.1 indicates that primary appraisal is shaped by a complex interplay of person and environmental factors. Stated briefly, a range of relatively stable personal features including values, goals, learned requirements, personal abilities, skills and state of physical health collectively serve as a perceptual lens through which a person appraises a situation and evaluates the relevant costs (Folkman, 1984; Folkman, Schaefer and Lazarus, 1979; Ostell, 1988, 1991). If for instance a person is sick and frail, this will affect appraisals as there is less energy to expend on coping than in the case of a healthy, robust person (Folkman et al., 1979). Generalized, abstract skills for problem-solving might include the ability to analyze situations, generating alternative courses of action or weighing alternatives with respect to desired or anticipated outcomes, whereas specific skills could include preparing for an examination or dealing with a life-threatening injury. Both levels of skills can affect appraisals. Similarly, general and specific beliefs can influence the appraisal process. Bandura (1977) for instance has emphasized the belief in self-efficacy as a general overarching resource that is critical in appraisal and coping, whilst Cvetanovski & Jex, (1994) examined the locus of control variable of unemployed people in relation to coping. On a broader sphere, enduring traits such as neuroticism can predispose the individual to appraise many situations as potentially problematic whilst at an even broader level, existential beliefs such as faith in God, fate and so on can exert yet further influences on appraisal.

Primary appraisal is also influenced by environmental factors. For instance, the nature and context of the situations or events themselves influence primary appraisal. Situations can occur in the context of work, or be concerned with the family, with personal relationships, or some combination of these. The situation itself may be concerned with staff conflicts at work, the death of a relative or marital problems, and so on. Antecedent factors such as whether or not the situation is familiar to the person, how likely the event is to occur, temporal concerns such as when it will occur, also exert a powerful influence on primary appraisal but cannot be uniquely attributed to the person or the environment. For example, the importance of unfamiliarity of events in the psychology of stress and emotions is highlighted by Bowlby (1970). In the general framework of his attachment theory, Bowlby described the problem of fear and its ontogeny and how unfamiliar events violate the cognitive structures or expectations that have developed often making the unfamiliar unassimilable. Similarly, unexpected events can bring about a sudden and often intense violation of expectancy which affects the appraisal process, particularly if unexpectedness is coupled with unfamiliarity (Lewis, 1970). The extent to which the individual is involved in other problem situations can also be an important antecedent situational factor which affects appraisal (Stone and Neale, 1984).

Initial stress reactions

When a situation is appraised as posing significant threat or cost(s) for the individual, initial stress reactions are aroused. These reactions represent changes in the person's psychological and physical states and are typified by distressing emotions (e.g., anxiety, anger, guilt, depression, etc.) each of which is mediated and sustained by a pattern of thinking peculiar to that particular emotional state (Hollon, Kendall and Lumry, 1986; Lazarus, 1966; Ostell, 1988). For example, a person who loses his or her job may experience anger at the perceived unfairness of the way things have turned out, be anxious about the well-being of other family members who will be affected by no longer having a financial income and depressed because the job loss is a blow to self-esteem. Irrespective of the type of initial stress reactions, however, it is important to note that if primary appraisal of a problem situation results in the arousal of initial stress reactions, then the individual is effectively faced with two problems, i.e., the original problem situation and their emotional reaction(s) to the situation. Of course, benign appraisals can occur, since not all situations will be at odds with a person's goals, values, etc., and, even if a situation is discrepant from a person's goals or values, the appraised costs may not be significant enough or so great as to arouse distressing emotions.

Secondary appraisal

Whether initial stress reactions are exacerbated or dispelled is largely determined by the cognitive processes of secondary appraisal as illustrated in Figure 1.2.

Secondary appraisal processes usually address the question 'What can I do?' whereby the individual evaluates what, if anything, can be done to deal with the situation. Available internal and external coping resources such as physical, psychological, social and material assets are evaluated with respect to the demands of the situation. Physical resources include health, energy and stamina; psychological resources may be drawn upon to sustain self-esteem, hope and effort for attempts at resolving the situation; both derive from the relatively stable features of the person. External resources, as Figure 1.2 indicates, derive from the environment. External social resources are the individual's social network and support systems from which can be drawn relevant information, tangible assistance and emotional support (Folkman et al., 1979). External material resources refer to money, tools, equipment and so on (see Folkman et al., (1979), for a full discussion of resources; see also Antonovsky (1979), for a related discussion on resource availability). Thus, both internal and external resources provide vital assets for the individual and exert a significant influence on cognitions in secondary appraisal which in turn affect coping options and emotional arousal (Folkman et al., 1979).

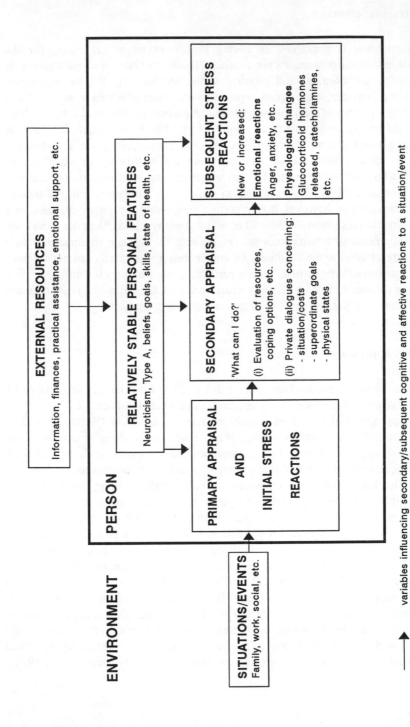

ENVIRONMENT

SITUATIONS/EVENTS
Family, work, social, etc.

PERSON

PRIMARY APPRAISAL AND INITIAL STRESS REACTIONS

SECONDARY APPRAISAL

'What can I do?'

(i) Evaluation of resources, coping options, etc.

(ii) Private dialogues concerning:
- situation/costs
- superordinate goals
- physical states

RELATIVELY STABLE PERSONAL FEATURES
Neuroticism, Type A, beliefs, goals, skills, state of health, etc.

EXTERNAL RESOURCES
Information, finances, practical assistance, emotional support, etc.

SUBSEQUENT STRESS REACTIONS

New or increased:
Emotional reactions
Anger, anxiety, etc.
Physiological changes
Glucocorticoid hormones released, catecholamines, etc.

→ variables influencing secondary/subsequent cognitive and affective reactions to a situation/event

Figure 1.2   **Secondary appraisal & subsequent stress reactions**

However, as Ostell (1988, 1991) points out, in addition to considering available resources, cognition in secondary appraisal 'is frequently deflected to issues brought into consideration by the process of problem-solving which may have little to do with whether a person can cope with the specific problem as defined initially' (1988, p.200). Here, cognitive activity can be described as personal or private dialogues whereby the individual engages in internal thoughts about the situation.

The content of these dialogues may be concerned with self-image (How will I look if...? etc.), or the moral appropriateness of the situation (It's not fair that he treats me this way....etc.). Or, the dialogues may reflect the individual's concerns about his or her emotional states and physical reactions which s/he is experiencing as a consequence of primary appraisal (e.g., worrying about rapid heart-rate, feeling faint or sick, etc.). Moreover, the manner in which a person engages in personal dialogues is important. For instance, styles of thinking such as 'overgeneralization', 'polarization' (Beck, Rush, Shaw and Emery, 1979) and 'catastrophizing' and 'awfulizing' (Ellis and Harper, 1975) can have profound effects upon emotional arousal by distorting realistic appraisals of the situation and exaggerating its negative implications or possible consequences.

In the context of this study on stress, coping and situational and health outcomes therefore, these dialogues are particularly important for three reasons:

1. the dialogues can compete with situational appraisals or problem-solving considerations to the extent that they can not only detract the individual's thoughts away from problem-solving considerations but also can become a problem in their own right (e.g., when protracted anxieties about self-image cause sleep problems);

2. because the dialogues often reflect superordinate values and goals (e.g., I must always please everyone) they are frequently the key to understanding the person's emotional distress and are therefore of heuristic and diagnostic value;

3. these dialogues play a crucial role in generating psychological and physical distress and are therefore, a vital component of the stress, appraisal, coping and health relationship.

Subsequent stress reactions

As Figure 1.2 illustrates, in much the same way as primary appraisal engenders initial stress reactions, the secondary appraisal processes lead to subsequent stress reactions or changes in the person's mental and physical states. On the one hand, if the necessary resources are available for dealing with the situation, then initial stress reactions are likely to be dispelled or reduced and the person will probably engage in coping behaviour (Ostell, 1988). On the other hand, if the required internal and/or external resources are not available then initial stress reactions may be increased in both range and intensity depending upon the attendant cognitive processes. At this juncture reappraisals may occur involving further reflection on the problem situation, re-evaluations of coping options, available resources and coping actions already undertaken (Lazarus and Launier, 1978).

Again, as Figure 1.2 illustrates, not only can cognitive appraisal processes play a vital role in the arousal of negative, distressing emotions, but in addition to the cognitive component, emotional arousal brings about physiological changes. These include increased blood and urine catecholamines and corticosteroids, increased blood glucose levels and blood pressure, changes in respiratory rate, sweating, dryness of the mouth and so on (see Cooper, Cooper and Eaker (1988a) and Cox (1978) for comprehensive discussions). In other words, negatively toned emotions are not only experienced as unpleasant but they also have implications for health, particularly if a person is emotionally distressed over a period of time. In this regard, research on stress and the immune system, ulcers, hypertension and coronary heart disease is amongst the best known, a brief review of which will be useful in aiding understanding of the stress/health relationship.

Psychological stress and the immune system

Research has shown that physiological 'fight' or 'flight' responses which occur when a situation is appraised as 'stressful' typically involve the activation of portions of the brain stem which causes the pituitary gland to stimulate the adrenals to secrete glucocorticoid hormones into the blood. Individuals under prolonged or repeated stress have been found to have an excess of these hormones in their blood much of the time. An excess of these steroids impairs the effectiveness of the immune system because the hormones reduce the power of the inflammatory response and cause the body to manufacture fewer antibodies. Thus, the impaired efficiency of these two defences makes it not only more likely that an individual will contract a disease, but also that the illness lasts longer and is more severe. (For more detailed accounts see Solomon and Amkraut (1981) and Stein, Keller and Schleifer (1976)).

Psychological stress and ulcers

Research evidence indicates that psychological stress can lead to serious disorders of the digestive system. The enzymes and hydrochloric acid that aid digestion in the stomach are also secreted when an individual is experiencing negative emotional arousal yet when these substances are present for prolonged periods in an empty stomach they begin to digest the stomach lining itself burning a hole (i.e., an ulcer) in the lining of the stomach or duodenum (see Ader's (1971) review of research in this area and Quick and Quick (1984) for further details).

Psychological stress and hypertension

The research literature abounds with examples of the ability of psychological stress to produce a hypertensive pattern or high blood pressure (e.g., see Goldstein (1979) for a review and Melhuish (1978)). Briefly, this condition of increased fluid pressure within the coronary arteries can damage the heart and kidneys, is a direct cause of strokes and is a prime contributor to hardening of the arteries. Much evidence suggests that stress arousals produce temporary increases in blood pressure but that if stress reactions are intense and prolonged, the temporary elevation of blood pressure may be maintained after the stress is over and become permanently elevated.

The appraisal processes

At this point it is useful to summarize the discussion on cognitive appraisal. From the interplay of situational and individual factors, three forms of cognitive appraisal occur - primary, secondary and reappraisal, each process imbuing a situation with meaning for the individual and each bringing about changes in the person's emotional and physical states. The essential difference between primary and secondary appraisal lies in what is being evaluated, namely the appraisal of significant costs or the appraisal of coping resources and options. However, as Lazarus and Launier (1978) point out, primary and secondary appraisal are not discrete processes. The term 'secondary' does not necessarily mean that secondary appraisal follows primary appraisal either in time or importance and, the two forms of appraisal influence each other. For instance, the knowledge that resources are available to deal with a potentially dangerous situation may make that danger moot. At the same time, knowing that one is in danger typically mobilizes appraisals about available resources and what can or cannot be done. Therefore secondary appraisal plays a crucial role in shaping a person's coping activities when under psychological stress as well as shaping the primary appraisal process itself.

  Moreover appraisal processes may be conscious and reflective or so automatic that the individual is not immediately aware of cognitive activity, (Ostell, 1991). But whether conscious or unconscious, appraisal processes play a central role in the aetiology of emotional and physical stress reactions, which then not only feed back and have an adverse impact upon ongoing appraisal activity but also feed forward and affect coping behaviours.

Coping behaviour

Like stress, the concept of coping has generated much debate. The term coping is a commonly used catch-word for a whole concatenation of thoughts and acts used in different contexts. Indeed, much of the debate has been about which acts should or should not be classed as coping, since one can argue that virtually everything an individual does has adaptive significance and then, the scope of coping is coextensive with adaptation (Lazarus and Launier, 1978). In the past decade however, most researchers have distinguished the concept of coping from adaptation and preferred to define coping more narrowly - not as an automatic, well-established, readily available response (as when braking in a car to avoid a child) but rather, as a response to a situation for which the adequate response is unclear, not immediately available, is perhaps difficult to mobilize and/or its adequacy is doubtful.

Functions of coping

A considerable amount of research has provided strong empirical support for the idea that coping usually includes two main functions:

1. managing (i.e., mastering, reducing, altering) the problem person/environment relation causing the distress (problem-focused);

2. regulating the emotional reaction(s) to the problem situation (emotion-focused).

This distinction has long been implicitly recognized by clinicians (Folkman, 1984) as well as by numerous investigators including Folkman and Lazarus (1980), Kahn, Wolfe, Quinn, Snoek and Rosenthal (1964) and Mechanic (1962) although more recent research builds on these two broad distinctions to classify strategies as cognitive versus behavioural (Steptoe, 1991) or task-oriented, emotion-oriented and avoidance-oriented (Endler & Parker, 1990) or problem-focused, emotion-focused, reappraisal, denial and acceptance strategies (Carver, Scheier & Weintraub, 1989).

Focus of coping

Coping behaviour comprises a hugely diverse number of activities and processes (Parkes, 1994) and a full discussion of coping is outside the scope of this book. However, Coelho, Hamburg and Adams (1974), Lazarus (1966), Menninger, Mayman and Pruyser (1963), and Moos (1974) have written systematic and comprehensive works on the subject and, from a review of this and other literature, it is possible to categorize coping behaviours in the following way:

> Coping behaviour refers to overt and/or covert (intrapsychic) actions which a person takes in order to solve, manage or adapt to a problem and/or to manage emotional reactions to that problem.

> (Ostell, 1988).

Figure 1.3 illustrates nine foci towards which coping behaviours may be directed.

Overt coping responses can be directed at:

1. *Situation/events* - These responses involve direct behavioural attempts to change the problem situation such as negotiating, executing a plan of action, diffusing a situation and so on.

2. *External resources* - Utilizing available external resources such as relevant information, practical help/assistance from other people, finances, emotional support etc., to help solve the problem and/or to manage emotions.

3. *Relatively stable features* - Acquiring new skills to cope with the problem itself or similar situations in the future, e.g., attending an interpersonal skills training course.

4. *Stress reactions* - Overt behavioural attempts to manage/palliate emotional/physiological stress reactions. These responses might involve the individual undertaking physical exercise such as jogging, swimming, yoga, etc., or using biofeedback training to gain control of physiological functions. Or, an individual may indulge in excessive smoking, eating or taking medications such as anti-depressants in an attempt to palliate their emotional reactions to the problem.

5. *Leaving the situation* - Physically removing oneself from the problem context altogether as a means of 'coping' with the problem and/or the emotional reaction(s).

Covert responses can be directed at

6. *Primary appraisal* - These responses involve reappraisal of the situation to verify or modify the conclusions of primary appraisal.

7. *Secondary appraisal* - Reappraisal of available coping resources and options and/or further private dialogues (e.g., what will others think if...? etc.).

8. *Stress reactions* - These responses involve covert attempts to manage emotional and/or physiological reactions to the problem such as positive reappraisals of the situation or denial whereby the person 'copes' with the problem and/or their emotional reaction by deliberately avoiding or refusing to think about the situation.

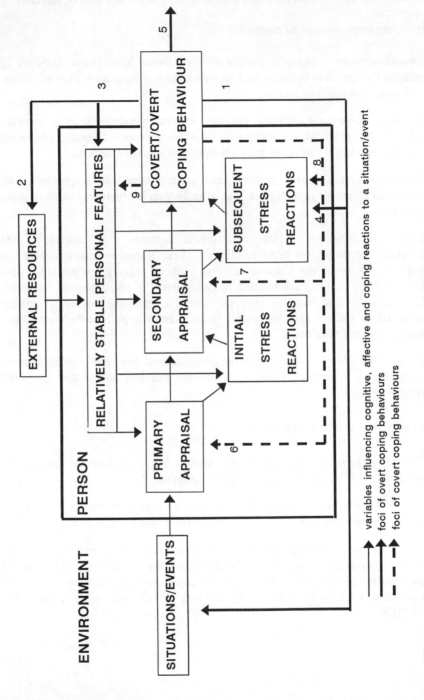

Figure 1.3   Various foci of overt/covert coping behaviours

variables influencing cognitive, affective and coping reactions to a situation/event

foci of overt coping behaviours

foci of covert coping behaviours

9. *Relatively stable features* - These covert responses are efforts to change long term goals and/or beliefs so that the perceived costs of the situation are reduced or no longer exist (Lazarus and Launier, 1978; Ostell, 1988, 1991). This mode of coping bears an analogy to Piaget's (1952) adaptive process of accommodation whereby children modify cognitive schemata or needs to conform to the environmental demands.

Thus, although the range of coping processes which can be simultaneously or sequentially employed is extensive, they can be broadly categorized according to whether they are overt or covert, their function (i.e., to manage the problem and/or the emotion) and their focus (e.g., on changing the situation, changing beliefs or goals, moderating the distress, and so on.) But irrespective of type, function or focus, a crucial factor in this process is, of course, the effectiveness of the chosen coping response(s). If a person is successful in dealing with a problem situation, then stress reactions are likely to be diminished (Lazarus and Launier, 1978; Ostell, 1991). Conversely, if a person fails to manage a situation effectively then the whole process of appraisal and coping is usually reiterated, involving re-appraisal of the costs, the available resources, viable coping options and actual coping responses. Often the whole process is undertaken on a trial-and-error basis until an acceptable resolution is found (Ostell, 1991).

At this juncture, it is worth noting two important points, both of which concern ways of studying the stress/health relationship. First, in any stressful encounter, as well as being a respondent to the environment, the person is also an active agent of change on the environment. For example, initial coping efforts may exacerbate a situation making it more difficult to cope with and perhaps even generating further problems. Moreover, when subsequent coping attempts are ineffective it is common for individuals to become increasingly distressed and engage in dysfunctional modes of thinking which feed back and affect ongoing appraisals, feed forward and affect further coping efforts and ultimately have a deleterious effect on psychological well-being and physical health (Felton and Revenson, 1984). Thus, although much of the above discussion about appraisal, emotion and coping has perhaps suggested unidirectionality within the process, in reality it is, congruent with the definition of stress, a bidirectional and transactional process. If we are to fully understand this process therefore it would seem that research methodologies should, at least in part, be able to explore and accurately represent the dynamic nature of the stress, coping and health relationship.

The second point to note in terms of studying stress and coping is that in any given situation which is perceived as having significant costs, the individual must strive for a balance between

- controlling the situation as effectively as possible, and

- maintaining internal homeostatic balance to sustain bodily health.

In other words, in order to cope, a person has to strive to manage both the situation and their emotional reactions to that situation effectively. Whilst a great deal of emphasis is placed upon direct action/problem-solving skills in the stress management literature, relatively little attention is given to managing emotions.

Thus, it is useful if an individual can find ways of controlling or reducing the emotion not merely by attempting to manage the problematic situation but by directly regulating the emotional state itself. Further, as we have seen, reactions such as anxiety, anger, guilt, sadness and so on are not only psychologically distressing in the short-term but also, if severe and protracted can result in physical illness. Given this, the ability to handle emotions is a vital element of effective coping and should, therefore, be of pivotal interest to any study of stress, coping and health.

1.4   A transactional model of stress and coping

In this chapter a transactional, cognitive-phenomenological perspective on stress, coping and health has been described. The chapter began by defining psychological stress as transactional in nature, whereby the individual transacts with or appraises a situation and perceives that the situation poses significant costs (real or imagined). This recognition then leads to initial stress reactions such as anger, anxiety or fear which are either exacerbated or diminished following secondary appraisal processes. These processes consider feasible coping options, available resources and also involve private dialogues relating to either the specific situation, to superordinate values, or both. In turn these appraisal processes feed forward affecting subsequent emotional reactions, reappraisals and attempted coping behaviours.

Cognitive and/or behavioural coping responses may be directed at the problem, the emotional reaction to the problem, or both. The actual responses might involve changing the situation, changing beliefs, values, goals, etc., utilizing external resources to help manage the problem and/or the emotions, reappraisals of the situation and options for coping and so on. Depending upon the effectiveness of coping efforts and the individual's motivation to persist, the appraisal processes and coping behaviours may be reiterated cyclically until such time as an acceptable solution is reached.

Having identified some of the key components in the stress, coping and health relationship, Figure 1.4 represents a transactional model of stress and coping which can be used to both illustrate and amplify those components of the process which merit research attention.

Looking at Figure 1.4 it can be seen that situations or events, external resources, the individual's relatively stable features, appraisal processes, stress reactions and overt and covert coping behaviours are the major components of the transactional model. The various relationships between the main features of this model have been detailed in this chapter and we have seen that stressful transactions are a product of two interacting systems, the person and the environment with which the person has continuing commerce. There is a constant interplay between these two, mediated by complex, ongoing cognitive appraisal processes which not only affect each other in a continuous flow of events unfolding over time, but also generate and are influenced by the person's stress reactions.

In contemplating areas worthy of research attention therefore, it would seem that the stress, coping and health relation cannot be fully understood until these mediating cognitive processes and their interplay are spelled out in some detail. Since stress reactions can have deleterious effects on coping and health outcomes then ultimately, we need to be able to describe the kinds of appraisal or the dialogues that lead to each emotion or pattern of reaction.

In assessing coping behaviours, it would be of value to not only describe actual coping strategies but also understand how appraisals and situational factors affect strategy selection, implementation, and perhaps most importantly, coping effectiveness. Moreover, since emotional reactions can have such adverse effects upon appraisals, coping and ultimately, on health, then coping studies should be focused as much on the ways in which people attempt to manage their emotions as on their attempts to manage the problem situation(s).

The individual's relatively stable features - beliefs, values, personality, etc., act as a perceptual lens through which any situation is appraised and predispose the person to react to situations in certain ways. Consequently, these features need to be considered in assessments of stress and coping. External resources also play an important role in the stress process. Thus, we need to understand why and how external resources affect appraisals, coping options, selection of coping responses and ultimately, situational outcomes. In sum, the model indicates that a person's relatively stable features, along with appraisal processes, external resources and coping behaviours, are important components of the stress and health relation and that these components warrant research attention.

Above all, the model of stress enforces a transactional, time-oriented and process-oriented perspective for studying stress and coping. Quite clearly, the stress process is a dynamic, unfolding process, not a static, unitary event. The essence of this process model is change. Emotions are characterized by flux. At any given phase of a situation people are likely to experience complex and even contradictory emotions shaped largely by constantly changing appraisal processes.

Coping too is complex, reiterative and characterized by change, with individuals typically combining multiple forms of problem and emotion-focused strategies at different stages of a situation. Whilst models tend to imply a linear or one-way cause and effect relationship going from environment or situation, via the person (mediator) to the response, in reality there is reciprocity of causation: the person thinks and acts and thereby changes the person-environment relationship; information about this is then fed back to the person through cognitive activity, and so on.

21

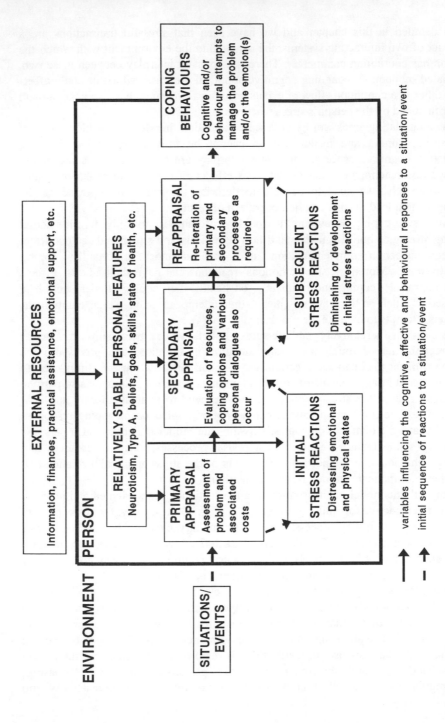

Figure 1.4 A cognitive, affective, behavioural process model of psychological stress

It is not wholly satisfactory therefore to try and encompass the continuous flow of such person-environment relationships in stress appraisals, emotions and coping within a linear causation model. Nor do we have statistical techniques which are readily amenable to modelling the true complexity of these processes. Such complexity might be best examined initially in descriptive terms because these variables and their salience are constantly changing with the flow of events as the person acts on the environment and in accordance with feedback from it.

In essence, the model indicates that in order to reach a full understanding of the stress, coping and health process, methodologies must be used which focus as much attention on describing transactional relationships and the processes involved in them as on empirically assessing their determinants.

Having identified in this chapter some of the key elements in the stress process, the purpose of the next two chapters is to review the literature on stress, coping and health and determine whether, and how these important components have been studied.

2 Conceptualization and measurement of coping

This chapter contains a critical review of the stress and coping literature. Different approaches to conceptualizing and measuring coping are examined and the advantages and limitations of each approach highlighted. The review will attempt to show that research in stress and coping, whilst prolific, has arguably reached an impasse, with continuing debate about conceptualization and measurement and many remaining, unresolved issues about the relationship between stress, coping and health.

2.1   Coping: conceptualization and measurement

There are many factors affecting how individuals cope with problem situations and the relative importance placed on a particular influence affects both the conceptualization of coping and its measurement (Aldwin and Revenson, 1987). For example, situational factors (Pearlin and Schooler, 1978), personality characteristics (Kobasa, 1979) cultural practices and preferences (Aldwin, 1985), and cognitive appraisal (Folkman and Lazarus, 1980) are just some of the many factors which can influence coping and the way it is conceptualized and measured. And there are many different ways of measuring coping strategies including standardized coping scales, interviewing protocols, observational techniques and personality or defense mechanism inventories (Dewe, Cox & Ferguson, 1993; Latack and Havlovic, 1992). Because of this diversity, most researchers therefore specify the conceptualization of coping and measurement method being used in a particular study which makes it easier to identify the major approaches currently being used for studying stress and coping.

There are five major approaches to conceptualizing coping: the psychoanalytic approach, personality-trait approach, situation-oriented approach, the stage-sequential approach and the methods-foci approach. What follows is a review of each of these approaches and discussion of their inherent limitations and advantages.

2.2   Psychoanalytic approach

The psychoanalytic approach conceptualizes coping in terms of defense mechanisms or primarily intra-psychic processes. These mechanisms include processes such as denial, repression and intellectualization by which an individual's emotional functioning is protected from external and intrapsychic threat. Typically, the defense mechanisms are organized hierarchically on an evaluative dimension. Vaillant, for example, presents hierarchical descriptions of defense processes ordering them from 'primitive' to 'mature' according to their 'relative theoretical maturity and pathological import' (1977, p.80). Here, coping represents the highest level of adjustment whilst processes further down the hierarchy represent inferior or less reality-oriented methods of adjustment. In his longitudinal study of Harvard graduates, Vaillant demonstrated how these adaptive mechanisms change through adulthood. Similarly, Haan (1977) placed ego processes on an evaluative dimension as indicating ego-failure, defense or coping according to their adherence to an 'objective reality'. In her psychodynamic study of managerial/professional subjects, Firth (1985) reported detailed qualitative case studies which described the personal meanings of occupational stress and showed stress to be a very individual process arising from an interaction of individual and situational variables whilst more recently, Firth-Cozens (1992) used a similar approach to examine the relationship between early family experiences and perceptions of organizational stress.

The main advantage of psychoanalytic approaches to studying coping is that they usually yield a rich source of data with vivid descriptions of the coping process. There are, however, a number of potential disadvantages with this approach. First, some studies using the psychoanalytic approach are rather narrowly focused because they give an inordinate amount of attention to defensive coping modes at the expense of other modes of coping (Lazarus and Launier, 1978; White, 1974). Further, the preoccupation with defense mechanisms has the effect of creating an overemphasis on failure and pathology rather than on effectiveness with the result that these studies can tell us little about effective coping (Folkman and Lazarus, 1980). Another problem with the psychoanalytic approach is that the ego processes are ranked according to their adherence to an 'objective reality'. Yet studies have shown that the **denial** of reality can be an effective means of coping (Hamburg and Adams, 1967; Miller and Grant, 1979; Suls and Fletcher, 1985), whereby the denial of an uncontrollable situation may help to reduce stress reactions. A final problem associated with this approach is that coping is viewed as a defense system whose purpose is to reduce tension and restore psychological equilibrium. Thus not only is attention focused primarily on anxiety reduction to the exclusion of other emotional states but also, relatively little attention is given to dealing with the problem situation. Yet as we saw in chapter 1, although maintaining psychological equilibrium is an important function of coping (Cohen and Lazarus, 1979), so is problem solving (Janis and Mann, 1977; Mechanic, 1962). A comprehensive definition of coping, therefore, needs to include both emotion regulation and problem solving functions (Folkman and Lazarus, 1980).

2.3   Personality approach

Many studies have characterized coping as determined by a personality trait and examined the impact of trait measures such as locus of control (Cvetanovski and Jex, 1994; Lefcourt, 1985) or Type A behaviour (Cooper, Watts, Baglioni and Kelly, 1988b; Suls and Sanders, 1988), or hardiness (Kobasa, Maddi and Courington, 1981; Schmied and Lawler, 1986) on the relation between stress and well-being. Implicit in this approach is the assumption that individuals with certain predispositions (e.g., those with high hardiness in respect of control beliefs, commitment and challenge) are behaviourally, attitudinally and cognitively consistent across situations. Individuals high on hardiness, control or exhibiting Type B behaviour, for example, are assumed to be better able to cope with stress and suffer less psychological distress relative to their counterparts.

Even though this approach seems intuitively appealing, the idea that stable coping styles exist has aroused some controversy. The personality approach to coping implicitly assumes that coping is unidimensional and stable across time and situations. Yet Folkman and Lazarus (1980, 1985) have repeatedly emphasized that coping should be thought of as dynamic and multidimensional. Characterizing coping as a single, stable, personality dimension has been criticized therefore for being overly simplistic (Folkman and Lazarus, 1985; Parkes, 1994).

Others have criticized this approach to coping because there is limited empirical evidence that personal traits are good predictors of actual situational appraisals and coping behaviours (Cohen and Lazarus, 1973; Nelson and Cohen, 1983). For example, in a study examining the relationship between stressful life events and symptomology as mediated by the impact of locus of control, little correspondence was found between control orientation (internal versus external) and actual appraisals of control over stressful life events (Nelson and Cohen, 1983). Likewise, Cohen and Lazarus (1973) found no support for the hypothesis that Byrne's (1961) personality dimension of regression versus sensitization would predict the course of recovery from surgery. The null findings in studies such as these have led some researchers to conclude that traditional personality dispositions are unlikely to be useful as predictors of coping (e.g., Folkman and Lazarus, 1980).

However, it is a moot point whether these objections to the personality approach to coping are well-founded enough to discount entirely the notion that personality affects coping and health. As Carver, Scheier and Weintraub (1989) pointed out, the fact that personality measures in the past were poor predictors of coping may be more indicative of the poor predictive value of the particular personality measures used than of personality measures in general. It is possible, therefore, that trait measures other than repression-sensitization and locus of control may be good predictors of coping. Moreover, another reason for not entirely discounting a possible personality/coping relationship is, as Edwards (1988) notes, that in most personality and coping studies, actual coping processes are only inferred but never measured. Kobasa (1979) for example, **assumes** that 'hardy' persons react to stress with a sense of commitment, challenge and control but does not actually measure coping responses. Indeed, in a review of relevant literature, Cohen and Edwards (1988) were unable to find a single study where coping behaviours of hardy and non-hardy individuals were actually measured. It is debatable then whether traditional personality trait measures are useful as predictors of coping and stress. It could be that by:

- using trait measures not used in previous research, and

- by assessing rather than inferring coping behaviours,

significant relationships may emerge between personality, coping and health outcomes.

2.4   Situation-oriented approach

Many studies have adopted a situation-oriented approach to coping and described the ways in which people cope with specific (and often unusual) situations such as spinal cord injury (Frank, Umlauf, Wonderlich, Askanazi, Buckelew and Elliott, 1987) breast cancer (Taylor, 1983) or academic (doctoral) examinations (Mechanic, 1962). For example, Frank et al., showed that subjects with spinal cord injury who evidenced external attributions of control and relied on health care providers were more psychologically distressed than subjects who evidenced internal attributions or beliefs regarding personal control. Along this line, Taylor (1983) found that attributional processes were related to psychological adjustment to breast cancer and argued that the adjustment process centred around three themes:

- a search for meaning in the experience;

- an attempt to regain mastery over the specific event;

- attempts to restore self-esteem through self-enhancing evaluations.

In such studies, the coping strategies are described in terms of the particular function they serve, e.g., seeking information, maintaining self-esteem, positive appraisal, and so on. Although the coping strategies often include defense mechanisms, they are not organized around defense theory (as in the psychoanalytic approach) and, consequently, this approach allows a more inclusive and comprehensive description of coping, because the concept of coping is not limited to defensive processes (Folkman and Lazarus, 1980). Mechanic's (1962) study was a particularly good illustration of this since it yielded a detailed description of how students coped with preparations for doctoral examinations by using strategies such as developing test-taking skills, making favourable social comparisons, using comforting cognitions and seeking support from faculty and friends.

Much can be learned by assessing the coping efforts of persons who are faced with unusual problematic events or have sustained catastrophic injury or who face life threatening illness. Not only are such studies of great heuristic value but also the observed differences in coping strategies can direct the development of effective psychological interventions such as behaviour modification and cognitive therapy. However, a major problem with situation-specific approaches to coping is that situation-specific approaches identify situation-specific coping responses which are limited in terms of their generalizability to other contexts. In other words, situation-specific studies usually focus on unusual situations and the coping responses identified are, therefore, limited in terms of generalizability to coping with more everyday-type problem situations.

Nevertheless, one situation-oriented study by Pearlin and Schooler (1978) differed in important ways from previous situational studies. Rather than focusing on unusual situations, Pearlin and Schooler asked subjects how they coped with everyday specific stresses in four social roles: marriage partnership, household finances, parenting, and work. Pearlin and Schooler looked at the efficacy of a number of coping behaviours and considered the relative contribution of personality characteristics (self-esteem, self-denigration and mastery) and coping responses to psychological well-being. The efficacy of various coping behaviours was judged in relation to the amelioration of distress in each of the four role areas. The results showed personality characteristics and coping responses had different effects relative to each other, depending on the nature of the stressful conditions. Individual coping interventions, for example, were most effective in areas such as marriage and child-rearing, where the subject's efforts could bring about change. In contrast, individual coping interventions were least effective in areas where there was little opportunity for control, such as work.

Seventeen coping responses were identified which the authors described as having three overall functions in coping:

1. to change the situation

2. to control the meaning of the stressful episode

3. to control the stress once it had emerged.

Of these three, the most frequently used responses were those which functioned to control the meaning of the problem situation. The most common type of coping response involved the making of positive comparisons, a response captured in such idioms as 'We're all in the same boat' or 'Count your blessings'.

Certain coping responses, such as engaging in selective comparisons, were identified in all four social roles, whereas other responses were apparent only in one area. These differences are important because they help to describe the complexity of coping responses in everyday, specific situations and suggest that there may be both consistency and variability when coping is studied across situations.

Of the situation-oriented approaches to coping then, Pearlin and Schooler's findings were more generalizable because they studied everyday as opposed to unusual situations. However, the main limitation of the Pearlin and Schooler study is that they asked the subjects how they usually coped with the everyday stresses at home and work and not how they actually coped. For instance, representative questions were:

How often do you

1. tell yourself that marital difficulties are not important?

2. try to overlook your spouse's faults and pay attention only to good points?

How strongly do you agree or disagree that

1. you cannot completely be yourself around your spouse?

2. your marriage doesn't give you enough opportunity to become the sort of person you'd like to be?

The analyses in this study were based on questions like these which either assessed how the respondents usually coped (questions 1 and 2) or defined situational stress in terms of a general abstract quality, in this case, opportunity for self-expression (questions 3 and 4) but do not yield information about the specific demands with which the person is coping (Folkman and Lazarus, 1980). The problem with general questions about behaviour is, as a number of authors recognize (Folkman and Lazarus, 1980; Newton, 1989; Parkes, 1994) that they are likely to elicit information about how the person thinks s/he copes rather than how s/he does in reality cope. Thus, the information may be so strongly influenced by the person's self-image that it more closely resembles a personality-trait than a coping behaviour.

In essence, the basic distinction here is between actual coping behaviour(s) and perceived coping style, and the distinction is an important one in coping research. The relevance of the differentiation can be supported and illustrated with two theoretical distinctions. The first derives from Argyris and Schon (1974) who distinguished between a person's espoused behaviour and actual behaviour thus:

> When someone is asked how he would behave under certain circumstances, the answer he usually gives is his espoused theory for action for the situation.... However, the theory that actually governs his actions is his theory-in-use, which may or **may not be** compatible with his espoused theory.
>
> (Argyris and Schon, 1974, p.7, added emphasis)

Tulving's research into human memory provides the second theoretical distinction which is relevant here. Tulving (1983) distinguished between episodic memory (memory of events, episodes, incidents) and semantic memory (knowledge, facts, concepts) and argued that the two are functionally different. This distinction is directly relevant to coping research because, if respondents are asked to recall how they **actually** coped with stressful incidents, they access their episodic memory. In contrast, if respondents are asked how they **usually** cope with stressful incidents, they access their semantic memory (Newton, 1989). Moreover, researchers argue that actual coping behaviours are unrelated to coping styles (Newton, 1989) and compounding this, research has found little correspondence between actual responses and preferred styles of coping (Carver, Scheier and Weintraub, 1989; Edwards, 1988). In sum, although assessing coping styles may occasionally be useful, it would seem that the best way to learn about situational demands and how people cope with them is to ask subjects how they actually cope with specific everyday situations.

2.5   Stage-sequential approach

A number of researchers have conceptualized coping as a stage-sequential process through which the individual passes in response to stress. This approach is particularly common in research on reactions to severe or extreme situations such as death of a loved one (Horowitz, 1976) or life-threatening illness (Kubler-Ross, 1969) or physical disabilities (Shontz, 1975). For example, Horowitz (1976) formulated a sophisticated stage-sequential model of stress responses to the death of a loved one. Stated simply, the model described how the memory of trauma can neither be excluded from consciousness nor fully integrated, such that information that is 'unacceptable' to the individual is prevented from being completely processed but remains in active memory, exerting a constant pressure toward processing. He showed that oscillating periods of denial (characterized by numbness, avoidance of reminders, etc.) and intrusion (e.g., nightmares, waves of feelings and being reminded of the stressor by almost any stimulus) over time become less intense, with an eventual 'working through' of the stressful material (Horowitz, 1976). Likewise, Kubler-Ross (1969) described how terminally ill patients pass through stages of denial, anger, bargaining, depression and acceptance. Shontz presented a similar model of coping with severe illnesses and physical disabilities. In his model, retreat (avoiding thinking about the trauma) and encounter (cognitive and emotional response to the stressor) alternate in a cyclical pattern. The ideal resolution of this pattern is acknowledgement, in which the threat is safely incorporated into an 'integrated self-structure' (Shontz, 1975, p.115). Thus, the common feature of stage approaches to coping is to assess a series of discrete responses which occur in a specific sequence.

This approach presents several distinct advantages. First, the data are usually obtained from individuals responding to authentic and extreme cases and a great deal can be learned by observing and assessing their coping efforts. Second, this approach usually involves multiple assessments of coping efforts over time, thereby tapping into the multidimensional and dynamic aspects of coping. Third, the stage -sequential approach addresses the often neglected processes underlying the selection and implementation of strategies (Cummings and Cooper, 1979; Edwards, 1988) to give a more comprehensive account of coping as a dynamic, bidirectional transaction between the person and the situation.

Despite these advantages, the stage-sequential approach to coping does have a number of disadvantages. Like the situation-oriented approaches, stage-sequential approaches are usually adopted for studying severe or unusual situations and the findings are, therefore, limited in terms of their generalizability. Another disadvantage is that when repeated measures of coping over time are used, the researcher's initial interventions are liable to cause reactivity in the respondents and thereby influence subsequent measures. Further, it is questionable whether individuals coping with stress actually do pass through predictable stages. Instead, as many studies suggest (e.g., Pearlin and Schooler, 1978) it seems more reasonable to assume that individuals select from a diverse array of coping strategies and implement these strategies in a wide variety of sequences. To date, there is little supporting empirical evidence that coping behaviour does occur in a specific sequence (Silver and Wortman, 1980). As Silver and Wortman point out, stage approaches to coping do not specify either, the exact duration of each stage or, the dimensions which influence transition from one stage to another. The sheer complexity and variability in coping responses is such that identifying the conditions under which transitions from one stage to another take place has, so far, proved impossible. The lack of empirical support for stage-sequential coping may be attributable, therefore, to the enormous difficulties in identifying conditions under which certain permutations of coping stages occur and to the sheer complexity and variability of individual and situational factors (Edwards, 1988). Thus, until stage models can specify stage duration and particularly the factors affecting stage transition, it will be difficult to gather empirical support or otherwise for the stage-sequential approach to conceptualizing coping.

2.6   Methods / foci approach

A widely used approach is to conceptualize coping in terms of either specific methods of coping or specific foci of coping efforts. Typically, this approach involves the development of a taxonomy of coping items which categorizes coping efforts according to the method used or the focus or target of the responses. Several investigators have presented their own categorization schemes (Billings and Moos, 1984; Carver et al., 1989; McCrae, 1984; Folkman and Lazarus, 1980) but for the most part, these schemes are modifications of the best known coping taxonomy, 'The Ways of Coping Checklist' (WCCL) which was originally developed by Lazarus and his colleagues (Aldwin, Folkman, Schaefer, Coyne and Lazarus, 1980) and later revised by Folkman and Lazarus (1985).

Since its development, the WCCL (and adaptations of it) have been and continue to be widely used in coping studies (Aldwin and Revenson, 1987; Carver et al., 1989; Edwards, Baglioni and Cooper, 1990; Folkman and Lazarus, 1980, 1985, 1988; Folkman, et al., 1986a, 1986b; McCrae, 1984; Patterson, Smith, Grant, Clopton, Josepho and Yager, 1990; Solomon, Mikulincer and Habershaim, 1990; Stone and Neale, 1984).

The Ways of Coping Checklist, as presented in Lazarus and Folkman (1984, pp. 328-333), consists of 67 items that describe a broad range of cognitive and behavioural coping strategies people might use to manage internal and/or external demands in stressful situations. Thus, embedded in the WCCL is the distinction between efforts focused on the problem and efforts focused on emotional reactions to the problem.

Attempts to establish the construct validity of the WCCL by factor analyzing data from samples with different demographic characteristics have yielded inconsistent results (Aldwin et al., 1980; Collins, Baum and Singer, 1983; Folkman and Lazarus, 1986; McCrae, 1984; Vitaliano, Russo, Carr, Maiuro and Becker, 1985). However, most factor solutions have identified between six and nine factors, which represent both problem-focused and emotion-focused strategies such as:

- *Instrumental action* - representing efforts towards managing the problem with items such as 'Made a plan of action and followed it'.

- *Negotiation* - another problem focused tactic directed at bargaining or compromising to get something positive from the situation.

- *Exercising caution* - holding back actions which may do more harm than good, expressed by items such as 'Tried not to burn my bridges but leave things open somewhat'.

- *Escapism* - an emotion-focused factor related to wishful thinking, fantasizing or excessive indulgence in drugs, sex, alcohol, etc.

- *Self-blame* - intropunitive strategies directed at the self rather than the problem and represented by items such as 'Realized that I brought the problem on myself'.

- *Seeking meaning* - an emotion-focused strategy concerned with attempts to discover new faith or turning to religion.

- *Minimization* - conscious coping efforts to refuse to dwell on the problem and expressed in items such as 'Refuse to get too serious about the situation'.

- *Social Support* - efforts to mobilize advice, information and emotional support to help with either the problem and/or the distress experienced.

Although modes of using and scoring the WCCL vary somewhat from study to study, most commonly, respondents describe their coping responses to a problem situation by indicating how often each way of coping was used cn the following scale: 0=Not used/Not applicable; 1=Used somewhat; 2=Used quite a bit; 3=Used a great deal. Ratings for the 67 items are factor analyzed so that distinct but more general strategies of coping (as described above) can be identified. These strategies are then used as predictors of such measures as situational outcomes (e.g., Folkman et al., 1986a), psychological symptoms (e.g., Aldwin and Revenson, 1987) and somatic illness (e.g., Solomon et al., 1990).

Studies based on this approach have made some valuable contributions to our understanding of the stress, coping and health relation. For example, using the WCCL, Aldwin and Revenson (1987) explored the relation between coping strategies and psychological symptoms and found that the strategies most strongly related to symptoms were escapism or fantasizing and self-blame, whereas problem-directed instrumental action functioned as a stress buffer. Similarly, in their study of adults with unipolar depression, Billings and Moos (1984) devised a 32-item coping inventory within three domains of coping:

1. **Appraisal-focused coping** - appraising and reappraising the stressful situation

2. **Problem-focused coping** - active efforts to deal with the stressor

3. **Emotion-focused coping** - attempts to handle the emotions aroused by the stressor.

Respondents were asked to indicate a recent stressful event and then rate the frequency of use, on a 4 point scale, of the 32 coping responses. The findings from this study indicated that coping responses directed toward problem solving (e.g., Made a plan of action and followed it) and affective regulation (e.g., Tried to see the positive side of the situation) were associated with less severe dysfunction, whereas emotional-discharge responses such as 'Took it out on other people when I felt angry or depressed' were linked to greater dysfunction.

Because of the broad range of coping activities included in typical methods/foci measures, investigations based on this approach usually give a fairly comprehensive assessment of actual coping behaviours. For instance, Folkman et al., (1986a) examined the relation between appraisal, coping and psychological symptoms. Primary appraisal was assessed with 13 items that described various stakes people might have in a problem situation (e.g., losing self-respect, or harm to a loved one's health, safety or well-being or a strain on financial resources) and subjects indicated the extent to which each stake was involved on a 5-point Likert scale. Secondary appraisal was measured with four items where subjects indicated on a 5-point scale the extent to which the situation was changeable, had to be accepted, required more information or needed restraint of action. Bivariate correlations were found between the primary appraisal/stakes variables and psychological symptoms indicating that in general, the more the subjects had at stake over diverse situations, the more they were likely to experience symptoms. In addition, significant correlations between coping and psychological symptoms were confined primarily to the problem-focused forms of coping, such that planful solving was negatively correlated with symptoms whereas confrontive coping was positively associated.

In the same study, Folkman et al., (1986a) went some way towards describing the relation between appraisal, coping and outcomes. Primary appraisal was found to influence choice of coping strategies. For example, when threat to self-esteem was high, subjects used more confrontive coping, self-control, accepted more responsibility and used more escape-avoidance, compared to when threat to self-esteem was low. In addition, the relation between secondary appraisal and coping was examined and showed that subjects used more distancing and escape-avoidance in encounters they appraised as having to be accepted or 'uncontrollable'. Moreover, the relation between secondary appraisal and encounter outcomes in terms of improvement, no change or a worsening of the situation was examined. This revealed that satisfactory outcomes were associated with higher levels of situational changeability.

Using an adaptation of the WCCL, McCrae (1984) also indicated some of the relations between appraisal and coping. McCrae examined the situational determinants of coping responses and found rational action, positive thinking, perseverance and self-adaptation to be used primarily by subjects facing challenge, as opposed to loss or threat. (Most of these mechanisms are considered by theorists (e.g., Vaillant, 1977) as examples of mature, non-neurotic coping.) Further, meaningful differences were found between reactions to loss and to threat, whereby individuals facing a threat to their health or well-being more often took concrete action, sought help, or persevered in a course of action. This is also consistent with Billings and Moos (1981) who found that 'active-behavioural' coping was used more by subjects who were dealing with illness (threat) than by subjects who were dealing with death (loss).

From just a brief review of some studies using the methods/foci approach then, there is little doubt that this approach has some advantages over other approaches. Coping inventories such as the WCCL are easy to use, require little training and are not confined to defense mechanisms but include comprehensive lists of items which assess both problem and emotion-focused strategies. Such measures permit the respondent to characterize his or her thoughts with some degree of complexity and, because of the broad range of coping activities included, studies based on this approach usually give a fairly comprehensive account of coping behaviours.

The findings from many of the studies based on the methods/foci approach have served to increase our understanding of the relationship between contextual features of specific situations and coping processes as well as the relationship between various modes of coping and adaptational outcomes such as somatic and psychological well-being. The advantages of taking a methods/foci approach to studying coping undoubtedly account for its extensive and continued use in coping research.

Nevertheless, in spite of its heuristic value and wide usage, the methods/foci approach to conceptualizing and measuring coping is not without limitations. Consider, for example, some of the results of the methods/foci studies which have been reviewed in the foregoing pages. On the basis of these findings it is tempting to make a number of deductions. One may deduce for example that:

- Planful problem solving appears to be used more in situations which are appraised as changeable or challenging and by and large, is associated with favourable outcomes in terms of health, whereas confrontive coping tends to be related to unfavourable health outcomes.

- Emotion-focused efforts appear to be used most frequently when situations are appraised as unchangeable or when the stakes are loss or threat.

- Although their primary function is to facilitate coping, it would seem that many emotion-focused efforts (e.g., distancing, avoidance, fantasizing) are frequently related to unfavourable health outcomes.

Deductions such as these, however, assume that coping strategies can be labelled as 'effective' or 'ineffective' and applied wholesale regardless of differences between individual and situational variants. Yet there are many inconsistencies and contradictory findings in the literature which indicate that coping strategies cannot be labelled thus. For example, studies of coping among cancer and tuberculosis patients (Calden, Dupertuis, Hokanson and Lewis, 1960; Rogenstine, van-Kemmen, Fox, Docherty, Rosenblatt, Boyd and Bunney, 1979) have shown confrontive coping to be adaptive whereas Folkman et al., (1986a) found it related to increased symptoms. In their classic study of coping with stress at Three Mile Island, Collins et al., (1983) showed that distancing can be an adaptive response to an outcome that is seen in negative and unalterable terms, but Folkman et al., (1986a) found the reverse. Horowitz (1979) recognized that avoidance may be good coping if avoidance of highly stressful information allows the person to 'dose' him or herself strategically with the needed information, thereby avoiding extreme and dysfunctional emotional responses. Similarly, Hamburg and Adams (1967) have observed that denial can be constructively employed by a helpless victim of spinal injury or polio as a means of effectively coping through the early stages of debilitation, but turn to more reality-based appraisals and actions aimed at rehabilitation when the victim is physically and emotionally stronger. A number of the studies reviewed earlier, however, (e.g., Folkman et al., (1986a) found avoidance and denial-type strategies were related to poorer psychological adjustment.

A further notable example of inconsistent results is in the recent study by Folkman and Lazarus (1988) on how coping affects emotion. They found that positive reappraisal was associated with a decrease in distress (i.e., disgust/anger) in one group of younger subjects, but with a worsened emotional state (i.e., worry/fear) in an older group of subjects. In the same study, seeking social support was associated with increased positive emotions with the older group, but showed no association in the younger group. Similar contradictory findings were apparent concerning the use of confrontive coping strategies.

In summary, what these contradictory and inconsistent findings suggest is that a particular coping strategy cannot be valued and labelled as 'effective' or 'ineffective' without reference to the context in which it is used. Given this, the most we can deduce from studies using coping checklists is that some forms of coping, such as planful problem solving or positive appraisal or seeking support, will have salubrious effects on certain personal and situational outcomes, in certain circumstances involving certain individuals. Or, strategies such as confrontive coping, denial or escapism will have deleterious effects in some populations and in some contexts. But the extent to which these effects are context and/or individual specific is still not clear, because typical coping measures take only static snapshots of what is essentially a dynamic, bidirectional relationship between the individual and the situation (Oakland and Ostell, 1995).

It is feasible, of course, as Aldwin and Revenson (1987) point out, that the apparent inconsistencies and contradictory findings may, in part, be due to methodological variances in measures and varying sample characteristics. However, they may also be a reflection of a number of inherent weaknesses in the methods/foci approach to coping. As discussed earlier, in studies using this approach, respondents are required to give details of their coping responses to a problem situation by indicating which strategies they used, and how often they used them. The frequency with which a particular strategy was used is then correlated with some outcome measure such as psychological well-being or physical symptoms. Yet the problem with simply correlating the frequency of use of a particular strategy with an outcome measure is that it assumes that using the strategy will have uniform effects regardless of other aspects of the situation and the person. In other words, a crucial intermediate step is omitted: whether the coping efforts were successful.

To elaborate, researchers ask whether respondents 'Made a plan of action' but do not ask 'Did the plan work?' or 'Were you able to carry it out successfully?' or 'Did the plan yield positive or negative outcomes?' As a result, the complex interaction of the use of coping strategies with perceptions of their efficacy is completely overlooked. This may be a crucial oversight in understanding the coping and health relation since whether a particular strategy such as 'Making a plan of action' is useful in reducing stress may depend on an additional factor: whether or not it worked. Thus, it is insufficient simply to inquire as to which strategies were used; more information is needed about their effectiveness (Newton, 1989).

Another weakness associated with conceptualizing coping in terms of foci or method, is that items within each of the coping categories suffer to a greater or lesser degree from a lack of clear focus (Carver et al., 1989). Often this occurs because an item does not describe fully why the response was made. For example, should the item 'Talked with others about the problem' be classified as seeking emotional support, information seeking or direct action problem solving? It is quite feasible of course that a single coping act may involve a variety of foci whereby the individual 'Talked with others about the problem' to get more information, which will help solve the problem and also allay fears. Or, someone who takes a tranquilizer before a major exam may do so to simultaneously dampen their emotional response **and** control their anxiety to improve exam performance. Thus, a single act may be classified as both problem and emotion-focused coping, but lack of clarity in some coping items does not permit this distinction (Edwards, 1988).

Carver et al., raised the same criticism of typical coping items. For example, they considered the item from the WCCL: 'Took a big chance or did something risky' and pointed out that doing something risky may mean taking drugs to avoid thinking about a problem. Alternatively, doing something risky could mean taking action which may not work, but if it does, will solve the problem. It is important therefore to differentiate between the reasons for certain behaviours because those reasons can have very different implications. Thus, items like 'Took a big chance or did something risky' describe a coping response but because the focus of the response is ambiguous, the intentions behind the response remain unclear.

Stone and Neale's (1984) attempt to develop a new measure of coping further highlights the lack of clarity in typical coping items. They developed a measure of daily coping by asking subjects to describe how they had handled a problem from a list of 55 possible responses. Next, in an attempt to understand what the subjects were doing, the investigators asked subjects to sort their coping responses according to function - namely, distraction, situation redefinition, direct action, catharsis, acceptance, social support, relaxation and religion. But, on checking the subjects' categorization of responses, Stone and Neale found that items they had earlier classified as 'situation redefinition' were classed by some subjects as 'direct action' and others as 'acceptance'. Items the researchers thought represented 'direct action' were classed by some subjects as 'seeking social support'. Relaxation items were sometimes classified as catharsis and sometimes as distraction.

This lack of conceptual clarity in many coping items may also explain some analytical problems which researchers have encountered. Folkman et al., reported high intercorrelations of coping strategies where, for instance, escape-avoidance had a .51 zero-order correlation with symptoms but was also correlated with confrontive coping at .52. Yet whilst the authors admit that this multicollinearity poses analytical problems and that it 'may also mask important relations' between coping strategies (1986a)p.578) the coping inventories continue to be widely used and quantification procedures of analysis adhered to unswervingly (see Oakland and Ostell, (1995) for a more detailed review and critique of methods/foci research). In summary, it is feasible that the inconsistencies and analytical problems encountered in many coping studies reflect the fact that different coping behaviours or thoughts can be used in different ways or with different intentions and with differing degrees of efficacy. These issues cannot be addressed in typical quantitative assessments of coping.

2.7   Chapter summary

In this chapter the five main approaches to conceptualizing and measuring coping have been reviewed. Whilst these approaches have provided a substantial contribution to our understanding of the stress, coping and health relationship, they also present certain conceptual and methodological problems. Psychoanalytic approaches provide a rich source of descriptive data about the coping process, but are limited because they give an inordinate amount of attention to defense mechanisms and maintaining psychological equilibrium at the expense of other modes of coping directed at the problem. Personality approaches to coping are controversial because to date, there has been mixed evidence regarding the predictive value of traditional personality trait measures for coping behaviours.

Situation-oriented approaches have contributed greatly to our understanding of situation-specific coping responses, but because they are typically concerned with severe, unusual situations, the generalizability of their findings is limited. Studies which ask how subjects actually cope with everyday problems, therefore, are more generalizable. Stage-sequential approaches to coping have increased our knowledge about coping with trauma and crises but underrepresent the variability and complexity in coping by attempting to place coping behaviours in discrete categories or stages for which, as yet, there is little empirical support.

The methods/foci approach has a number of distinct advantages over other approaches. Because it is not restricted to defense mechanisms, it usually involves easily administered inventories of a wide range of cognitive and behavioural responses and provides, therefore, a fairly comprehensive description of actual coping behaviours (e.g., Folkman and Lazarus, 1980, 1985). However, the rigid adherence to quantified measures of coping has resulted in potentially crucial factors in the stress, coping and health relation being overlooked. These measures only ask how often certain strategies were used but do not ask 'Why did you choose that strategy?', or 'Did the strategy work?'. Consequently, all that can be said confidently from these studies is that some strategies are effective, some of the time, for certain individuals in certain situations. The factors influencing the individual's selection of coping methods and foci are largely overlooked and the effectiveness of strategies is never addressed.

Having reviewed the major approaches to conceptualizing and measuring coping, it is clear that every approach has some advantages and some limitations and, in spite of the recent burgeoning of stress and coping research, there are still many unresolved issues concerning the mechanisms through which stress and coping might affect health. It is to some of these important issues that the discussion now turns in the next chapter.

3 Stress, coping and health: Research issues and objectives

In chapter 1, various personological and environmental variables were identified as major components of the stress, coping and health process. Foremost in this regard were internal factors such as personality, an individual's skills, perceptions of control and self-efficacy, cognitive appraisal processes, emotional reactions and overt/covert coping behaviours. Important external variables were the stressful situations or events themselves and the availability and adequacy of external resources for coping. Research reviewed in chapter 2 showed that most studies have either focused on stress and coping with specific, unusual events or, have used theoretically-derived coping checklists to examine the stress, coping and health relationship. It was argued that a preoccupation with the situational determinants of coping has resulted in studies adopting research methods which mask the subtleties of the stress process, producing results which are often contradictory and of limited generalizability and leaving many important issues unresolved.

In this chapter, further review of the literature demonstrates that some crucial variables in the relationship between stress and health have been largely overlooked in previous research. Throughout, a rationale is developed for the design of a research study which attempts to circumvent the weaknesses and build upon the advantages of previous studies. This chapter therefore clarifies some of the important issues to be addressed by the research, establishes a basis for the major objectives of this research and provides a rationale for the methodological design.

3.1   Cognitive appraisal processes

In chapter 1, stress was conceptualized as transactional, whereby the person and the environment are viewed as being in a dynamic, mutually reciprocal relationship (Lazarus, 1966; Lazarus and Launier, 1978). According to this stress and coping paradigm, stress reactions occur when an individual appraises an event and recognizes that environmental or internal demands (or both) tax or exceed their adaptive resources. Thus, a central feature of this definition are the processes of cognitive appraisal which clearly warrant research attention. However, as a number of researchers recognize (Dewe, 1991, 1992; Newton 1989; Oakland, 1991; Schwartz and Stone, 1994), whilst the central importance of appraisal is acknowledged theoretically, most studies on stress overlook the process of appraisal empirically.

Consider the transactional definition of stress outlined above. The basis of this stress definition was developed by Lazarus from Arnold's (1960) theory of emotion and personality. Arnold distinguished emotional responses from the objects with which they were associated, seeing appraisal as the intervening process between the two:

> To arouse an emotion, an object must be appraised as affecting me in some way, affecting me personally as an individual with my particular experience and my particular aims. If I see an apple, I know it is an apple of a particular kind and taste. This knowledge need not touch me personally. But if the object is of my favourite kind and I am in a part of the world where it does not grow and cannot be bought, I may want it with real emotional craving.
>
> (Arnold, 1960, p.171)

This quotation indicates clearly that appraisal is the crucial, mediating process between the existence of an object and the arousal of emotion. But the problem with a lot of stress research is that it fails to make this basic distinction between the existence of an object (or a demand) and the evaluation of that object or demand. For example, as was apparent from the literature reviewed in chapter 2, in many stress studies the predominant research paradigm has involved analyzing whether there are associations between certain stressful situations, various coping responses and psychological and/or physiological measures (e.g., Folkman and Lazarus, 1980, 1985; McCrae, 1984). While this research can indicate that certain situations are associated with certain strains or that certain coping responses are associated with certain adaptational outcomes, it can tell us nothing about why such associations exist, since nothing is known about how or why the individual evaluated a certain situation as stressful. Without this information, understanding of the stress process is severely limited because knowledge about a central variable, cognitive appraisal, is lacking.

That the appraisal process is acknowledged theoretically but largely ignored empirically is borne out by many occupational stress studies. Here, the predominant research paradigm has involved analyzing whether there are associations between work demands such as role ambiguity or role conflict and psychological and/or physiological strains (e.g., Kahn, et al., 1964; Rizzo, House and Lirtzman, 1970). Whilst this research goes some way to indicating that certain job demands are associated with certain strains, it tells us nothing about why such associations exist, since nothing is directly known about how or why an individual evaluated certain demands as 'stressful' (Brief and Atieh, 1987).

To elaborate, the design of many occupational stress studies can be characterized as follows: Questionnaire respondents are asked to report the frequency with which they encounter various job conditions such as 'I receive incompatible requests from two or more people' (role conflict item from Rizzo et al., 1970). Next, respondents are asked to report their job-related affective states. The relationship between the 'stressful' job conditions and job-related affective states is then statistically ascertained and, so long as the detected relationship is statistically significant, the researcher concludes that a source of job stress has been identified. This description captures the bulk of occupational stress studies (Brief and Atieh, 1987).

However, as several authors have recognized, these studies are seriously flawed (Brief and Atieh, 1987; Dewe, 1989; Glowinkowski and Cooper, 1985; Newton, 1989); they use traditional rating scales that imply demand rather than measure it, since the job demands or conditions have been a priori labelled as stressful by the researcher (Glowinkowski and Cooper, 1985). Thus, if a respondent answers 'very frequently' to the item 'I receive incompatible requests from two or more people', this is interpreted as an indication of high role ambiguity pressure. Yet it is quite feasible that a respondent who very frequently receives incompatible requests from two or more people feels no ambiguity or pressure at all but finds it easy to cope with that particular condition of the job (Newton, 1989). In other words, the existence of a demand must be distinguished from the individual's appraisal of the demand, but many typical job studies fail to make this distinction (Dewe, 1989).

This has prompted a number of authors (Brief and Atieh, 1987; Dewe, 1989; Glowinkowski and Cooper, 1985; Jackson and Schuler, 1985; Newton, 1989) to question whether the bulk of occupational stress studies are really measuring stressors in the workplace. Consider, for example, the two constructs - role conflict and role ambiguity - which have generated considerable research attention (Van Sell, Brief and Schuler, 1981) as sources of job-related stress. In a meta-analysis of role conflict and role ambiguity research, Jackson and Schuler (1985) identified more than 200 studies which had utilized the occupational stress design outlined above. Yet, based upon the average observed (i.e., unadjusted) correlations, Jackson and Schuler found that role conflict and role ambiguity explained only 7 per cent of the variance in reported distress, as indexed by various job-related affective reactions. Are these studies then, which make a priori assumptions concerning work demands and fail to assess the individual's appraisal or evaluation of those demands, really measuring stressors in the workplace?

A study by Payne, Jabri and Pearson (1988) adds credence to the argument that the existence of a demand is not necessarily equivalent to stressful appraisal of the demand. These researchers asked about the frequency of work demands and how satisfied respondents were with the level of the demands. Simple product moment correlations between demand level and demand satisfaction showed that certain demands were indeed related to dissatisfaction, and the authors duly labelled these 'attritional demands'. However, other job demands were found to be strongly related to satisfaction and these they labelled 'attractional demands'. Findings such as these demonstrate further that studies which do not tap into the individual's appraisal of a given situational demand are limited in their explanatory power, since they lack information about a central variable in the stress process, namely - cognitive appraisal. This limitation points to the need for semantic relabelling of typical questions in quantitative assessments of stress and such questions should be targeted at the individual's evaluation or appraisal of specific situations or events. However, in considering designing quantitative measures which tap into the appraisal of situational demands, it is pertinent to digress here and review a body of literature in personality psychology which has implications for any study attempting to assess stressful appraisals.

3.2   Negative / positive emotionality and appraisal

It has been suggested already that a substantial part of the literature on job stress is based on observed relationships between presumably stressful conditions of work and various indices that are purported to gauge the levels of distress experienced by workers using self-report measures for both stressors (the predictors) and strain (the criterion). Indeed, reliance on low job satisfaction scores as indicators of job-related distress pervades the literature (Brief and Atieh, 1987) and a number of authors (Brief and Atieh, 1987; Parkes, 1990; Payne, 1988) have questioned whether these self-report measures might be confounded by the personality disposition of negative emotionality (or negative affectivity or trait neuroticism, depending on the measure used). More specifically, work in personality psychology suggests that a tendency to experience negative affective states and view the self, others and the world in negative terms is reflective of a pervading disposition called negative emotionality (NEM) (Watson and Clark, 1984). Thus, high levels of NEM are associated with a type of cognitive style through which people approach and interpret their life experiences accentuating the negative aspects. Various empirical studies have illustrated this accentuation to show that high NEM subjects generally interpret ambiguous stimuli in a negative or threatening manner (Watson and Clark, 1984) are more likely to interpret normal symptoms and sensations as painful or pathological (Costa and McCrae, 1985) and report higher levels of perceived stress (Watson, 1988) than subjects low in NEM.

Findings such as these have prompted some researchers to question whether the dispositional trait NEM might influence how people experience and evaluate both their jobs and their reporting of health and symptoms. Indeed, a number of studies have demonstrated that NEM does confound relationships between work-stress and health measures (Brief, Burke, George, Robinson and Webster, 1988; Parkes, 1990; Payne, 1988). For example, Brief et al., (1988) using partial correlation analyses, found markedly reduced relationships between work-stress measures and affective outcomes when NEM was controlled for. They found a significant positive relationship between negative job stress and somatic complaints at work (r = .21, <.01, n = 327) but when NEM was controlled for the partial r coefficient was .03. Parkes (1990) and Payne (1988) demonstrated similar effects.

Assuming these results generalize to other studies of stress/strain relationships, questions arise regarding the current state of much of the job stress literature and future methodological approaches. It would seem that typically reported stress-strain relationships cannot be confidently relied upon because correlations between the perceptions of stressors and the reporting of strain (i.e., psychological symptoms) may be inflated by the pervading dispositional trait of negative emotionality. Consequently, it was considered necessary to include a measure of NEM in this study of stress and health and to investigate its potential confounding effects. It is also important to point out that, apart from the confounding effect of NEM upon the measurement of the 'stressor-strain' relationship, high NEM probably also plays a substantive role in distress generation and maintenance processes (Depue and Monroe, 1986; Watson, 1988). In other words, NEM is not simply a generalized way of perceiving environmental circumstances and personal experience but it also can result in chronic, though possibly fluctuating or intermittent, emotional and physical disturbance. Unfortunately it is difficult in most studies to partial out the separate effects of measurement problems from those substantive distress generation and maintenance processes.

In the original report of this research (Oakland, 1991), the positive analogue of NEM - positive emotionality (PEM) was also considered. According to Watson (1988), positive emotionality reflects enthusiasm, mental alertness, energy and determination or more generally, the individuals 'pleasurable engagement with the environment' (1988, p.1020). Yet Watson emphasizes that when assessed with factor-analytically derived scales, NEM and PEM are largely independent dimensions of affect or mood and further, insists that whilst NEM is correlated with self-reported stress, PEM is not. However, since negativity has attracted much recent research attention, only the analyses relating to NEM are reported in this book, but interested readers should refer to Oakland (1991) for the findings relating to PEM.

So far in this chapter, reasons have been given for designing quantitative measures which assess **appraisal** of situational demands and for examining the potential confounding effects, on appraisal, of the dispositional trait NEM.

However, because cognitive appraisal has been shown to play such a vital role in the stress process, what is also required is a methodology which will permit open-ended questions to be directed at the cognitive processes involved in appraisal (Dewe, 1991; Oakland, 1991; Oakland and Ostell, 1995). Questions need to be asked such as 'Why is X a problem for you?' or 'What is it about situation X which makes it seem difficult for you?' and 'How does that make you feel?', etc., because, as pointed out in chapter 1, it is the evaluation or appraisal of costs inherent in a problem situation which are a necessary and sufficient condition for the arousal of stress reactions in a person (Lazarus, 1966; Lazarus and Launier, 1978; Ostell, 1988, 1995b). Hence, until these cognitive processes in appraisal are studied empirically, explored and described, our understanding of the stress, coping and health relationship will be limited (Dewe, 1991, 1992; O'Driscoll and Cooper, 1994; Oakland, 1991). For one can argue that even if more empirical attention were given to certain conditions of work or certain situational variants, understanding the aetiology of stress would remain impaired because data relating to a crucial variable, appraisal, would still be missing.

In other words, what is needed is a predominantly qualitative methodology which will identify the cognitive processes or private dialogues people engage in when they appraise the potential costs of and their options for coping in situations, because these dialogues are the key to understanding the stress reactions (disturbances of emotion, cognition and behaviour) which if protracted, can have deleterious effects on the person's psychological and/or physical health (Ostell, 1988; Stone, Reed and Neale, 1987). Consequently a major objective of this study was to design a methodology to identify these cognitive processes or private dialogues which play such a vital role in the aetiology of stress reactions.

3.3   Cognitive processes, coping and health

The conception of cognition as a private dialogue can be first traced to Socrates who, in Theaetetus, described thinking as 'a discourse that the mind carries on with itself' (Hamilton and Cairns, 1961, p.895). Contemporary writers refer to this as either self-talk (Ellis, 1962) or internal dialogues (Meichenbaum, 1977) or private dialogues (Ostell, 1988) or silent soliloquy (Ryle, 1949), but despite the differences in terminology, a growing body of empirical research agrees that private dialogues bear a relationship to psychological health and disorder. For example, the pioneering work of Ellis (1962), Meichenbaum (1977) and Schwartz (1986) amongst others, has demonstrated that private dialogues are an inevitable and basic aspect of the human condition which can influence human actions, feelings and well-being in both facilitatory and inhibitory ways. Thus, the role of private dialogues is important in the context of stressful appraisals, coping and health outcomes.

The content of private dialogues can be classified along a variety of dimensions such as unrealistic/realistic, rational/irrational, appropriate/inappropriate expectations of self, negative/positive and so on. But because terms such as 'unrealistic', 'irrational' or 'inappropriate' are notoriously elusive, empirical studies involving private dialogues ultimately base judgements on the adaptive or functional value of the dialogues (Schwartz and Gottman, 1976). Several investigators, for example, have used a positive-negative dichotomy for private dialogues in terms of their functional impact on coping with a specific situation or problem (e.g., Kendall, Williams, Pechacek, Graham, Shesslak and Herzoff, 1979; Schwartz and Gottman, 1976). In a study of assertiveness, where subjects were faced with refusing an unreasonable request, Schwartz and Gottman (1976) defined a positive self-statement such as 'I'll be sorry later if I give in and say yes' as one that facilitated the goal behaviour (in this case, refusing an unreasonable request). A negative coping thought such as 'I might get embarrassed if I say no' was defined as dialogue that interfered with the goal behaviour (i.e., made it harder to refuse the unreasonable request). Similarly, Kendall et al., (1979) operationalized the positive-negative dimension in terms of private dialogues that would help or hinder coping behaviour of patients undergoing a cardiac catheterization procedure. In this study, thoughts such as 'This procedure could save my life' were identified as positive and functional, whereas thoughts such as 'The doctor looks too young and inexperienced', were classed as negative and dysfunctional. Thus, in both studies, the positive and negative dimensions used related to the functional role of the private dialogues with respect to coping with a specific situation.

Of primary interest to this study are the cognitive processes or private dialogues which people engage in when appraising and attempting to cope with problematic situations. These will be studied by asking open-ended questions about the process of appraisal directed at:

- **Primary Appraisal** and the perceived costs in a given situation

- **Secondary Appraisal** and the options for coping

- **Reappraisal** as the situation develops and perhaps is resolved/unchanged/worsened, etc.,

- **Emotional Reactions** and the private dialogues associated with each emotion.

The qualitative data from these questions will then be used to explore and describe some of the underlying themes in the private dialogues in order to reach a deeper, fuller understanding of the relationship between appraisal, emotions, coping and health. Moreover, a review of the literature suggests that two particular areas are worthy of attention in this respect:

46

1. dialogues pertaining to attributions the individual makes about the outcome of a situation

2. dialogues relating to when an individual holds beliefs/values in an absolutist manner and a situation threatens to or actually does violate or contravene these beliefs/values.

3.4   Attributional styles in appraisal

Individuals coping with problematic situations must inevitably encounter successful and unsuccessful outcomes, both of which are of interest to this study. Research has indicated that success is usually considered to be due to one's own personal characteristics, whilst failure is seen as caused by situational factors (Arkin, Gleason and Johnston, 1976; Gooding and Kinicki, 1995; Greenberg, Pyszczynski and Solomon, 1982). These attributions are described as internal and external attributions respectively. Such attributions can be understood as attempts to explain one's own behaviour, either to others as a self-presentational tactic (Goffman, 1959) or to oneself if its meaning is not immediately clear (Bem, 1972). On the one hand, researchers studying the self-concept recognize that maintaining self-esteem is one of the primary motivators of human behaviour and cognitions (Rosenberg, 1979) whereby attributions offered to oneself about behaviour can serve an egocentric function by protecting, maintaining or enhancing self-esteem. On the other hand, students of the dramaturgical perspective (people are essentially 'actors') begin with the premise that people convey impressions to others that are as favourable as possible (Goffman, 1959). But, in either case, attributions can be biased by the idiosyncratic perspective of the individual offering them, resulting in self-serving explanations for behaviour.

Through the years there has been a steady interest in the attributional concomitants of various individual difference variables. This work has demonstrated that certain attributional styles are related to psychological well-being. More specifically, causal attributions have been examined in relation to self-esteem (Ickes and Layden, 1978; Tennen and Herzberger, 1987) depression (Anderson, Horowitz and French, 1983; Janoff-Bulman, 1979; Kuiper, 1979; Peterson, Schwartz and Seligman, 1981; Seligman, Abramson, Semmel and von Baeyer, 1979) unemployment (Ostell and Divers, 1987) and personal problem solving (Baumgardner, Heppner and Arkin, 1986).

Kuiper (1979), for example, found differences between depressed and non-depressed subjects primarily in causal attributions for failing performances; depressed subjects viewed their failing performances as due more to their own personal responsibility than did non-depressed subjects. Baumgardner et al., (1986) found that whilst self-appraised effective problem solvers did not differ from their counterparts in their ability attributions for successful performances, they did for failing attempts. Following failure, self-appraised effective problem solvers attributed their failing performances less to ability and more to external factors or lack of effort.

To elaborate on Baumgardner's findings mentioned above - ability is a property of the person, and although environmental factors may augment or deplete ability, it essentially describes the person and not the environment (Heider, 1958). Because ability is an internal, stable and relatively uncontrollable factor, individuals who make attributions to poor ability believe that there is little they can do to control the situation and succeed (Baumgardner et al., 1986). In contrast, attributions to external factors allow the individual to disown the failure and not feel personally responsible. Effort attributions lead the individual to believe that as long as s/he tries harder, s/he will be able to exert control over the situational outcome. Effort offers a unique opportunity for self-serving attributions (Elliott, 1989). As an internal, variable and potentially controllable factor, the amount of effort expended ranges from none to as much as possible and is entirely at the individual's discretion. Further it is possible to disguise the actual amount of effort given by appropriately managed impressions, e.g., making a great show of exerting effort (or not). Furthermore, it is possible to make claims about effort without much fear that they will be contradicted by other performance-relevant information since there are few independent checks on a subject's claims about effort that cannot be manipulated to his or her advantage (Elliott, 1989). Finally, as Baumgardner et al., (1986) point out, internal, controllable and variant attributions regarding efforts about problem solving would seem to increase the possibility of evoking task-oriented responses when confronted with a problem situation. But whether attributions are made to external, uncontrollable or internal, controllable factors, one implication of this self-serving pattern of attribution is that it allows the individual maximum reinforcement in evaluative settings: In cases of success, confidence is bolstered; in cases of failure, confidence is protected.

The work of Janoff-Bulman (1979) also shows evidence of a self-protective attributional bias. She posits that there are two different types of self-blame:

1. **Behavioural** self-blame representing an adaptive, control oriented response

2. **Characterological** self-blame, a maladaptive, self-deprecating response generally related to harsh self-criticism and low evaluation of one's worth.

The nature of the focus of the blame is the primary distinction between these two attributions. On the one hand, behavioural self-blame focuses on behaviour - an internal, variable, controllable source and is associated with a belief in future avoidability of other negative outcomes in similar situations. Characterological self-blame on the other hand is esteem-related and involves attributions to an internal, stable and non-controllable source, i.e., character or disposition, and is associated with a belief in personal deservingness for past and present negative outcomes. Utilizing this distinction, Janoff-Bulman (1979) found that depressed college students engaged in more characterological self-blame than non-depressed students. Using the same internal behavioural/characterological distinction, Ostell and Divers (1987) found that unemployed managers making characterological attributions for negative events had poor mental health and those managers making behavioural attributions had better mental health.

At this point, two themes emerge which are of relevance to the current study. First, these findings suggest that causal attributions for failing attempts may most clearly differentiate subjects as regards health. In other words, it is possible to hypothesize that subjects, irrespective of health, would attribute the successful outcome of a problem situation to their own abilities or skills. Second, since studies have demonstrated a relationship between various characterological/behavioural attributions and mental health, subjects in poor health would be expected to make more internal-characterological attributions for an unsuccessful problem outcome than subjects in better mental health. Conversely, those in better mental health (relative to their counterparts) would be expected to make either, more internal-behavioural attributions or more external attributions (in other words, self-serving) for their failed attempts at problem solving. In sum, a major objective of this study was to identify the dialogues associated with attributional tendencies individuals have when appraising situations with both successful and unsuccessful outcomes.

3.5   Absoluteness in appraisal

A review of other literature indicates that an attempt to identify the private dialogues associated with beliefs which are held in an absolutist manner may also prove valuable in a study of stress, coping and health. Of particular interest to this research is the way in which individuals can become distressed psychologically when situations or events threaten to or actually do contravene their beliefs or values.

The impetus for identifying this research issue derives mainly from the Rational-Emotive Therapy work of Ellis (1962), and theorists such as Horney (1950), Woolfolk and Richardson (1978) and most recently, Ostell (1988, 1992). These authors share the central assumption that emotions and behaviour are primarily a function of how environmental events are construed. But of special interest to this study is the emphasis these writers place on the private dialogues and ensuing emotional and/or behavioural disturbances which can arise when environmental events are appraised as contravening a person's absolutist beliefs or values. The potential value of identifying these dialogues in a study of stress, coping and health can be illustrated by elaborating further on the nature and emotional and/or behavioural consequences of absoluteness.

Nature and consequences of absoluteness

Ostell (1992) describes absoluteness as a learned mode of thinking which influences a person's emotional states and behaviour. In essence, it is an absolutistic outlook whereby the individual insists upon or demands conformity to certain standards of belief and/or behaviour - such demands being made either of themselves, of others, of the environment, cosmic forces, fate, etc. For example, individuals may demand that they succeed in all tasks and be approved of by everyone. Or, they may insist that others treat them fairly, or dictate that the world be more pleasant. Thus, someone who demands success in every task s/he undertakes may become very anxious about their personal abilities in a situation with an unsuccessful outcome. Similarly, someone who insists on having everyone's approval may become extremely angry if they discover that malicious gossip is being spread about them. Emotional consequences of absolutist thinking arise then, when the individual engages in a private dialogue about the events which threaten to or actually violate his or her absolutist beliefs or values. It is these dialogues and emotional consequences which are of interest to this study.

Although there is a paucity of literature in this area, a review of the existing theories suggests there are a number of themes, any one or more of which typically underpin absolutist thinking. These themes include:

Victimization/persecution complex

The person who holds beliefs in an absolutist way will sometimes evidence a persecution complex or feel victimized in the sense that they or others are being compelled to experience something unpleasant or are the victims of negative interference (Woolfolk and Richardson, 1978). This particularly applies when another person is the agent of the misfortune, and even more so if the offending actions are construed as intentional. Actions which are perceived as both unjustified and intentional are likely to arouse especially strong emotions, particularly anger (Woolfolk and Richardson, 1978).

A sense of injustice

Closely related to feelings of victimization are the perceptions of injustice or inequity characterized by the shoulds, oughts and 'musturbatory' beliefs which can underpin absoluteness (Ellis, 1962; Horney, 1950). This moralistic way of thinking typically results in the individual legislating, demanding or insisting upon certain standards of behaviour of themselves and/or other people. For instance, someone who shares a confidence with a trusted friend may react angrily on discovering that the confidence has been broken because the friend has violated that person's beliefs about keeping confidences. The subject feels they have been unjustly or unfairly treated and may 'demand' that the offending party rectifies matters in some way (Ostell, 1992).

Demands for perfectionism or infallibility

Absolutist beliefs about standards of belief and/or behaviour are often underpinned by a demand for or an insistence on perfectionism (Ellis and Harper, 1975). Perfectionistic standards may be demanded of their own or other people's behaviour or performances in a given situation such that any behaviour(s) or performances which fall short of perfection lead to self-deprecatory thoughts, self-blame or ruminations about other people's shortcomings. These dialogues then engender emotions such as anger, anxiety, guilt, shame and so on. Along this line, demands for perfectionism are closely allied to demands for infallibility. This makes it difficult for the individual to accept their own limitations and/or the fallibility of human beings in a more general sense. Thus, a person might demand that situations they are coping with should always be resolved satisfactorily or that other people should always be able to cope effectively.

Unwillingness/inability to be flexible

The demanding, dogmatic nature of absoluteness frequently entails that the individual is unwilling and/or unable to see a situation from another person's point of view (Woolfolk and Richardson, 1978). Typically, the absolutistic nature of the beliefs and values held are adhered to so unswervingly and rigidly that the individual displays an unwillingness and/or inability to identify with and understand a frame of reference other than their own. Their point of view or perspective is thus inflexible and resistant to change.

To summarize, feeling victimized, demands for perfectionism, a sense of injustice and the inability/unwillingness to change beliefs and/or behaviours are some of the cognitive/behavioural consequences of absoluteness. Also, because every individual has certain personal beliefs and values, shaped by cognitive development and varying cultural emphases, it seems reasonable to assume that absolutist thinking will be present to a greater or lesser degree in everyone. However, the discriminating factor is the extent to which the private dialogues associated with absoluteness are functional in terms of appraisal, coping and health. Essentially, it is the magnitude of the discrepancy between what is actually happening and what the individual demands should or ought to be happening that influences the private dialogues in appraisal, which in turn influences the level of emotional arousal and ultimately, coping behaviour and health. Indeed, it is important to restate here the point made in chapter 1, that although the dialogues originate from appraisal of the problematic situation, they are often deflected to other superordinate goals and concerns and may become a problem in their own right. In this study of stress appraisals, coping and health, therefore, it is both the dialogues and the consequences of the dialogues relating to absoluteness which are of particular interest.

At this juncture it is worth noting that although absolutist thinking can lead to a variety of emotional reactions, anger is said to be a particularly common emotional reaction to situations where an individual's experience is discrepant from their expectations. (Braham, 1994; Novaco, 1979; Ostell, 1988, 1992; Woolfolk and Richardson, 1978.) This is noteworthy for two reasons: First, in stress research there is a tendency to focus predominantly on anxiety-type emotional reactions with other affective responses like anger and frustration being largely overlooked (Keenan and Newton, 1984, 1985; Newton, 1989; Spector, 1975; Storms and Spector, 1987) even though hostile reactions such as anger and frustration may be as common, if not more common, responses to stress than anxiety. Second, anger is commonly viewed in negative terms because of its role as an affective stress reaction that has adverse implications for health and behaviour (Novaco, 1979). For instance, anger can have enduring negative effects on the individual, including increased blood pressure, a tightening of muscles and changes in respiratory rate (Braham, 1994). Sometimes, an individual who is angry may be inclined towards aggressive behaviours and then, the enduring effects can be on others as well as the individual and cause impairment to social relationships (Novaco, 1976). Hence, anger can have deleterious consequences that go beyond the experience of a negative emotional state and have adverse implications for health, performance and social relationships. This reflects the severity of anger as a stress reaction and highlights its potential as a predictor of psychological health and physical symptoms. Given this, the potential value of attempting to identify the private dialogues associated with and emotional consequences of absoluteness is further increased.

So far in this chapter, it has been argued that whilst many studies place great theoretical emphasis on the central role of appraisal, empirically it is largely ignored. The rationale has been developed for designing a study which attempts to redress this balance by identifying the cognitive processes or private dialogues relating to inherent costs in a given situation, emotional reactions, attributions about the situation's outcome as well as the dialogues associated with absoluteness. These data should permit exploration and description of the interplay between situational and environmental factors and facilitate understanding of both the aetiology of stress reactions and the appraisal, coping and health relationship. In addition, reasons have been given for assessing the impact of environmental demands with measures which tap into appraisal of the demands whilst controlling for the potential confounding effects of negative and positive emotionality.

In the next section of this chapter, this literature review remains focused on the process of appraisal, but refers particularly to the assessment of internal and external resources and the important role they can play in stressful appraisals and coping.

3.6   Appraisal, coping and resources

In this study, stress is conceptualized as a dynamic, bidirectional relationship between the person and the environment, with stress reactions occurring when the person appraises the situation as being problematic with important costs and recognizes that the environmental demands tax his or her coping resources (Lazarus and Folkman, 1984).   This cognitive theory of psychological stress highlights the interplay between demands emanating from the environment and the resources which the individual can bring to meet those demands.   It also acknowledges how coping resources may moderate psycho/physiological strain and health as well as affect stress appraisals (e.g., Lazarus and Launier, 1978). According to this theory, coping resources can be drawn from within the person (internal resources such as locus of control, beliefs about self-efficacy, skills, health and energy, etc.,) or from the environment (external resources such as information, financial assistance, practical help, etc.).   Such resources are a crucial component of the stress, appraisal and coping process for two reasons.   First, they provide a key set of data for the person to evaluate when appraising any transaction for its impact on well-being.   Second, they provide the basis of coping action depending, of course, on knowledge about them and how they can be used (Folkman, Schaefer and Lazarus, 1979).   Theoretically then, both internal and external coping resources are acknowledged as a vital component of the stress and coping process. However, in the discussion that follows it is the contention that whilst the importance of internal and external resources has been emphasized theoretically, empirical studies have:

- tended to focus only on internal resources using quantitative assessments which have limited explanatory power, and

- have largely overlooked the primary role which external resources can play in the stress process.

3.7   Internal resources: control and self-efficacy

Turning first to consider internal resources, two cognitive constructs have generated much interest: perceived control and perceived self-efficacy (Turk, Meichenbaum and Genest, 1983) and these are of special concern to this study. Perceived control refers to the belief that one has at one's disposal a response that can influence the aversiveness of a situation (Thompson, 1981).   Perceived self-efficacy refers to confidence in one's ability to adequately carry out the necessary behavioural and cognitive strategies required to produce a successful outcome (Bandura, 1977).   Thus, perceived control relates to perceptions of the availability of a response, whereas self-efficacy relates to confidence in being able to effect that response. Several writers agree that perceptions of control and self-efficacy play a prominent role among internal coping resources (e.g., Kobasa, 1979; Folkman, 1984; Moos and Billings, 1982; Pearlin and Schooler, 1978) and consequently, these constructs were considered worthy of attention in this study. Both are discussed in relation to why and how they were assessed in this research.

Perceived control

The concept of perceived control has generated much research and speculation, particularly as a mediator of the impact of aversive events (e.g., Miller and Grant, 1979). Writers usually distinguish between two different forms of control - generalized and situational appraisals of control. Both are of interest in the context of coping. Generalized beliefs about control are likened to Rotter's (1966) locus of control and, because internal locus of control is associated with the tendency to assume that one can affect outcomes, generalized control beliefs may reduce the likelihood of primary appraisal as threatening or harmful. Situational appraisals of control are part of secondary appraisal when attention is focused on identifying appropriate responses rather than evaluating the stressor (Folkman, 1984).

Many studies have indicated that the presence or absence of control can have profound effects on behaviour and health, but the relationship between perceived control and these outcomes is complex. Some studies, for example, have shown that when certain situations are appraised as uncontrollable, a host of physiological changes can occur including increased heart rate, excess production of adrenocortical and adrenomedullary hormones and decreased immunological activity (Glass, Reim and Singer, 1971). Lack of control has also been shown to promote 'helplessness', a syndrome of cognitive, motivational and emotional deficits produced by the belief that events are uncontrollable (Cvetanovski and Jex, 1994; Seligman, 1975). Losing control (relative to never having had control) has been associated with frustration and prolonged depression (Krause and Stryker, 1984).

Other studies have indicated that demanding situations in which there is the opportunity for control can lead to reduced physiological arousal. The majority of studies manipulating behavioural control have found that it affects both physiological arousal and self-report of discomfort in the anticipatory period before an aversive event (Thompson, 1981), such as receiving shock (Szpiler and Epstein, 1976) or exposure to loud noise (Glass et al., 1971). The importance of control in facing demands has also been recognized by 'stressful life events' researchers. Kasl (1983) in reviewing the literature, suggested that 'the controllability and predictability of life events have been especially singled out as important qualities which can modify events' (1983, p.95). Hence, anticipated life events such as retirement, which are within the subject's control, are associated with more positive appraisals and health outcomes than life events such as the death of a spouse or close family member.

However, other studies have shown the obverse to be true. Mills and Krantz (1979) for example showed that having control can be stress inducing when having control is antagonistic to an individual's preferred style. In their study of blood donors, Mills and Krantz found those individuals who received more detailed information (i.e., more control) about the blood drawing procedures **than they would have preferred**, were more distressed than subjects who received limited information (i.e., less control). Here, increased choice and participation (control) in the blood drawing procedure apparently heightened stress. Along this line, Folkman (1984) theorized how control can be stress-inducing when the exercise of control yields negative social consequences, e.g., when the control to take particular actions is potentially damaging to interpersonal relationships. Or again, as Folkman points out, the potential for control can have ambiguous outcomes for the individual. Consider a cancer victim who is given the option of control over the malignancy through chemotherapy. On the one hand the option of control may result in the disease being contained. On the other hand, that control may exact a cost on the person's physical and psychological well-being by causing nausea, hair loss, depression and so on. In this case, the potential for control can have conflicting outcomes for the individual.

There are, then, many complex sub-themes underlying the relation between appraisals of control, coping and outcomes which are determined by the interrelation between cognitive, situational and dispositional characteristics in specific situations. But it is the nature of this interrelation that is still not well understood (Folkman, 1984). Consequently, beliefs about control, whether they are shaped by generalized beliefs or by situational variants, need to be examined in the context of specific stressful encounters in order to facilitate understanding of the personal meaning or significance of control in relation to what is at stake for the individual and what the costs/benefits of exercising control might be (Folkman, 1984).

Questions need to be asked about perceptions of control in relation to specific situations and the data should then permit exploration of the question 'Control over what?' so that we might better understand which facets of the situation are the targets of control. Furthermore, the data should allow description of the fit between appraisals of controllability and situational contingencies and coping behaviours. In sum, the data should go some way towards increasing understanding of how perceptions of control ultimately influence appraisal, coping behaviours and stress-related adaptational outcomes.

Perceived self-efficacy

The other internal resource which was considered worthy of exploration in this study is perceived self-efficacy. Related conceptually to the locus of control variable, self-efficacy refers to the belief that one can adequately carry out the necessary behaviours and cognitions required to produce a successful outcome in a given situation (Bandura, 1977). So, whereas perceived control relates to the availability of an effective coping response, self-efficacy relates to having confidence in being able to carry out the necessary response. In this sense, self-efficacy is a self-generated evaluation and represents a person's confidence in his or her ability to behave in such a way as to produce a desirable outcome. Like control, self-efficacy beliefs can be both generalized and specific, for although self-efficacy was primarily conceptualized as a situation-specific belief, there is evidence that experiences of personal mastery, over time, contribute to efficacy expectations more generally (Bandura, 1977).

According to self-efficacy theory, expectations of personal mastery are based on four main sources of information:

1. **Performance accomplishments**
    This source of efficacy information is particularly influential because it is based on experiences of personal mastery whereby repeated successes raise efficacy expectations and repeated failures lower them.

2. **Vicarious experiences**
    These efficacy expectations are derived from vicarious experiences; seeing others cope with events successfully without adverse consequences, which then generates expectations in the observer that they too should be able to deal with a similar situation successfully. Relying as it does on social comparisons, vicarious experiences are thought to be a less dependable source of information about personal capabilities than is direct evidence of personal accomplishments (Bandura, 1977).

3. **Verbal persuasion**
    Efficacy expectations can be induced by verbal persuasion whereby people are led, through persuasive suggestion, to believe they can cope successfully with given situations. Like vicarious experiences though, efficacy expectations induced by verbal persuasion lack an authentic, experiential base and are, therefore, likely to be weaker than expectations arising from personal accomplishments (Bandura, 1977).

4. **Emotional arousal**
    Emotional arousal is the fourth constituent source of information that can affect perceived self-efficacy in coping with problem situations. States of emotional and accompanying physiological arousal can have informative value concerning personal competency, since individuals are more likely to expect success when they are not experiencing aversive arousal.

In the context of stress and coping, this construct is of interest because self-efficacy theory asserts that personal mastery expectations can exert powerful influences on behaviour. For instance, someone who judges themselves incapable of managing a situation may react with fear and avoidant-type coping strategies and have little if any motivation to deal with the problem directly. Conversely, someone who is confident about their capabilities of managing a situation may react assuredly and be motivated to utilize direct action problem solving strategies and be persistent in their efforts if they are not initially successful (Bandura, 1977). Thus, self-efficacy can influence both the choice of coping activities and whether or not coping behaviour will be attempted in the first place. Through expectations of eventual success, self-efficacy can affect persistence of coping efforts, how much effort a person will expend when dealing with a problem situation and the emotional reactions to the problem (Bandura, 1977; Moos and Billings, 1982; Moriarty, Douglas, Punch and Hattie, 1995).

A large body of empirical research is congruent with this theory and has indicated that self-efficacy beliefs predict behaviours across a wide range of situations. The behavioural domains that have been examined have tended to be in laboratory settings involving severe or unusual situations and have included increased tolerance and decreased distress in response to pain (Litt, 1988), agoraphobia (Williams and Rappoport, 1983), reducing anxiety during a final exam (Houston, 1977), and postsurgical recovery (Cohen and Lazarus, 1973). For example, Litt (1988) showed that manipulating efficacy expectations brought about changes in the subjects tolerance of pain in a cold-pressor task. Williams and Rappoport (1983) reported that female agorophobic patients with high self-efficacy levels performed better on a behavioural test than subjects low in self-efficacy.

Relatively little research, however, appears to have examined self-efficacy beliefs in the context of everyday-type coping with problematic situations. Aldwin and Revenson (1987) assessed coping efficacy by asking respondents how well they had handled a given situation and the findings indicated that when coping efforts were perceived as successful, physical symptoms markedly decreased. But to date, it seems no studies have attempted to explore the factors which influence self-efficacy beliefs of individuals coping with everyday-type problem situations. Yet these factors are the key to understanding how self-efficacy expectations affect appraisal, motivation and persistence in coping, actual coping behaviours, emotional reactions and ultimately adaptational outcomes.

Open-ended questions about self-efficacy or confidence need to be asked, therefore, in relation to subjects attempting to cope with everyday problem situations. These questions need to be directed at three main objectives to determine:

- the magnitude or strength of the self-efficacy beliefs

- the factor(s) which influence the strength of the self-efficacy beliefs

- what impact the perceptions of self-efficacy have on appraisal, motivation, coping options and responses and emotional reactions.

3.8   External resources

Turning now to examine the role of external resources in the stress, coping and health relation, let us first consider the theoretical emphasis on coping resources. In their discussion of cognitive appraisal, Lazarus and Launier (1978) distinguished between primary appraisal - the evaluation of whether the situation constitutes a threat to self-esteem, goals, physical health, etc., and secondary appraisal - the evaluation of coping resources and viable coping options with respect to the demands of the situation. Then, to illustrate the interrelatedness of primary and secondary appraisal and how they affect the coping process, Lazarus and Launier give a detailed account of how five individuals with access to different coping resources might appraise the same situation in vastly different ways, with different coping options, different coping choices and differences in emotional distress.

Stated briefly, the authors discussed how five people might appraise the same situation - an upcoming job interview. They theorize that in terms of primary appraisal, all the individuals appraise it as threatening because they all anticipate being rejected. But the degree of threat is affected by secondary appraisal. Differing secondary appraisal results in different coping options, different coping responses and different distress levels. For example, one individual thinks that he will probably be rejected, doubts his interview abilities, can get no advice, has no-one to help in the situation and reacts with hopelessness and despair. In contrast, another individual also thinks that he will probably be rejected, but knows the personnel manager, thinks he might be able to help in finding alternative employment, and reacts with determination and hope. Thus, secondary appraisal for the first individual not only reinforces the threat but also results in feelings of despair and hopelessness, considerably reduces viable coping options, and results in a decision not to bother with the interview at all. However, the individual who has access to practical assistance/emotional support/help from the personnel manager, feels only mildly threatened by the potential rejection, sees a number of possible coping options available and is motivated to deal with the situation.

Here, Lazarus and Launier's intention is to illustrate how secondary appraisal, oriented as it is to possible coping resources and options, not only influences primary appraisal itself, mitigating or enhancing threat or the sense of harm, but also shapes coping activity. Elaborating on this theme, the authors say that

> The central reason why secondary appraisal has so much to do with primary appraisal of harm-loss, threat and challenge is to be found in the definition of psychological stress itself. A potential harm is not a harm if

the person can master it easily, and if it is appraised as such there is little or no threat. The resources a person believes are available are arranged psychologically against the dangers and harms being faced, and are **a crucial cognitive factor** in the generation of the psychological stress response.

(Lazarus and Launier, 1978, p.308, added emphasis)

This example and quotation illustrate the theoretical emphasis on the primary role of the individual's internal and external resources in influencing appraisal and shaping coping activity. Nonetheless, whilst the importance of resources is stressed theoretically, most studies conceptualizing stress as a person-environment transaction appear to have largely ignored the importance of external resources empirically (Newton, 1989; Oakland and Ostell, 1995). In chapter 2, for instance, a review of the literature showed that many studies typically use coping inventories containing items such as 'Sought more information about the problem' (Folkman and Lazarus, 1980) or 'Tried to get emotional support from friends or relatives' (Carver et al., 1989) or 'Asked for advice' (McCrae, 1984). But these studies never ask, 'Was the information available and adequate?' or 'Was the advice forthcoming and helpful?' or 'Do you have access to emotional support, and if so, what is the quality of that support?' Instead, most empirical studies tend to focus on internal resources and fail to consider that appraisal and coping may be as much shaped by the availability and adequacy of **external** resources which are available (Newton, 1989).

Take a simple example. Consider an individual who has been made redundant after 25 years loyal service with an organization. How that person appraises, reacts to and copes with this situation will be shaped by the availability of resources s/he has to meet the situational demands. Aside from personological resources (such as self-esteem, hardiness, Type A behaviour, etc.) the availability and adequacy of external resources such as finances, emotional support, advice, information and practical help will affect appraisal, possible coping options, actual coping responses and the amount of stress experienced. For instance, someone with adequate financial resources might appraise their redundancy as only a minimal threat relative to someone who has no available finances. Adequate information and expert advice about future employment could broaden the range of coping options, motivate the individual to seek alternative work and thereby effectively buffer the level of stress experienced. Without adequate information and advice, the individual may be at a loss regarding viable options for coping, not be motivated to look for another position at all, and become depressed at the hopelessness of the situation. Consequently, how the individual copes with being made redundant will be a function of internal personal resources (personality, health, etc.) but it will also be shaped by the availability and adequacy of external resources. Studies which attach primary salience to internal resources but overlook external resources are, therefore, ignoring a critical variable in the stress, coping and health relation.

There are some exceptions, whereby some person-environment studies do acknowledge external resources (Billings and Moos, 1981, 1984; Buunk and Peeters, 1994; Morrissey, Becker and Rubert, 1990; Roy and Steptoe, 1994; Sarason, Levine, Basham and Sarason, 1983; Schuler, 1982; Sheffield, Dobbie and Carroll, 1994; Solomon et al., 1990). For example, Billings and Moos (1981) found in a study of individuals coping with stressful events, that mood and symptom levels were related to both coping responses and measures of social resources. Similarly, Solomon et al., (1990) studied the relationship between life-events, coping strategies and social resources on the one hand and somatic complaints of Israeli soldiers on the other. Their findings indicated that the severity of somatization among the soldiers was related to life-events, social resources and coping strategies, and that even when life-events and coping strategies were controlled for, social resources made a direct and unique contribution to somatization.

However, even in the studies which do acknowledge external resources, there is a tendency to place the emphasis on **social** resource adequacy (e.g., emotional support or help from colleagues, friends or relatives) such that other external resources like financial resources, tangible assistance or help , advice or more information are overlooked. Indeed, of the studies mentioned above which acknowledge external resources, only the recent work by Morrissey et al., (1990) has assessed the adequacy of both social and financial external resources. Of course, some studies choose to ignore personological variables and focus only on external environmental factors in the stress/strain relationship (e.g., Karasek, 1979; Payne and Fletcher, 1983) but are necessarily deficient in explanatory power (Newton, 1989; Oakland and Ostell, 1995).

In order to reach a better understanding of stress appraisals, coping and health, therefore, it was necessary to design a methodology which quantitatively assesses the adequacy of external resources. This would help to redress the apparent imbalance between theory and practice and allow the importance of external resources to be stressed theoretically and their adequacy to be studied empirically. For it would seem that Lazarus's (1966) highly influential cognitive theory of stress, which has been used as the basis for much research, has oriented stress research towards the perspective of the individual and how s/he perceives and evaluates events, and away from considering how environmental factors may determine both how an individual copes with stressful situations and the amount of psychological distress experienced (Newton, 1989; Oakland and Ostell, 1995). Take, for instance, Schuler's (1982) study which does consider environmental factors. Even here it is apparent that the locus of coping is still viewed as lying with the individual. Schuler suggests that 'individuals who have socially supportive relationships are more physiologically capable of dealing with stress because of the acceptance shown by others' (Schuler, 1982, pp.11-12). Yet he goes on to describe social support as an 'individual characteristic' and does not address the question of whether social support is available as an environmental, variable characteristic. This theoretical emphasis on individual characteristics is also reflected in a comment from Lazarus and his colleagues (Lazarus, Cohen, Folkman, Kanner and Schaefer, 1980) on research attempts to link stressful phenomena to longer term health problems:

> What is left out here is the possibility that recurrent or stable psychological characteristics, **regardless of the environmental situation**, entail physiological consequences which might eventually result in disease.

> (Lazarus et al., 1980, p.100, added emphasis)

Quotations such as this reflect the theoretical emphasis on personological variables in coping which has seemingly oriented much research towards studying individual characteristics, but away from empirically assessing salient factors such as the adequacy of external resources. This constitutes a major limitation since external resources can play a crucial role in determining appraisal, coping options, coping responses and magnitude of affect arousal (Oakland and Ostell, 1995).

Quantitative measures need to be developed therefore to assess the adequacy of external resources such as information, advice, emotional support, finances and practical assistance whilst open-ended questions must be asked to explore **how** external resource availability affects appraisal, coping options, coping responses and experienced stress.

3.9   Summary of research issues and objectives

A number of important research issues have been identified in this chapter. Foremost in this regard is the need to study cognitive appraisal which, it has been argued, is theoretically emphasized as a crucial part of the stress, coping and health relationship but, tends to have been empirically overlooked. It has been suggested, therefore, that when situational demands are being quantitatively assessed, efforts should be made to design measures which tap into appraisal of those demands. Further, since the dispositional trait measures of negativity and positivity have been highlighted as potentially confounding influences on both situational appraisals and subjective reporting of health status, recommendations have been made for partialling out their effects before arriving at conclusions about stressor/strain relationships. Furthermore, the private dialogues in appraisal, particularly those relating to absoluteness and attributional styles have been suggested as potentially valuable research issues for increasing understanding of the stress, coping and health process. These dialogues will be best studied using a methodology which can explore, describe and assess their role in the process. Finally, attention has been drawn to the potentially powerful influence on appraisal and coping of internal resources such as perceptions of control and self-efficacy and external resources such as finances, more information, practical help and so on. Again, these issues need to be explored and described if we are to progress in our understanding of their function in the stress process.

The above research issues, when integrated with some of the main points arising from discussion in chapters 1 and 2, gave rise to the following research objectives:

- To study stress and coping with everyday-type problem situations at work. *(Because studies of coping with unusual situations are limited in terms of generalizability and there are relatively few studies of coping at work).*

- To ask subjects how they actually coped with the situations. *(Because asking how people usually cope accesses their semantic, rather than episodic, memory).*

- To examine problem and emotion focused coping strategies and whether or not they were effective. *(Both problem and emotion focused strategies are important for coping and health and previous studies have not assessed coping efficacy).*

- To quantitatively assess the relationship between occupational demands and health outcomes using a measure which taps into appraisal of those demands. *(Many job stress studies make a priori assumptions about appraisal directionality).*

- To explore the potentially confounding effects on appraisal of occupational demands and reported health status of negative and positive emotionality (NEM and PEM). *(NEM/PEM may influence environmental and subjective appraisals).*

- To explore and describe the dialogues in appraisal associated with attributional biases and absoluteness and to examine their role in the aetiology of stress reactions, in affecting coping behaviours and ultimately, situational and health outcomes. *(Theory suggests these dialogues are a crucial part of the stress/health process, but empirically, these dialogues have been overlooked).*

- To examine the role of perceptions of control and self-efficacy in appraisals and coping. *(Previous research has not examined the factors which underlie these perceptions).*

- To explore, describe and measure the impact on stress appraisals and coping of in/adequate external resources.
  (Theoretically, resources play an important role in the coping process but most studies focus on resource availability and fail to address resource adequacy).

- To design a methodology which permits exploration and description of stress, coping and health as a dynamic, multi-dimensional process.
  (Most studies adhere to predominantly quantitative approaches which mask the subtleties of a process).

The overarching objectives of this study therefore were to explore, describe and assess the ways in which headteachers react to and attempt to cope with stressful situations at work and to determine the implications for situational outcomes, psychological well-being and somatic health. The methods used to achieve these objectives and the reasons why headteachers were chosen for this study are described in the next chapter.

4 Research design and data collection

This chapter focuses on the reasons for choosing the sample and the methods used in designing the questionnaire and semi-structured interview schedule which were used in this study (both of which could be used, with only minor modifications, by anyone undertaking research into stress, coping and health in virtually any sample group). Issues of reliability, validity and data analysis are considered along with access to the sample and data collection.

4.1   Stress and education

Since the early 1970's, education in England and Wales has been characterized by rapid and almost continuous changes (Maclure, 1988). Comprehensivization, new systems of public examinations and the raising of the school leaving age have all resulted in radical changes in teaching methods and curricula.

Changes have also occurred in the public demands made on education. Since the introduction of Personal and Social Development in 1970, headteachers and their staff have responsibility for teaching about such matters as road safety, morality, sex education, smoking, alcoholism, current social issues, politics, pollution, careers education and other areas not previously considered to be in the school's province. Employers have become more involved with the state educational system and teachers and heads are required to co-operate with Work Experience Schemes. Education, which used to be the exclusive province of teachers, is now the concern of the nation as a whole, with Central Government taking a very active role in the formulation of the curriculum. As a result, education in general, and teachers and headteachers in particular, are much more publicly accountable for their work. This increasing clamour for public accountability was exacerbated by the 1981 Education Act (Walford, 1994) requiring the publication of all written reports made by H M Inspectors after an inspection of a school as well as the compulsory publication of a prospectus for every school and all the examination results.

A major consequence of these changes is that they have necessitated radical changes in teaching methods, in the curriculum taught, in the administration required to maintain schools generally, and particularly in the duties headteachers are expected to perform. As a result, there has been increasing professional and public interest in issues relating to stress and education and for more than a decade, researchers have attempted to describe the problems faced by educationalists and the effects of those problems on both their well-being and work performance (Boyle, Borg, Falzon and Baglioni, 1995; Burke and Greenglass, 1995; Cooper, 1995; Cox, 1977; Cox, Boot and Cox, 1989; Dewe, 1986; Dunham, 1984; Fontana and Abouserie, 1993; Kyriacou, 1987; Kyriacou and Pratt, 1985; Payne and Fletcher, 1983; Pithers and Fogarty, 1995; Proctor and Alexander, 1992; Pullis, 1992; Sheffield, Dobbie and Carroll, 1994).

A review of the occupational stress literature in education indicates that teachers are the popular target for such research. Low pay, heavy workload, long hours, low morale throughout the profession, increasing pupil behavioural problems and decreasing rights for punishment have emerged as some of the main causes of teacher stress and job dissatisfaction. These causes of teacher stress have been so widely publicized that they are familiar not only to occupational stress researchers, but also to the public at large. Interestingly however, relatively few occupational stress studies have targeted **head**teachers (Cooper and Kelly, 1993; Oakland, 1991; Sihera, 1989). Generally speaking, most studies of headteachers are concerned with the recruitment and retention of headteachers (Earley and Baker, 1989) or with examining the headteacher's role in innovation (Hughes, 1975) or the head's role in change (Burgess, 1983) or with monitoring and evaluating headteacher duties and performance (Morris, 1981; Wolcott, 1973). For example, Wolcott's pioneering ethnographic study of one elementary school principal and the research of Morris, in eight primary and six secondary schools where the headteachers were shadowed for up to 12 days over a 2-year period, showed that most time was taken up with one-to-one personal interactions, meetings and telephone calls. Yet few studies have been concerned with headteacher health and well-being and it was this lack of attention in previous studies to headteacher stress and occupational health which prompted the focus, for this research, on headteachers as opposed to teachers.

The focus on headteachers is indeed timely since the 1988 Education Reform Act (ERA) has brought about profound changes in education generally, but particularly to the role of headship. Under this legislation, many of the head's traditional educational powers, over the curriculum and school standards for example, have been taken over by the Government. In return, heads have been given new managerial and financial powers in abundance, powers for which as trained educationalists, they had little if any training. Since the inception of the Act there has been prolific media coverage about the deleterious effects of these changes on schools, on head recruitment figures and the increase in the number of headteachers taking early retirement on the grounds of stress and ill-health (Earley and Baker, 1989). A brief overview of the Education Reform Act will make it easier to understand why it is bringing about such profound changes in schools and how it is compelling headteachers to undertake major changes in their role.

4.2   Education Reform Act (ERA) 1988

The 1988 Education Reform Act has been described as 'a watershed in the history of education in this country' (Scott, 1994) and 'the most important and far-reaching piece of educational law-making for England and Wales since the Education Act of 1944' (Maclure, 1988). The controversial Act has also been called 'a Gothic monstrosity of legislation' (*The Independent*, 4/9/1989). With its 238 clauses and 13 schedules, the Act is effectively five Acts rolled into one and, as Maclure (1988) notes, few other Acts have attempted so ambitiously to entirely re-design a major public service. Kenneth Baker, the then Secretary of State for Education, said he saw it as an attempt to raise standards by freeing schools from professional and bureaucratic straightjackets, by creating a service that responds to its consumers' needs. Many critics, pointing to Baker's 415 new powers, saw it as an irreversible shift of power to the centre, the biggest attack on local democracy this century.

The five major facets of the Reform Act can be summarized as follows:

1.   *National Curriculum*

Described as the 'corner-stone' of the reforms, the National Curriculum requires that maths, English, science, history, geography, technology, music, art and physical education are taught to children of all ages. The Government no longer require that particular periods of time should be allocated to particular subjects. New clauses make it clear that schools are solely responsible for delivery of the curriculum. Her Majesty's Inspectors must assess the children and the school and publish all critical reports. Local authorities must set up complaints procedures for parents dissatisfied with how schools are carrying out the curriculum and assessments.

2.   *Opting out*

All secondary schools and those schools with more than 300 pupils are able to opt out of local authority control and become grant-maintained schools funded directly from Whitehall. Though the paymaster will be different, grant-maintained schools receive money for current spending on the same basis as those schools under local education authority control. However, the governors' powers to control admissions and to hire and fire staff is greater and there are no local authority nominees on governing bodies.

3.   *Open enrolment*

With open enrolment, parents may enrol their children at any school which has the physical capacity for them, providing that the school caters for the appropriate age range and aptitude of the child. The local authorities and governors, but not the headteachers, can agree to increase the 'standard' number (i.e., the maximum acceptable number of pupils for that school).

4.   *Local management of schools*

All secondary schools and primary schools with more than 200 pupils receive budgets from the local authority which they are free to spend as they wish. Technically, local authorities will continue to employ headteachers; in practice, heads and governors make the decisions. Schools now decide how money will be spent and operate as if they are small businesses. Income depends on the school's success in attracting 'customers'.

5.   *Religious education*

Although religious education is not included in the national curriculum, schools must now provide it for all pupils. In some respects, schools have more freedom than under the 1944 Act because the daily act of worship can take place at any time of the day - not just at the beginning - and it need not involve all pupils simultaneously. However, in other respects, requirements are tightened. 'Broadly Christian' worship is specified for the first time, although heads who have large numbers of pupils from minority religions can apply to the local Standing Advisory Council for a waiver from the 'in the main' Christian worship requirement. But on this, heads must consult governors who may, in turn, consult parents.

4.3   Headship and the Education Reform Act

What then are some of the main implications the Education Reform Act has for headteachers? Perhaps the most notable change is the local management of schools (LMS). With LMS, control of the school budget is passed from local education authorities to headteachers and governors. This demands an enormous change in role since before 1988, headteachers typically had control of around 4% of their school budget; by 1990, this had risen dramatically to up to 97% (*Financial Times* 4/6/90). An average-sized secondary modern school of between 600-800 pupils, for example, will have an annual budget of about one million pounds.

Thus, heads are now facing a specialist learning curve as their school takes on all the basic computer requirements of a small commercial business, such as accounting, payroll and stock control. There is also a need to adopt sophisticated financial modelling facilities so headteachers can work out the implications of different spending patterns for the most efficient use of resources. In addition, heads now have to plan ahead to cope with demographic changes like falling pupil rolls which will have an effect on the budget and staffing requirements.

Heads are now responsible for overspending on their budgets but have no control over the amount they receive, most of which comes from Local Education Authorities on a per capita basis. Although more pupils means more money, schools have little flexibility over how it is spent and, basing the budget on pupil numbers has already been shown to widen social inequalities (Edwards, Fitz and Whitty, 1989; Walford, 1994). Schools in wealthy towns can attract monies and are more likely to be able to recruit financial experts onto their board of governors and get contributions from parents.

Moreover, basing the budget on pupil numbers has inevitably caused tension between local schools competing for children in areas of falling rolls. This happened in Peterborough, where the first LMS pilot schemes were held (*Financial Times*, 4/6/1990). Thus, the desire to attract more pupils and increase the budget requires a change in the educational ethos; heads now need to be increasingly conscious of the way they market the school. They must think of the school as a commercial enterprise where the end products are people (i.e., children). This fundamental change loads every other shift in the headteacher's role with crucial importance: success breeds success and earns money; failure is automatically followed by loss of resources and ultimately, closure of the school. Thus LMS is demanding a cultural change of headteachers, many of whom are temperamentally opposed to the very idea of marketing. For instance, in a report from the National Association of Headteachers (NAHT), some heads claimed they felt they were running a business where the people controlling the money flow (the councillors) did not care about the finished product (the pupils) (*The Guardian*, 27/3/1990).

The changes relating to the National Curriculum and assessment of pupils also have many implications for the role of headteachers. Under the 1988 legislation, the National Curriculum is determined by statutory orders made by the Secretary of State for Education. This has been the subject of continued political debate ever since the inception of the ERA. Traditionally, the school curriculum has always been regarded as 'the teacher's secret garden' (*The Independent*, 4/9/1989) and as Wilby and Crequer (1989) point out, until the Act it would have been almost unthinkable for the Government to dictate on such matters as grammar's place in English, the role of the calculator in mathematics or the emphasis on British heritage in history. Moreover, prior to the Act, Local Authorities adopted a largely non-interventionist policy too; only Her Majesty's Inspectors offered guidance and advice to schools. Now, the Government determines the curriculum, children must be assessed and critical reports on schools and children made publicly available.

There is evidence that this increased clamour for public accountability is pressurizing some headteachers (Halstead, 1994). Only months after the beginning of the Act, the National Association of Headteachers (NAHT) reported that some heads 'are being pushed to the verge of suicide' when they are publicly shamed by the publication of HMI's critical reports on their schools. As one head put it, when condemning the Government's decision to publish HMI reports,

> In a small community where everybody knows everybody else and their business, a teacher and in particular senior teachers and heads, cannot separate professional life from social and personal life. Public criticism of professional life has a devastating effect on the whole of that person's life and on his or her family. The hurt, the pain which is caused, is totally inappropriate, totally negative, totally appalling.

(Walter Ievers, Primary school head in Bangor)

More recently a similar knock-on effect of public accountability is that many schools are increasingly reluctant to accept children with behavioural problems because of the impact these children may have on the school's published examination league tables (*The Times,* 30/1/1995).

In summary, the Education Reform Act is demanding of heads not just a role change, but a role reversal. Prior to the Act the authorities determined resources, number of teachers and their pay scales, the pupil-teacher ratio, spending on buildings, money for books and equipment and so on. Heads were responsible for educational decisions, the subjects to be taught and their content, when and how to assess children and what to tell parents. In the 1990's roles are almost exactly reversed. Syllabuses and assessment are largely determined by the Government. There are precise regulations about child assessment and about informing parents. Heads are responsible for maintaining the school building, paying the fuel bills, and deciding how much is spent on books and how much on teachers.

In view of this, it is hardly surprising that a survey by the National Foundation of Educational Research on behalf of the NAHT reported that headteachers and their deputies are 'punch drunk' at having to introduce so many changes in schools, so fast, and that morale is 'very low' with heads having insufficient time to cope with administrative work or prepare themselves for an increasingly managerial role in their school (*The Guardian*, 28/9/1990). Nor is it surprising that increasingly there are headship recruitment problems and headteachers are opting out of the pressures of headship by taking early retirement (*The Guardian,* 24/1/1995). In the early 1980's, premature retirement and illness accounted for two out of ten heads who left schools. In contrast, the NAHT reported that seven out of ten heads who left schools had taken early retirement or retired because of stress and illness (*The Independent*, 24/5/1989).

Prompted by the far-reaching implications on schools of the ERA as outlined above, headteachers were chosen as the sample for this study of occupational stress, coping and health. However, the real focus of the study was concerned primarily with exploring and assessing cognitive appraisal and coping processes in a general sense. This study was, therefore, only concerned with situational factors such as external resourcing, LEA involvement, financial budgets etc., to the extent that these influenced appraisals and coping. The research objectives detailed in chapter 3 and practical considerations concerning the sample chosen, guided the design of the research methodology.

4.4   Research design

Eighty headteachers from the Bradford Local Education Authority in England took part in the study. Each headteacher was interviewed for approximately two hours about two 'stressful' work situations they had coped with recently, one with a successful outcome and the other with an unsuccessful outcome. In addition, the heads were asked to complete a questionnaire assessing how they perceived certain aspects of their job, personal beliefs and psychological well-being and physical symptoms. (Full details of the questionnaire and interview schedule are given later in this chapter).

Any research design is necessarily an interplay of resources, practicalities, methodological choices, personal judgements and creativity (Patton, 1987). Having determined the research objectives and the sample, the different options and methods of data collection had to be considered. On the one hand, qualitative data from interviews would give the desired in-depth information about events, emotional reactions, cognitive processes and coping responses. On the other hand, a questionnaire would enable quantitative, standardized data to be collected relating to personality, job demands and mental and physical health. Consequently, the research objectives could best be met by using both methods of data collection. However, both qualitative and quantitative methods have strengths and weaknesses which had to be considered prior to research design.

The major advantages of qualitative data are that they provide depth and detail through direct quotation about situations, events, interactions and behaviours and the data are not constrained by predetermined categories of analysis as in a questionnaire. However, qualitative responses are usually much longer and variable in content than questionnaire responses and, because the replies are not systematic or standardized, analysis can be difficult and comparisons imprecise. By contrast, quantitative data fit diverse opinions and experiences into predetermined response categories. The advantage of the quantitative approach is that it facilitates comparison and statistical aggregation of data and gives a broad, generalizable set of findings. The disadvantage of this standardized approach is that respondents must fit their experiences into predetermined categories which can distort what they really mean or have experienced. However, even though the purposes and functions of these two methods of data collection are different, it is possible to use them in a complementary way by incorporating both methods into a research design (Henwood and Pidgeon, 1995; Patton, 1987). Thus, the statistics from quantitative data make summaries, comparisons and generalizations relatively easy and precise. Qualitative data provide a forum for elaborations, explanations and descriptions of events in context and frequently lead to meaningful and new ideas (Patton, 1987).

4.5   Design of the interview schedule

For this study, face to face interviews were chosen as the primary method of qualitative data collection. The interview is widely used in the social sciences and its popularity is understandable since it is an effective way of obtaining data about attitudes, opinions, motivations, feelings and other characteristics that are not directly observable (Gummesson, 1991; Patton, 1987). The presence of an interviewer has the advantage (over mailed questionnaire, for example) that the certainty is increased that it is the respondent who answers the questions. Further, the respondent's performance can be controlled (to a certain degree) and clarifications can be given if necessary. The co-operation of the respondent is usually greater, so the proportion of 'refusals' will be less and the number of questions that can be posed is greater (Kahn, 1957).

However, the popularity of the interview does not mean that it should be uncritically accepted as a means of data gathering. Criticisms concerning the quality of interview data stem from studies which show that respondents' answers should not always be taken for granted. Responses can be distorted by the formulation of the question, expectations of the interviewer, motives of both the interviewer and the respondent, social desirability and instructions for response behaviour (Gummesson, 1991; Richardson, Dohrenwend and Klein, 1965; Sudman and Bradburn, 1982; Weiss, 1975). Such distortions or 'response effects' alter the respondent's opinion or attitude, that is, the variables the interviewer is interested in (Sudman and Bradburn, 1982).

Further, much of the data required from the interview in this study were to relate to events, actions, feelings and cognitions or cognitive processes as reported retrospectively by the interviewee. Yet, Nisbett and Wilson (1977) have pointed out that humans are not particularly adept at reporting their own cognitive processes. They argued that people base their reports on a priori causal theories rather than reporting from memory about cognitive processes. Similarly, Loftus and Loftus (1980) reviewed evidence regarding the processes associated with memorial recall. This evidence suggested that, in at least some instances, subjects' recollection of past events were so altered by subsequent information, that the altered construction was accepted and reported uncritically as the 'true' construction of earlier events. In summary then, it was necessary to heed all of these criticisms of interviewing outlined above because they had important implications for the design of the interview schedule to be used in this study if the data were to be reliable and valid.

Interview format: some considerations

Initially, the three major types of interview format were considered:

- highly structured

- informal/conversational

- semi-structured

A highly structured interview format containing a predetermined set of closed questions was considered unsuitable for this descriptive, exploratory study since respondents must fit their experiences and feelings into predetermined categories. Such a rigid structure may be perceived by the respondent as impersonal, mechanistic and irrelevant to their personal experience and distort what they really mean or have experienced (Patton, 1987).

An informal, conversational interview format which allows the interviewer to be highly responsive to individual differences and situational changes was also rejected. The strength of this approach lies in the richness of the data which can be gathered. The weakness is that it requires a great deal of time (i.e., repeated interview sessions with the same respondent) to collect systematic information. Given the hectic working schedule of the headteachers in the sample, the informal interview format was rejected on pragmatic grounds.

Consequently, a semi-structured interview schedule was decided upon where the topics and issues to be covered were specified beforehand in outline form and the sequence of questions was determined in advance. The outline served to increase the comprehensiveness of the data and made much of the data collection systematic for each respondent. However, where necessary, the exact wording of some questions was designed to be flexible so that the interview remained conversational and situationally appropriate (Kahn, 1957). This flexibility also allowed logical gaps in the data to be anticipated and closed.

The semi-structured interview format necessitated the use of both open and closed questions. The open-ended questions permitted a detailed study of selected issues such as feelings, thoughts and behaviours since the responses were not constrained by any predetermined categories of analysis. The richness of the respondents' experiences were thus captured in their own terms. At the same time, the open-ended questions allowed the respondent to give not only question-specific information about thoughts, feelings and behaviours, but also to recall other past relevant behaviours, thereby enhancing the validity of the data (Markus, 1977; Regan and Fazio, 1977). Markus, for example, used the concept of self-schemata to refer to cognitive generalizations about the self. He presented evidence that showed if a person is encouraged to recall schematic personal dispositions relevant to the behavioural dimension about which the self-reports are being elicited, then validity of the self-report data is enhanced. Similarly, Regan and Fazio demonstrated that self-reported attitudes and behaviours of people instructed to recall their past behaviour showed a better fit with later actual behaviours than was true for people who were given no such instructions. The open-ended format of the questions in the current study therefore allowed respondents to recall past, relevant behaviours and thereby increased the consistency of the self-report data.

A good proportion of the schedule was comprised of open-ended questions followed by a series of probes. The probes were used frequently throughout the interview to deepen the responses to questions and to increase the richness of the data. In addition, probes were used to give cues to the interviewee about the level of response that was desired as well as to provide the interviewer with a means of maintaining control over the flow of the interview (McCracken, 1988; Millar, Crute and Hargie, 1992; Wright and Taylor, 1994). The probe questions could not be written out in the schedule since a major characteristic that separates probes from general questions is that they are flexible and must be used sensitively in response to the open-ended answers provided by the person being interviewed. Throughout the interview schedule detail-oriented probes were used when appropriate (i.e., 'who', 'what', 'when', and 'how' questions) to get a complete and detailed picture of some experience or activity. Elaboration probes were used to cue the interviewee to keep talking (e.g., 'Tell me more about that') as well as clarification probes on any unclear responses to elicit more information or more context (Wright and Taylor, 1994). To maintain rapport, however, attempts were made to keep the probes conversational (Kahn, 1957).

A number of closed questions were also incorporated into the schedule. These closed questions facilitated interviewer control over the salience and pace of responses (Randell, 1979) and were used as a means of gaining quantitative data which were succinct, parsimonious, standardized and easily aggregated for statistical analysis (Patton, 1987). For each of the closed questions, corresponding scale cards were designed to be shown to the respondent not only to focus their reply, but also because this is a useful interviewing device which breaks up the routine of the interview and effectively motivates respondents to answer questions further on in the interview (Sudman and Bradburn, 1982).

Whilst it is not possible to completely eliminate response effects (Dijkstra and Vander Zouwen, 1982) efforts were made in the design of the interview schedule to considerably reduce this potential limitation of interviewing. Firstly, the schedule was designed so that a large proportion of the questions and instructions were formulated in exactly the same way for each respondent thereby reducing the possibility of distorted responses. Secondly, the same schedule was administered in the same order, by the same interviewer, to all the respondents. This standardized the interview procedure so that it can at least be assumed that the effects of the interviewer were constant over respondents and, relations between variables of interest to the research were minimally affected. Thirdly, to encourage the respondent to answer honestly and counteract the social desirability bias of the responses, potentially threatening words such as 'stress', 'coping', 'psychological health' and so on, were purposefully avoided throughout the interview schedule. Instead, more neutral terms like 'difficult situation', 'handle or deal with', and 'feelings and behaviour' were used. Moreover, in the introductory section of the interview schedule, the interviewee was assured that the study was not an evaluative exercise but rather, aimed to increase understanding of the different ways in which people think, feel and react to various responsibilities and duties at work. Finally, reassuring words of praise, thanks, encouragement, etc., were used throughout the interview to maintain rapport and to establish the interview as an interactive process rather than an interrogative process (Kahn, 1957).

Details of the semi-structured interview schedule
(A copy of a completed interview schedule can be seen in Appendix A).

A single interview lasting approximately two hours, was to be arranged with selected headteachers in the Bradford Local Education Authority district. Because of the limited time with each subject, it was important to design the schedule such that rapport was quickly established and maintained throughout the interview (Randell, 1979). This would ensure that good quality data were elicited on the topics of interest, many of which were of a personal, sensitive nature.

The introductory page of the schedule was designed to familiarize the subject with the nature of the study, explain possible implications for results from the study, and reassure the interviewee of confidentiality.

Next, questions were formulated to elicit biographical and demographic details. According to Patton (1987), it is preferable to space such questions strategically and unobtrusively throughout an interview schedule since these questions epitomize what people do not like about interviews. For this study, however, distributing the biographical data randomly throughout the schedule would have interrupted the flow of the interview and inhibited data collection. Consequently, as many personal and demographic details as possible were obtained from the school's secretary prior to the interview. The remainder of personal details required were kept to an absolute minimum and placed at the beginning of the schedule.

At this point in the interview a request was made to tape-record the interview. This not only ensured accuracy and completeness of data but also permitted maximum attentiveness to the subject's reactions, facial expressions and replies (Kahn, 1957; Patton, 1987; Randell, 1979).

74

To establish rapport quickly, three open-ended, non-controversial questions were designed asking for relatively straightforward accounts of the main responsibilities, rewards and difficulties of headship. These required minimum effort and recall and encouraged the respondent to talk descriptively, thereby establishing a context for moving on to subsequent questions which were more sensitive and required the expression of opinions, attitudes, feelings and descriptions of and reasons for behaviours (Kahn, 1957).

Section A of the schedule began with a question asking the respondent to describe a recent problem situation, at work, which they had dealt with in the six weeks prior to the interview and which had turned out successfully. Asking for information about **recent** events had a two-fold purpose in terms of data validity: first it maximized the likelihood of accurate recall thereby enhancing data validity (Osberg, 1989); second, the information about recent events linked consistently with the two health measures used in the questionnaire, which were also pertaining to a period of six weeks prior to the interview.

To set the events in context, respondents were then asked to briefly describe who else was involved in the problem situation. Next, questions about the antecedent conditions which can affect appraisal were asked relating to the unexpectedness, unfamiliarity and the unpleasantness of the event. Respondents were also asked to rate their replies on the six-point scale shown in Table 4.1, where 1=Extremely familiar (expected or pleasant) and 6=Extremely unfamiliar (unexpected or unpleasant).

Table 4.1
Rating scale for the un/expectedness, un/familiarity and un/pleasantness of the problem situation

	Expected			Unexpected		
	Familiar			Unfamiliar		
	Pleasant			Unpleasant		
1	2	3	4	5	6
Extremely	Very	Somewhat	Somewhat	Very	Extremely

In each case, 6 represented the maximum negative impact in terms of appraisal. A six-point scale was chosen for these variables because situations are often complex and comprise familiar and not so familiar elements, pleasant and not so pleasant elements and so on. But it was important to ascertain whether respondents appraised the situation as predominantly pleasant or unpleasant or predominantly familiar or unfamiliar and so on. Consequently, the even number of categories in

75

the six-point scale served to indicate the direction in which respondents were leaning (Sudman and Bradburn, 1982). The interval level data were also suitable for statistical procedures such as correlation and regression analysis.

Next, questions were asked about the extent of other problems, control over being able to deal with the problem situation, and how confident respondents felt that they would be able to deal with the situation satisfactorily. The respondents were asked to rate their answers on the 7-point scale shown in Table 4.2 where 1=Not at all, 4=Moderately, and 7=Very much so. A seven-point scale was chosen for measuring these variables in order to provide a middle option for respondents (Sudman and Bradburn, 1982) and to yield data suitable for correlation and regression analyses. Having given a quantitative answer, respondents were then encouraged to elaborate on their answers, since one of the main research objectives was to explore and describe the factors that lead to perceptions of high/low control and confidence.

Table 4.2
Rating scale for extent of other problems, control, confidence,
external resource adequacy and how well the problem situation was handled

1	2	3	4	5	6	7
Not at all			Moderately			Very much so

At this point in the interview, the major issues and themes were summarized by the interviewer to facilitate understanding and clarify any uncertainties before proceeding further (McCracken, 1988; Wright and Taylor, 1994). Then, a number of relatively sensitive questions were asked relating to why the problem was appraised as difficult, how the respondent felt, what they were thinking to make them feel angry or anxious, etc., and what, if anything, they did to handle their emotional reaction(s). A prompt card of emotions, shown in Table 4.3, was shown to the respondents since studies have shown that individuals often differ in their ability to convey such information (Osberg, 1989).

Table 4.3
Prompt card of emotional reactions to the problem situation

Sad	Embarrassed
Angry	Happy
Agitated	Frightened
Frustrated	Delighted
Dejected	Determined
Anxious	Confident
Guilty	Panicky
Proud	Worried

Questions about coping responses followed next, and respondents were encouraged to report their coping behaviours and thoughts in a chronological order as the problem situation unfolded. Subjects were asked not only what they did to cope, but why they chose those strategies, whether or not the strategies worked, and whether any alternatives were considered and tried or considered and rejected. A coping response prompt card, shown in Table 4.4, was also used to facilitate memorial recall and encourage the interviewee to elaborate about the coping process.

Table 4.4
Prompt card of coping responses to the problem situation

- Refused to get too serious about the situation
- Made a plan of action and tried to follow it
- Did something with the specific intention of relaxing
- Turned my back on the situation
- Bargained or compromised to get something positive out of the situation
- Vented my emotions/took my feelings out on others
- Decided things were due to chance, luck or fate
- Engaged in smoking, drinking or taking medications more than usual
- Considered the problem carefully and tried not to act hastily
- Refused to believe it had happened
- Sought more information about the problem
- Acquired or developed the necessary skills for handling the problem
- Had wishes or fantasies about how I would like things to be
- Looked for or found spiritual comfort
- Accepted the situation because I decided nothing could be done about it
- Criticized or blamed myself for things
- Sought or found emotional support
- Changed my ideas about what was sensible, reasonable or possible

In drawing section A to a close, questions were asked about the outcome of the situation, external resources, and how the subject felt about the outcome. The replies about outcome were standardized on the prompt card shown in Table 4.5 and pre-coded as follows: 1=Resolved, 2=Improved, 3=Unchanged and 4=Worsened.

Table 4.5
Prompt card for outcome of the problem situation

1 = Resolved
2 = Improved - but not resolved
3 = Unchanged
4 = Worsened

Questions about external resource availability and adequacy were answered first, quantitatively on the 7-point scale detailed earlier in Table 4.2, and then, qualitatively to explore and determine the effects of external resources on both the situation and the appraisal process. Finally, interviewees were asked to rate, again on the 7-point scale, how well they had handled the situation, and were then encouraged to elaborate further and say why the situation had turned out successfully.

Section B of the interview comprised the same questions as section A, except that the respondent was asked to describe a recent, problematic situation with an unsuccessful outcome.

4.6   Design of the questionnaire

Designing the questionnaire for this research involved a number of practical, theoretical and analytical considerations. Before the questionnaire was developed, discussions with various educationalists indicated that headteachers frequently complain about their 'ever-growing' administrative tasks, a large proportion of which involve questionnaire completion and form-filling.   It was important, therefore, that the questionnaire to be used in this study was brief, easy to complete and non-threatening in nature. Brevity and acceptability were also important because the respondents were to be asked to complete the questionnaire having already given two hours of their time in an interview.

The questionnaire, entitled 'A Profile of Health, Behaviour and Personal Characteristics', can be seen in Appendix B and consisted of a:

- personality measure of Negative and Positive Emotionality (NEM/PEM),

- job demands measure called Affective Job Experience (AJE),

- General Health Questionnaire (GHQ),

- physical symptoms inventory (SYMP),

- yes/no question about visiting the doctor.

Of these, the NEM, PEM and GHQ were well established, validated scales. The AJE and SYMP scales were designed specifically for this study.

NEM/PEM measures

According to Watson and Clark (1984) one of a number of scales can be used to assess the negative affectivity construct. Some studies for instance have used the 23-item Neuroticism scale of the Eysenck Personality Questionnaire (Parkes, 1990; Payne and Hartley, 1987) whilst Brief et al., (1988) used the 50-item Taylor Manifest Anxiety Scale (TMAS, Taylor, 1953). But as was argued in chapter 3, it was important in this study that both negative emotionality **and** positive emotionality were examined concurrently in order to extend understanding of the aetiology and implications of subjective emotional experience (Watson, 1988). Consequently, two scales from the Multidimensional Personality Questionnaire (MPQ, Tellegen, 1982) were used to assess the subjects' negative and positive affective levels.

The 11-item Positive Emotionality (PEM) and the 14-item Negative Emotionality (NEM) scales are brief measures of trait positive affectivity and negative affectivity. Unlike many other negative affectivity scales, the NEM focuses on the experience of negative affect and is an especially good trait measure for health research since it contains no somatic complaints. Thus NEM's correlation with physical symptom reporting is uncontaminated by content overlap (Watson, 1988).

Representative items from the NEM measure are, 'My feelings are hurt rather easily', 'My mood often goes up and down', and 'I often find myself worrying about something'. Typical items from the PEM scale are, 'It is easy for me to become enthusiastic about things I am doing', 'In my spare time I usually find something interesting to do' and 'I always seem to have something pleasant to look forward to'.

The PEM and NEM scales are true-false inventories and respondents indicate whether each of the 25 items is true (or largely true) or false (or largely false) as applied to them. The scales contain negatively and positively worded statements to minimize the effects of subject response sets. All the items are 'true' keyed, coded accordingly and then summated to give a total NEM score and a separate PEM score. Variables measured in this way are suitable for many statistical analyses including the techniques which were to be used in this study, e.g., T-tests, correlation and regression procedures.

Affective Job Experience (AJE)

The Affective Job Experience measure was designed specifically for this study. The 17 items in the measure were developed by both adapting items used previously in occupational stress research (Burke and Belcourt, 1974; Cooper and Marshall, 1978; Kahn, et al., 1964) as well as developing items of interest which the educational literature and preliminary talks with educationalists suggested were particularly salient to the headteacher's role.

Some of the items measured the extent to which the respondents' work environment allowed control over job-related decision-making. Representative items were 'Choosing your own method of working' and 'Having authority to influence school management methods and procedures', and these closely modelled items used by Karasek (1979) on decision latitude. Other items were devised from Cooper and Marshall's (1978) discussion of sources of executive stress at work relating to interpersonal duties. In this study representative items were 'Dealing with staff related issues, e.g., motivation' and 'Making decisions that affect others'. Another group of items were adapted from Burke and Belcourt's (1974) role conflict measure and items used in this study were 'Trying to equate perceived objectives of the school with external demands and constraints' and 'Handling some aspects of your job for which you feel you have inappropriate training'. Finally, a number of items were especially developed for this study to assess the impact, on headteachers, of the educational changes in schools. Examples of these items were 'Planning ahead amidst organizational and curricula changes' and 'Preparing for increased financial responsibilities'.

Since it was the appraisal of the above aspects of headship which was of primary salience to this study, each item was on a 6-point scale ranging from 1=Extremely pleasant, 2=Very pleasant, 3=Somewhat pleasant, 4=Somewhat unpleasant, 5=Very unpleasant, 6=Extremely unpleasant. Scores were summated to give an overall AJE score for each individual, the higher score representative of individuals experiencing various facets of headship unpleasantly.

In order to increase construct validity, each construct within the scale (e.g., role conflict, role changes, etc.) was assessed by a minimum of 3 items (Sudman and Bradburn, 1982). The interval level data from the 6-point scale meant that factor analysis as well as correlation and regression analyses would be possible.

General Health Questionnaire (GHQ)

The 12-item General Health Questionnaire (GHQ) (Goldberg, 1978) was used to assess current mental health. The GHQ-12 is a shorter version of the original 60-item General Health Questionnaire which was designed as a self-administered screening test for detecting minor psychiatric disorders, but the shortened version was developed particularly for use where respondents' time is at a premium. However, the GHQ-12 was chosen not only for its brevity but also because it has been validated against clinical ratings (Banks, 1983), and because its psychometric characteristics are well established (Banks, Clegg, Jackson, Kemp, Stafford and Wall, 1980). For example, Banks et al., advocated the use of the GHQ-12 in employment studies because scores are not sensitive to age or marital status and because of its high internal consistency and unidimensional factor structure across three different samples.

Each item consists of a question asking whether respondents have recently experienced a particular symptom or item of behaviour on a scale ranging from 'less than usual' to 'no more than usual' to 'rather more than usual' to 'much more than usual'. Representative items ask respondents if they have recently 'lost much sleep over worry?', 'felt constantly under strain?', and 'been feeling unhappy or depressed?'

Two main scoring methods are advocated for the GHQ: the 'GHQ-method' and the 'Likert-method'. With the GHQ-method, individuals score 0 if endorsing either of the first two categories, or 1 for endorsing either the third or fourth category. Here, the GHQ is treated as a bimodal response scale which has the advantage that it eliminates any errors due to 'end users' and 'middle users', although this scoring method does produce a somewhat skewed distribution (Goldberg and Williams, 1988). Those people scoring above the designated cut-off point, which is 2 with the GHQ-12 version, are more likely to be suffering from poor mental health than those scoring below. Because there is a designated cut-off point with the GHQ-method of scoring, across-study comparisons can be made.

With the Likert-method, responses are given weights of 0, 1, 2 and 3 and scores on individual items are summed to produce a total score, higher scores indicating higher levels of distress. There is no designated cut-off point for the GHQ scored by this method and across-study comparisons therefore are limited. However, the Likert-method of scoring has the advantage that it produces a wider and less skewed distribution of scores more appropriate for parametric multivariate techniques (Banks et al., 1980). Consequently, to draw on the advantages of both methods of scoring, the health questionnaire was scored by the GHQ and the Likert-method.

Physical symptoms (SYMP)

A brief, easy to complete, measure of physical symptoms was designed especially for this study, largely because existing measures were considered to be either too lengthy and laborious to complete (e.g., Derogatis's 90-item Symptoms Checklist, 1973) or not unidimensional measures of physical symptoms (e.g., Langner's, [1962] 22-item Screening Score).

The 17-item physical symptoms measure (SYMP) contained questions about a variety of stress-related conditions and specific somatic symptoms. The items were developed from a review of the literature and from existing physical symptoms measures. The measure assessed:

- sleep-related problems with items such as 'Feeling unrested following a night's sleep' and 'Lack of energy, apathy or constant tiredness';

- general nervousness with items such as 'Acid stomach, nausea or indigestion' and 'Nervousness or shakiness inside (e.g., 'butterflies');

- respiratory problems with items such as 'Breathing difficulties or shortness of breath';

- general bodily discomfort with items such as 'Feelings of heaviness or weakness in your arms and legs'.

Respondents were asked to indicate the frequency of occurrence of each item (over the past six weeks) on a response scale ranging from 1 = Never, 2 = Very infrequently, 3 = Infrequently, 4 = Sometimes, 5 = Frequently, 6 = Very frequently. The responses to each item were then summed to give a total physical symptoms score for each respondent. Because the individual item scores were measured on an interval level scale, the physical symptoms measure was suitable for use in correlation and regression analysis (Cohen and Holliday, 1982) as well as factor analysis (Kim and Mueller, 1982).

Visit to general practitioner (GP)

The last item on the questionnaire offered a Yes/No response format to the question 'Have you visited your doctor recently in relation to any of the above physical symptoms?'.

The headteachers were assured of confidentiality for their responses.

4.7   Access and data collection

In order to forge important links with the major organizations invo!ved in headship in the Bradford LEA district, preliminary discussions were held with a variety of educationalists including members of the Schools Advisory Service, the Occupational Health Unit for Education, the Educational Research and Planning Division, educational psychologists and the chairman of the National Association of Headteachers. All these contacts reacted favourably to the proposed research. For reasons of propriety, the Director of Education in Bradford, Mr Richard Knight, was informed by letter of the proposed study and his reply was also favourable. (See Gummeson's [1991] discussion on securing access.)

To increase the likelihood of respondent participation, a succinct and persuasive telephone preamble was designed (Frey, 1983). Headteachers were selected from an alphabetical listing of schools in the Bradford LEA District, contacted by telephone and asked if they would be willing to participate in the study. Eighty-seven headteachers were contacted and of these, eighty (92%) agreed to take part in the study. This represented an excellent response rate (Frey, 1983).

The interviews were purposefully arranged to take place during the Summer term between April and July, since it has been shown that teacher stress levels vary at different points of the school year (Kinnunen and Leskinen, 1989). For maximizing reliability, therefore, it was important to collect data from the headteachers during the same school term.

Following each interview, the respondents were asked to complete and return the questionnaire. In addition, each respondent was sent a handwritten letter of thanks, largely standard in format, but which also permitted some special reference to each individual's interview (Kahn, 1957). Seventy-eight usable questionnaires were returned, again representing an excellent response rate of 98%.

From a methodological viewpoint it is worth noting that the high response rates to both the interview and the questionnaire may have been due to one or a combination of factors. First, in spite of prolific media coverage about the Education Reform Act, education generally and headteacher stress, the headteachers in this study had not previously been involved in stress research and hence their involvement in and time commitment to a study of this nature was novel. Second, the study was confidential and not associated in any way with the Local Education Authority. It is possible to speculate therefore that this was an influential factor in the headteachers' readiness to take part in the study. Third, the questionnaire was specifically designed to be non-threatening, easily understood and quick to complete (completion took approximately 8-10 minutes). Again, these factors may have influenced response rates. Finally, the content of the interview schedule was such that many respondents were encouraged to say the interview was 'informative', 'thought-provoking', 'helpful', 'awareness-raising', 'therapeutic', 'enjoyable' and so on. Indeed, some headteachers returned their questionnaire with their own letter of thanks. Any one, or a combination of these factors may have contributed to the excellent questionnaire and interview response rates in this study.

5 Preliminary data analyses and results

In this chapter, details are given of the methods used to assess the reliability of the questionnaire measures and the results of the preliminary analyses of the quantitative and qualitative data. Throughout, attention is drawn to the preliminary findings which are of pivotal interest not only to the study, but also to subsequent analytic procedures detailed in the next chapter.

5.1 Assessing reliability of questionnaire measures

Cronbach's alpha test was used to assess reliability for the measures used in the questionnaire. This is a technique which, unlike the test-retest method, uses only a single test administration and provides a unique estimate of reliability for a given test. Cronbach's alpha is calculated from the average inter-item correlation and the number of items in the scale. Thus, as the average correlation among items increases and as the number of items increases, the value of alpha increases, so that the addition of more items to a scale (that do not result in a reduction in the average inter-item correlation) will increase the reliability of the measuring instrument (Carmines and Zeller, 1982).

The internal consistency of items within the negative and positive emotionality measures, (NEM and PEM), the affective job experience scale (AJE), the psychological health measure (GHQ) and the physical symptoms index (SYMP) was evaluated by obtaining reliability estimates from the average correlation among items in each index with coefficient alpha:

$$R = \frac{(kr)}{(1 + [k-1])r}$$

where k is the number of items and r is the average inter-correlation among all items in each index (Cronbach, 1984). The results are shown in Table 5.1.

Table 5.1
Reliability of questionnaire measures

	Alpha
Negative Emotionality	.83
Positive Emotionality	.84
Affective Job Experience	.89
General Health Questionnaire	.91
Physical Symptoms	.89

Although coefficient alpha is commonly used and reported in the literature, no standards or guidelines exist on what magnitudes of the coefficient are adequate for measurement scales (Van de Ven and Ferry, 1980). But if, along with Carmines and Zeller (1982) we assume that as a general rule of thumb, reliability coefficients should not be below .80 for widely used scales, then the alpha coefficients reported above indicate that all the measures were acceptably reliable.

The significant reliability coefficient for the General Health Questionnaire was 'expected' in the sense that it is a well-established scale which has been used extensively in UK research. Nevertheless, in spite of the cultural difference, the NEM and PEM measures also yielded acceptable alphas. But it was particularly important to assess the reliability of the job stress (AJE) and physical symptoms (SYMP) measures, since these were constructed specifically for this study. For this reason, the reliability results for the AJE and SYMP measures are given in detail below.

Affective Job Experience (AJE)

Only one of the job stress items, AJE 7 'Not being able to influence some decisions and actions that affect you' had a non-significant item-total correlation of $r = .10$. The remaining sixteen items were significant at the .01 level having item-total correlations ranging from $r = .35$ (AJE 9 'Exercising independent thought and action in your job') to $r = .54$ (AJE 16 'Managing or adapting to organizational changes'). The AJE items then, yielded consistently moderate correlations indicating that each one was related to the total score. It was therefore a sufficiently reliable measure to justify use in further analyses.

Physical symptoms (SYMP)

All of the Physical Symptoms item-to-total correlations were significant at or beyond the .001 level. The individual item-total correlations ranged from $r = .32$ (SYMP 15 'Pains in the lower back') to $r = .58$ (SYMP 17 'Feeling unrested after a nights sleep'). These consistently moderate to strong correlations indicated that the items in the scale were operational referents of the same construct - each item being related to the total score. Calculations of the coefficient alpha yielded a standardized correlation coefficient of $r = .89$, $p < .001$. Thus the physical symptoms measure was sufficiently reliable to justify use in further analyses.

5.2 Exploratory factor analysis of AJE and SYMP measures

In addition to assessing reliability for measures used in the questionnaire, exploratory factor analysis was used for the job demands and physical symptoms measures as a heuristic procedure for identifying orthogonal scales, selecting the best items within each scale and thus, imputing a post hoc theoretical meaning and definition to each scale.

Factor analysis requires that the variables be measured at least at the interval level (Kim and Mueller, 1982). This requirement is implied by the use of correlation or co-variance matrices as the basic input to factor analysis. Hence, it is sometimes advocated that factor analysis be avoided when the metric base for the variables is not clearly established, for example, when measuring attitudes, opinions and personality, which do not have a clearly established metric base, as was the case with the measures used here. However, as Kim and Mueller (1982) point out, it is generally assumed that many 'ordinal variables' may be given numeric values without distorting the underlying properties. The deciding answer to this question really hinges on two considerations:

- how well the arbitrarily assigned numbers reflect the underlying true distances

- the amount of distortion introduced into the correlations (which become the basic input into factor analysis) by the distortions in the scaling.

Fortunately, the correlation coefficients are fairly robust with respect to ordinal distortions in the measurement. Hence, as long as one can assume that the distortions introduced by assigning numeric values to ordinal categories are believed to be not very substantial, treating ordinal variables as if they are metric variables can be justified.

Factor analysis of the Affective Job Experience (AJE) measure

A principal components factor analysis with varimax rotation was performed on the 78 subjects' responses to the AJE scale. Since males and females did not differ significantly in terms of total scores, data from both sexes were included in the analysis. The factor solution and final statistics are presented below in Table 5.2.

87

Table 5.2
Rotated factor matrix: Affective Job Experience measure (AJE)

	Factor1	Factor 2	Factor 3	Factor 4
AJE11	.79853	.36820	.10922	-.09124
AJE9	.72787	-.13460	.31385	.01510
AJE13	.68970	.20502	.42646	-.03526
AJE8	.65746	-.00284	.30118	.27723
AJE12	.64763	.36131	.10749	-.07535
AJE10	.64519	.41718	-.08265	.21688
AJE16	.19987	.79824	.27237	.08180
AJE15	.06405	.75616	.23275	.12854
AJE17	.23025	.75392	.14399	.17225
AJE6	.20195	.23600	.75106	-.14343
AJE1	.10108	.26614	.72096	.17311
AJE4	.26143	-.00658	.54344	.28138
AJE3	.38018	.27507	.51902	.07257
AJE7	-.15261	-.02786	.02494	.81268
AJE5	.15542	.30453	.07754	.61867
AJE2	.07447	.37648	.51232	.53795
AJE14	.24207	.50255	.15682	.51030

Final Statistics:

Factor	Eigenvalue	% Variance	Cumulative %
1	6.38271	37.5	37.5
2	1.97690	11.6	49.2
3	1.29185	7.6	56.8
4	1.11284	6.5	63.3

AJE - Scale Items with Factor Loadings of ± .50

Four factors emerged with eigenvalues >1, accounting for a total of 63.3% of the variance. The first factor accounted for the bulk of the variance, 37.5%, while factors 2, 3 and 4 accounted for 11.6%, 7.6% and 6.5% of the variance respectively. Six items (AJE 8, 9, 10, 11, 12 and 13), loaded on the first factor and reflected the opportunities in headship to work independently. This factor was labelled 'Role autonomy'. The second factor consisted of three items (AJE 15, 16 and 17), relating to the educational changes which headteachers are currently facing and this was labelled 'Role changes'. On the third factor, which was labelled 'Interpersonal duties', the four items (AJE 1, 3, 4 and 6), reflected the requirements of headteachers to manage, supervise and interact with many different people. Items loading on the fourth factor (AJE 2, 5, 7 and 14), reflected the conflicting demands and pressures on headteachers from outside agencies such as the governing body and the Local Education Authority. This factor was duly labelled 'Role conflicts'. As Table 5.2 indicates, each item loaded ± 0.5 on only one factor except for items AJE 2 and 14 which load highly on factor 4 and also on factors 2 and 3 respectively.

Factor analysis of the Physical Symptoms (SYMP) scale

A principal components factor analysis was performed on the 78 responses to the physical symptoms measure and the principal factors with eigenvalues >1 were extracted from the correlation matrix and rotated with a varimax procedure giving the final solution as detailed below in Table 5.3.

Table 5.3
Rotated factor matrix: Physical Symptoms measure (SYMP)

	Factor 1	Factor 2	Factor 3	Factor 4	Factor 5
SYMP17	.85001	.13181	.14565	.12335	.08761
SYMP7	.75548	.03539	.42746	.20739	.11987
SYMP16	.69874	.05623	.00543	.11134	.41676
SYMP11	.58882	.47324	-.11667	-.10908	.28373
SYMP1	.53723	.33357	.21451	.29049	-.00473
SYMP3	.16102	.76460	.04409	.23267	.08423
SYMP2	.10096	.75824	.10027	.25459	.27367
SYMP9	.15529	.69682	.34187	-.05111	.15255
SYMP6	.30537	.52747	.28358	-.00371	-.07183
SYMP13	.08812	.07961	.86408	.16029	.15850
SYMP12	.27215	.33981	.58403	-.10044	.06401
SYMP8	.33566	.22171	.55728	.20546	-.06272
SYMP14	.26973	.03042	-.03108	.86048	-.03411
SYMP4	.01306	.43448	.31054	.63905	.26030
SYMP5	.11586	.39948	.15470	.61481	-.02592
SYMP15	.11661	.13580	.08839	-.03053	.80673
SYMP10	.12642	.12053	.07703	.06865	.74183

Final Statistics:

Factor	Eigenvalue	% Variance	Cumulative %
1	6.45045	37.9	37.9
2	1.68358	9.9	47.8
3	1.46843	8.6	56.5
4	1.20360	7.1	63.6
5	1.04017	6.1	69.7

Physical Symptoms - Scale Items with Factor Loadings ± .50

Five factors emerged accounting for 69.7% of the variance. Factor 1 accounted for 37.9% of the variance. The items (SYMP 1, 7, 11, 16 and 17) reflected sleep problems, eye discomfort and general apathy and the factor was labelled 'Physical exhaustion'. The items loading on Factor 2 (SYMP 2, 3, 6 and 9) accounted for 9.9% of the variance and were related to digestive problems and 'butterflies' - the factor was labelled 'Nervous stomach complaints'. Factor 3 was labelled 'Physical discomfort' since the items loading on this factor (SYMP 8, 12 and 13) related to aching, numbness and heaviness of the limbs and they accounted for 8.6% of the variance. Items (SYMP 4, 5 and 14) reflecting respiratory difficulties loaded on Factor 4 which accounted for 7.1% variance and was duly called 'Respiratory problems'. The fifth factor contained only two items (SYMP 10 and 15) which together accounted for 6.1% of the variance and were related to skin problems and lower back pain. Imputing a post hoc theoretical interpretation on this factor was considered to be of dubious value.

5.3   Demographical/biographical details of sample

The sample consisted of 80 headteachers of schools within the Local Education Authority area of Bradford, UK. Forty-three of the schools were First Schools with an intake of pupils ranging from three to nine years old. Thirty-seven were Middle Schools with pupils ranging from nine to thirteen years old. The size of school varied considerably from the smallest, with eighty pupils on the roll, three members of staff and three auxiliaries, to the largest school which had six hundred pupils on the roll, thirty-nine members of staff and thirty-six auxiliaries. Most of the schools (91%) had only one deputy, whilst the seven largest Middle Schools had two.

The proportion of male and female headteachers interviewed is shown below in Table 5.4.

Table 5.4
Proportion of male and female headteachers interviewed
from First and Middle Schools

	First	Middle	
Male	15	28	(43)
Female	28	9	(37)
	(43)	(37)	

The eighty headteachers were interviewed for approximately two hours using the semi-structured interview schedule described in chapter 4. Following the interview, each respondent was asked to complete and return the questionnaire, also detailed in chapter 4, entitled 'A Profile of Health, Behaviour and Personal Characteristics'.

Preliminary analyses of data from the interview yielded the following biographical details about the sample. The age of the headteachers ranged from thirty-six to sixty-three years (Mean (M) = 47.1 years). Thirty-eight male heads were married and of these, thirty-one had a partner who also worked in education. The remaining five headmasters were divorced or separated. Twenty-nine of the female heads were married and nine had a partner who also worked in education. The remaining eight headmistresses were divorced, separated or widowed.

Educational experience

The number of years teaching experience varied from eight to forty-two years (M = 23.3 years), whilst the experience of headship ranged from one to twenty-six years (M = 7.9 years). The average deputy experience was 4.5 years. The number of years the head had been in post at the current school varied between one and twenty-three years (M = 6.4 years).

Educational qualifications

Educational qualifications were as follows: 98% had 'O' Levels, 75% 'A' Levels, 48% had Degrees, 10% had a Higher Degree and 77% of the headteachers also held a Teaching Diploma or Certificate.

Previous work experience

Just over half of the sample (54%) had work experience other than in education. This experience included management, commercial, clerical, Public Services, accountancy, laboratory technician and farming experience.

Hobbies and interests

When asked about their personal hobbies and interests just over one-third of the headteachers (35%) played a sport. Outdoor activities such as hiking, camping, caravanning, walking and gardening were pursued by 58% of the sample. More passive interests such as reading, theatre-going, watching television, dressmaking and so on, were mentioned by 70% of the heads and 20% also had home and family interests including DIY and decorating; 35% of the sample were members of clubs or organizations related to their hobbies.

In the context of the question about hobbies and interests, twenty-five of the headteachers (31%) remarked either, that they had 'no time at all' for hobbies, or that their time for hobbies was 'very limited'. In contrast, the remaining fifty-five heads answered the question without stating that time was a problem in relation to hobbies and interests - indeed, eleven from this group of heads commented that they felt it was 'important to **make** time for hobbies'. These contrasting attitudes to hobbies and interests were noted for reference in subsequent analyses..

5.4   Preliminary analysis of biographical data

Some of the variables such as sex, school type, etc., were truly dichotomous and consequently, cross-tabulations were computed in order to calculate the phi ø coefficient as an appropriate measure of association between pairs of dichotomous variables. Cross-tabulations were computed between sex, school type, club membership and partner working in education. The significance of the phi coefficients was then tested using the following formula

$$X^2 = N\varnothing^2$$

(Cohen and Holliday, 1982)

Substituting the obtained phi coefficients into the above formula, the only significant association was found to be between sex and school type where ø = .408 and (X^2 =12.50 [d.f.1] p = >.01). Thus, significantly more First School heads were female and significantly more of the Middle School heads were male.

Preliminary analyses using T-tests showed no significant differences between male and female heads in age, number of pupils on the roll or teaching, headship and deputy experience. T-tests did reveal, however, that male heads had significantly more teaching and auxiliary staff than female heads (p = .021 and .029 respectively). This was expected, given that significantly more of the male heads were heads of Middle and hence, bigger schools.

T-tests showed no differences between First and Middle School heads in age, teaching experience or headship and deputy experience. Middle School heads did, however, have significantly more pupils on the roll (p = .015) and more teaching and auxiliary staff (p = .000 and .015 respectively), again a reflection of school size. (These analyses are reported in full in Oakland, 1991).

5.5　Main responsibilities, rewards and difficulties in headship

Following the biographical details in the interview, each respondent was asked to give details of the main responsibilities of headship, the most rewarding aspects, and the major difficulties of the job. Replies were subject to simple content analysis.

Main responsibilities

Headship responsibilities fell into two categories: responsibilities **for** and responsibilities **to**. Eighty-five per cent of the respondents referred to their responsibilities for the education, welfare, safety and general development of the children; 79% of the group referred to their responsibilities for the professional development and personal welfare of the staff. Other replies related to responsibilities for the general management and delivery of the curriculum (44%), monitoring and evaluating the school building in terms of structural maintenance and repairs (23%), and financial responsibilities for the school budget and Local Management of Schools (LMS) preparations (19%).
　Headteachers were also responsible to various groups of people closely connected to the school. Forty-one per cent of the heads spoke of their responsibilities to the parents, to the Governors (29%), the Local Education Authority (23%), the community surrounding the school (19%) as well as to external agencies such as the local Police and the Social Services (10%).

Rewards of headship

When asked about the most rewarding aspects of headship, almost all of the headteachers (88%) referred to the rewards of working with children, seeing them develop and being happy in school. Thirty-six per cent of the respondents said they found it rewarding working with staff and seeing them develop professionally. Almost one quarter (23%) found support and/or praise from parents, Governors, the LEA and external agencies a rewarding aspect of the job (although several respondents qualified this by saying praise in headship was all too infrequent). Ten per cent of the headteachers found managing the school rewarding and only one respondent mentioned salary as a rewarding aspect of headship.

Almost three-quarters (73%) of the heads stated that educational changes in recent years were a major source of difficulty in the job, referring in negative tones to the nature, rapidity and preparations for those changes. Thirty-three per cent of the respondents referred to the difficulties of not having enough time to either complete tasks or do a job well. Difficulties relating to administrative tasks, 'red tape' or bureaucracy were also mentioned by 32% of the headteachers, whilst lack of training for managerial duties was said to be another major difficulty (32%). Nineteen per cent of the heads referred to difficulties with interpersonal relationships and conflicts with children, staff, parents, Governors and LEA personnel. Inadequate resourcing and/or facilities to meet the demands of the school was expressed as a major difficulty in headship by some (16%) and 11% expressed dissatisfaction with their fast-declining teaching role. Six per cent alluded to difficulties of the job arising from disciplinary problems and special needs children.

5.6   Problem situations in headship

The one hundred and sixty problem situations described by the respondents covered a wide range of organizational and interpersonal problems in headship. The dynamic nature of the situations made mutually exclusive classification somewhat problematic. Nevertheless, for descriptive purposes the problems were grouped under the headings listed below and the frequencies are shown in parentheses.

Personnel performance (17)

Problems relating to the heads' dissatisfaction with teaching or non-teaching staff's work standards or performance, e.g. classroom organization, teaching ability, handling of the children, etc.

Behavioural/special needs (28)

Problems concerning behavioural problems or special needs children, including disabled children and abuse-related problems.

Motivation/morale (16)

Problems where the head's role is primarily supportive, e.g. encouraging staff development, motivation or morale.

Internal conflicts/complaints (24)

Problems involving staff opposition, complaints or conflicts.

External conflicts/complaints (30)

Problems arising from complaints, opposition or conflicts involving parents, Governors, outside agencies, etc., but not the staff.

Organizational (30)

Organizational/management problems pertaining to the school building or changing of school procedures, policies or organizing school functions, including preparations for LMS and National Curriculum changes.

Recruitment (11)

Problems concerning to recruitment or resignation.

Intrapersonal (4)

Problems involving only the headteacher.

5.7 Emotional reactions to problem situations

Following the description of a problematic situation, respondents were asked how they felt in relation to that situation. The open-ended responses resulted in a plethora of emotional adjectives which, for the purposes of content analysis, were clustered in groups of conceptually similar emotions. These groups were as follows:

Anger   -   hostile type reactions such as angry, furious, frustrated, annoyed and cross.

Anxiety   -   anxiety type reactions such as anxious, worried, concerned, panicky and frightened.

Depression - reactions such as sadness, depressed, fed-up and dejected.
Guilt   - reactions such as guilty, remorseful, ashamed and embarrassed.
Happiness   - positive reactions such as happy, pleased, delighted and relieved.

Simple content analysis then permitted a frequency count of emotional reactions to the one hundred and sixty problem situations. The results are given below in Table 5.5.

Table 5.5
Frequencies of emotional reactions

Emotions	No. of times reported	% Total responses
Anger	145	43.4
Anxiety	98	29.3
Depression	52	15.5
Guilt	28	0.08
Happiness	11	0.03

The most commonly reported emotional responses were anger, annoyance, and frustration, together accounting for 43% of the responses. Anxiety-type emotions were mentioned less frequently and accounted for 29% of the responses, whilst feelings of sadness, dejection and depression accounted for 16%.

Many studies of stress lead us to suppose that feelings of anxiety or worry are the predominant emotional reactions to stressful situations. However, in this study, hostile feelings of anger, annoyance and frustration were the most frequently reported emotional responses. Interestingly, in their study of young professional engineers, Keenan and Newton (1985) also analyzed open-ended responses about emotional strain and they too found anger-type reactions to be the most common emotional response to work stressors.

A possible explanation for anger-type reactions predominating in both the Keenan and Newton (1985) and this study is that in many other questionnaire-approach studies of stress, researchers have been content to limit their questions to anxiety-type reactions. Qualitative approaches, however, permit open-ended answers about emotions and can, therefore, yield richer information about reactions such as frustration and anger. Given that hostile reactions such as anger can have deleterious effects on health and well-being (as detailed in chapter 3) it may be argued that many studies using measures which focus mainly on anxiety-type reactions are overlooking crucial variants in the stress, appraisal, coping and health process. Note for instance, the prevalence of sadness, dejection and disappointment in this study. Again, this is not an emotional reaction which is usually reported in studies of stress. Yet, the qualitative approach used in this study has yielded information which indicates that feelings of sadness and dejection are commonly experienced emotional reactions in stress and coping. Also, because sadness, dejection, disappointment, etc., are often closely linked with lowered self-esteem, these emotional reactions represent an important component of the stress, coping and health process.

5.8   Preliminary analyses of questionnaire data

The questionnaire consisted of a:

- Negative/positive emotionality measure (NEM/PEM)

- Affective job experience scale (AJE)

- General Health Questionnaire (GHQ)

- Physical symptoms checklist (SYMP)

- Yes/no question regarding recent visit to GP (GP visit)

Basic descriptive statistics of the questionnaire data are presented in Table 5.6.

Table 5.6
Means, standard deviations and ranges for questionnaire measures

	M	SD	Range	Possible range	n
NEM	5.40	3.95	0-14	0-14	78
PEM	7.12	3.02	0-11	0-11	78
AJE	48.62	9.89	26-74	7-102	77*
GHQ (Likert)	13.95	6.30	4-33	0-36	78
GHQ (Goldberg)	3.60	3.54	0-12	0-12	78
SYMP	38.83	14.75	7-79	17-102	78
GP Visit	1.76	.43	1 or 2	1 or 2	78

GP Visit was coded 1 = Yes, 2 = No
*Slight variation in sample size due to missing data.

Basic descriptive data

Negative/Positive Emotionality (NEM/PEM)

Consistent with other research in this area (e.g. Watson, Clark and Tellegen, 1988), subjects tended to report higher levels of positive affect than negative affect. Across all subjects, the mean score for the 11 PEM items was 7.1 whereas that for the 14 NEM items was 5.4. Thus, the subjects typically reported more than moderate levels of positive affect and a lower level of negative affect.

Affective Job Experience (AJE)

In chapter 3, it was argued that many job stress measures are flawed because they fail to distinguish between the existence of a work demand and the individual's evaluation or appraisal of that demand. Put another way, the wording of many job stress items is such that the existence of a work demand is assumed, a priori, to constitute pressure or negative appraisal of the demand. Consequently, the 17-item AJE measure was especially designed for this study and the items were purposefully worded to tap into the headteacher's **appraisals** of various demands at work. Responses were rated on a 6-point scale ranging from 1=extremely pleasant to 6=extremely unpleasant.

The mean response on the Affective Job Experience measure was 48.6 on a scale of 17-102 indicating only a moderate reporting of headteacher duties which were experienced as pleasant. Item-analysis of the subjects' replies revealed that sixteen of the seventeen aspects of a headteacher's work environment were experienced by some as pleasant and others as unpleasant. This can be seen in Table 5.7.

The value of asking questions which give respondents the option of reporting either negative or positive appraisals of work demands is amply demonstrated in Table 5.7. It can be seen that the items relating to task variety, role autonomy and independent goal setting were experienced by most headteachers as pleasant, whilst items relating to inappropriate training, external constraints and lack of decision latitude were experienced by most headteachers as unpleasant. These results are not particularly surprising since other studies have shown that opportunities for autonomy and task variety are frequently associated with job satisfaction (e.g. Wall and Clegg, 1981) whilst having inadequate training or lack of involvement in decision making are associated with job strain (e.g. Karasek, 1979). But it is important to note that only one of the items, 'exercising independent thought and action', was experienced by all the respondents in the same way, i.e., as pleasant. In other words, when the respondents were given the option of reporting negative or positive appraisals, most aspects of the headteacher's role were experienced differently by different individuals. So whilst 78% of the respondents enjoy making decisions that affect others, 22% do not. These differences are important because they show that even on aspects of the job which were experienced by individuals those aspects will have different implications. However, the most striking example of this diversity is shown by the responses to items 2, 14, 15, 16 and 17. These items were experienced by approximately half the respondents as pleasant and the other half as unpleasant. For instance, the item relating to dealing with the governors and the LEA was rated in varying degrees of pleasantness by 47% of the respondents, but in varying degrees of unpleasantness by 53%. Planning ahead amidst the educational changes, managing the educational changes and preparing for financial responsibilities were rated as pleasant by 43%, 58% and 42% of the headteachers and correspondingly as unpleasant by 57%, 42% and 58% of the heads.

Table 5.7
Item-analysis of responses to AJE measure

Item No	Brief Item Description	% Pleasant (Score 1,2 or 3)	% Unpleasant (Score 4,5 or 6)
1.	Supervising the work of others	84	16
2.	Dealing with governors, LEA etc.	47	53
3.	Dealing with staff-related issues	78	22
4.	Wide variety of tasks	92	8
5.	Inappropriate training	18	82
6.	Making decisions that affect others	78	22
7.	No influence over decisions that affect you	4	96
8.	Choosing own method of working	98	2
9.	Exercising independent thought and action	100	0
10.	Keeping up with technological change	78	22
11.	Influence over school management methods	96	4
12.	Authority to delegate	71	29
13.	Responsibility for goal setting	96	4
14.	Equating objectives with external constraints	35	65
15.	Preparing for financial responsibilities	42	58
16.	Managing/adapting to educational changes	58	42
17.	Planning ahead amidst the changes	43	7

Hence, this inspection of response tendencies to individual AJE items demonstrates the value of designing a measure which assesses an individual's appraisal of work demands since it clearly reveals that different individuals appraise the same demand in markedly different ways. Moreover, it adds credence to the critique of many occupational studies (reviewed in chapter 3) utilising items which assume a priori that the existence of a work demand necessarily equates with negative appraisal of that demand.

Returning again to Table 5.7, it will be noted that descriptive statistics given for the General Health Questionnaire were scored in two ways, the GHQ method and the Likert method. This was done because the GHQ scoring method (Goldberg, 1978) permits comparisons of this study's data with normative data similarly scored, whilst the Likert scoring method is preferable for statistical analyses (Banks et al, 1980).

As Figure 5.1 illustrates, fifty per cent of the headteachers scored above the cut-off point of 2 which is indicative of poor mental health (M = 3.60, SD = 3.53). Almost twenty per cent of the headteachers scored more than 6, with five per cent scoring 12 which indicates severe psychological distress.

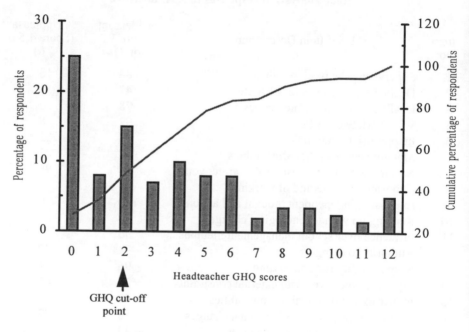

Figure 5.1   **Distribution of headteachers GHQ scores and cumulative percentage of respondents**

When compared to other studies of employed adults these scores are high. For example, compare the GHQ data in this study with that of four other occupational stress studies as detailed below in Table 5.8.

Table 5.8
Comparative General Health Questionnaire data

Study	Occupational Status	GHQ Data		% above cut-off point
		Mean	SD	
Oakland (1991) (study of headteachers)	Employed	3.60	3.53	50%
Wall & Clegg (1981)	Employed	.82	1.28	18%
Banks et al (1980)	Employed	.97	1.87	16%
Ostell & Divers (1987)	Unemployed	4.69	3.58	65%
Hepworth (1980)	Unemployed	4.68	3.52	62%

Looking at Table 5.8., it can be seen that in a study of engineers, Wall and Clegg (1981) found that only 18% of their sample scored above the GHQ-12 cut-off point and the mean GHQ score was 0.82 as against the headteacher mean of 3.60. Similarly, in their study of male and female employees in an engineering firm, Banks et al (1980) showed that only 16% of the sample scored >2 and the mean GHQ score was 0.97. Interestingly, however, studies of unemployed subjects have revealed GHQ scores similar to the headteacher results reported here. Ostell and Divers (1987) reported a mean GHQ score of 4.69 in their study of unemployed managers and 65% of these managers had GHQ scores greater than 2. Likewise, Hepworth's (1980) study of unemployed males yielded a mean GHQ score of 4.68 with 62% of the total sample scoring above the designated GHQ-12 cut-off point of 2. In summary, the headteacher GHQ scores and mental health status more closely approximates the GHQ scores and mental health status of **unemployed** subjects than employed subjects.

For the statistical analyses, the GHQ-12 was also scored using the 'Likert-method' where responses are given weights of 0, 1, 2 and 3 (Goldberg, 1978). GHQ scores from non-pathological samples are always negatively skewed (for obvious reasons) and thus the standard deviation is large relative to the mean value. Consequently, Banks et al (1980) advocated scoring GHQ responses on a Likert scale (0-3) since this produces a wider and less skewed distribution of scores more appropriate for parametric multivariate techniques. There is no official cut-off point for Likert-method GHQ scores but the headteacher mean of 13.95 (SD 6.30) is considerably higher than the GHQ mean of 9.13 (SD 5.21) reported by Parkes (1990) in her study of university graduates.

Physical symptoms (SYMP)

The mean response on the physical symptoms measure (SYMP) was 38.8 (SD 14.8) on a scale of 17-102, indicating a less than moderate level of reported physical symptoms. Because the physical symptoms measure was designed specifically for this study, across-study comparisons are not possible. However, as detailed in chapter 4, the measure was designed to tap into as diverse and comprehensive a range of respiratory, skeletal, visceral symptoms, etc., as possible.

Visit to general practitioner

Nineteen heads (24%) stated that they had visited their general practitioner or doctor in relation to physical symptoms on the checklist within six weeks prior to the interview. Phi coefficients were calculated to examine any possible relationships between sex, school type and a partner working in education and it was found that significantly more female than male heads had recently visited their GP ($\emptyset = .253$, $X^2 = 4.99$ [d.f.1] p = >.05 level). It is not possible to say that this represents a sample-specific trend since Government statistics also indicate that in England more females than males visit the doctor.

5.9 Preliminary analyses of quantitative interview and questionnaire data

First T-tests were performed to look for significant differences between the biographical and the questionnaire data and showed no statistically significant differences in means between male and female heads for Negative or Positive Emotionality, Affective Job Experience, the General Health Questionnaire or physical symptoms.

T-tests showed no significant differences between First and Middle School heads on the questionnaire measures, Negative and Positive Emotionality, Affective Job Experience, the General Health Questionnaire or physical symptoms.

No differences were found on any of the variables in relation to either having a partner working in education or being a member of a club or organization. But as might be anticipated, those heads who had recently visited their doctor had significantly higher GHQ (M's = 16.8, 13.0, p = 0.28) and physical symptoms (M's = 49.8, 35.3, p = .001)scores than heads not visiting their doctor. (See Oakland, 1991 for details of these analyses).

Associations between interview variables

Next, paired T-tests were used to look for differences between variables in the two separate sections of the interview: Section A, relating to a problem with a successful outcome, and Section B, relating to a problem with an unsuccessful outcome. The results are shown in Table 5.9.

Table 5.9
Paired T-tests of section A and section B variables

Variable	n[1]	Mean	SD	T	P<
A. Unexpected[2]		3.41	1.98		
B. Unexpected	80	3.71	1.82	-1.03	ns
A. Unfamiliar[2]		3.38	1.70		
B. Unfamiliar	80	3.31	1.67	0.25	ns
A. Unpleasant[2]		4.62	1.24		
B. Unpleasant	55	4.87	1.16	-1.02	ns
A. Other problems[3]		5.64	1.40		
B. Other problems	78	6.13	1.16	-3.86	.000
A. Control[3]		5.46	1.42		
B. Control	64	3.62	2.01	6.01	.000
A. Confidence[3]		5.27	1.32		
B. Confidence	70	3.91	1.91	5.92	.000
A. Advice[3]		6.00	1.21		
B. Advice	31	1.84	1.93	3.20	.003
A. Emotional support[3]		6.38	0.88		
B. Emotional support	42	5.36	1.59	4.36	.000
A. Financial[3]		3.86	2.19		
B. Financial	7	2.00	1.29	1.93	ns
A. Information[3]		6.07	1.17		
B. Information	30	3.87	2.08	5.63	.000
A. Help/assistance[3]		4.87	2.59		
B. Help/assistance	15	4.40	2.26	0.65	ns
A. Skills[3]		5.69	0.83		
B. Skills	65	4.15	1.54	7.79	.000
A. How well handled[3]		5.74	0.83		
B. How well handled	70	4.16	1.49	9.49	.000
A. Outcome[4]		1.69	0.57		
B. Outcome	69	2.32	0.87	-5.17	.000

Interpretation notes

1. *Range of n's due to differing external resource requirements (e.g. advice, finances, etc.,) in Sections A/B or missing data because respondents were unable to give a 'static' answer.*
2. *Unexpected, Unpleasant, Unfamiliar coded 1-6 where 1=Extremely Expected, 6=Extremely Unexpected and so on.*
3. *Variables measured on a 7-point scale where 1=Not at all, 4=Moderate, 7=Very Much So.*
4. *Outcome was coded 1=Resolved, 2=Improved, 3=Unchanged, 4=Worsened.*

Table 5.9 shows that highly significant differences were found between many of the variables common to both sections A and B of the interview. Since respondents were asked to describe a successful outcome problem in section A and an unsuccessful outcome problem in B, the significant difference on the 'outcome' variable was to be expected. Nevertheless, the highly significant differences found between the extent of other problems, control, confidence, adequacy of advice, emotional support, information, perceptions of personal skills and how well the situation was handled, are indicative of an intriguing trend, as depicted in Figure 5.2.

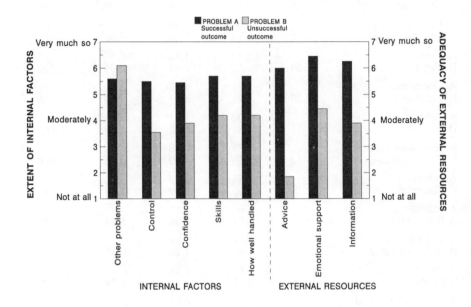

Figure 5.2   **Differences in extent of internal factors and adequacy of external resources for problem situations A and B**

Looking at Figure 5.2., it is clear that in section A, the situation with the successful outcome, internal factors such as confidence, control, adequacy of personal skills and perceptions of how well the problem was handled were all significantly higher than for problem B with the unsuccessful outcome. Further, the adequacy of external resources - advice, emotional support and information - was also significantly higher in the situation with the successful outcome. Furthermore, respondents reported significantly more 'other problems' when they were describing the unsuccessful outcome situation. This suggests that either, having lots of other problems to deal with can adversely affect outcomes or, that when situations turn out unsuccessfully this inflates people's perceptions of the extent of other problems at the time.

Further analyses were required, therefore, to determine the extent to which these interview variables were statistically associated with the situational outcome, with each other, and with the personality, job demands and health measures in the questionnaire.

5.10   Summary of the preliminary analyses

The preliminary analyses of the quantitative and qualitative data have been described in this chapter and can be summarized as follows.

1. All the measures used in the questionnaire are sufficiently reliable to justify being used in further analyses.

2. The demands of headship fall into four groups relating to role autonomy, interpersonal duties, role conflicts and role changes. Content analysis of the qualitative data indicates that of these, role changes (required of heads since the Education Reform Act) were mentioned most frequently as posing difficulties in headship.

3. Although many studies presuppose that anxiety, worry or tension are the predominant emotional reactions to stressful situations, more hostile reactions such as anger and frustration prevail in this study. Given anger's potentially dysfunctional effects on psychological and somatic health, these findings may have important implications for the health outcomes of headteachers.

4. The overall impact, on heads, of the various demands of headship, was experienced as modestly positive. However, this disguises the fact that individual heads reacted in vastly different ways to the same demand.

5. Compared to other studies of employed subjects, the GHQ scores of the headteachers are high. The headteachers' mental health status in this study more closely approximates that of **unemployed** subjects.

6. The experience of coping with situations which have successful or unsuccessful outcomes is not the same but involves significant differences in internal factors such as confidence, control and personal skills as well as significant differences in the adequacy of external resources such as advice, information and emotional support.

In view of the preliminary results summarized above, it was prudent to undertake more detailed analyses of all the quantitative and qualitative data in order to explore, describe and better understand the dynamics of headteachers reacting to and attempting to cope with work-related problem situations and the implications for their health.

6 Detailed qualitative and quantitative data analyses

In this chapter, content analyses of the qualitative interview data are described and the subsequent coding of the interview scripts. The qualitative interview data are then merged with the quantitative questionnaire data and the methods of statistical analysis used are detailed. The results of these analyses are tabulated and discussed briefly to highlight the findings of primary interest to the study and to form the basis of a more detailed discussion of the results in the next chapter. Since the use of qualitative data analysis is not as widespread or as well-documented as quantitative data analysis (Henwood and Nicolson, 1995; Miles and Huberman, 1994), this chapter begins by outlining some of the basic underlying principles and techniques used in this research.

6.1   Qualitative data analysis: basic principles and procedures

Qualitative data, in the form of words rather than numbers are a source of well-grounded, rich descriptions and explanations of processes occurring in context (Miles and Huberman, 1994). Qualitative data analysis or content analysis is a research methodology that utilizes a set of procedures for making replicable and valid inferences from text (Weber, 1985). A central idea in content analysis is that many words of text are classified into much fewer content categories. Each category may consist of one, several or many words, phrases or other units of text which, when classified in the same category, are presumed to have similar meanings (where 'meaning' refers to shared as opposed to private understandings).

In order to draw valid inferences from the text, it is important that the classification procedure used be reliable in the sense of being consistent; different people should be able to follow the classification procedure and code the text in the same way. However, the central problem of content analysis lies in this data-reduction process of text to categories, largely because of the ambiguity of word meanings, category definitions or other coding rules. Consequently, the most important procedure in content analysis is the definition, construction and testing of the codes or categories before they are applied to the whole text. From a review of the content analysis literature (Green, 1995; Henwood and Pidgeon, 1995; Holsti, 1969; Miles and Huberman, 1994; Van Maanen, 1979; Weber, 1985) this procedure can be summarized in the following steps:

Category definition

At the general level, the underlying principle of category construction is that categories should reflect the purposes of the research and be both exhaustive and mutually exclusive. (Since most statistical procedures require variables that are not confounded, then classifying a unit simultaneously into two or more categories may violate statistical assumptions and give dubious results). More specifically, the researcher must give clear conceptual definitions of the variables of interest and specify precisely the indicators which determine whether a given content datum falls within the category. In addition, the basic unit of text to be classified has to be defined, e.g., a word, a sentence, a theme, a paragraph, the whole text and so on.

Check coding validity

This stage involves checking the clarity of category definitions on a sample of text which usually reveals ambiguities in the coding criteria and leads to insights about revisions of the scheme.

Assess initial reliability

Next, the reliability of the coding procedure, as applied to a portion of the full data base, is assessed. Two types of reliability are pertinent to content analysis (Weber, 1985) - stability and reproducibility (often referred to as intra-rater and inter-rater reliability). Stability refers to the extent to which the results of content classification are invariant over time. Stability is ascertained when the same content is coded more than once by the same coder (intra-rater reliability). Inconsistencies or unreliability stem from a number of factors including ambiguities in the coding rules, cognitive changes within the coder, or simple error (e.g., recording the wrong code for a category). Since stability involves only one coder, it is the weakest form of reliability.

Reproducibility, or inter-rater reliability, on the other hand, refers to the extent to which content can be classified in the same way by more than one coder. Again, inconsistencies can arise from ambiguous text or coding rules, cognitive differences among the coders or from random errors. But because inter-rater reliability measures the consistency of shared understandings (as opposed to private) it is a much stronger form of reliability than intra-rater reliability (Miles and Huberman, 1994).

Revise coding criteria

If reliability is low, coding rules and/or category definitions are revised and then applied again to the text (as in stage two above) reiteratively until acceptable reliability is achieved. (Details for calculating reliability and criteria of acceptability are given later in this chapter).

Transform text to codes

When acceptable intra-rater and/or inter-rater reliability is reached, the rules can then be applied to all the text to transform it to codes.

Assess achieved reliability

When all the text is classified or coded, reliability is assessed and reported.

Whilst the procedures outlined above represent the underlying theory of qualitative data analysis, in practice, these procedures can vary tremendously from very simple to extremely complex. For example, content analysis may involve simply counting the number of times a particular word or phrase was used. Thus in chapter 5, simple content analysis enabled a frequency count of emotions, headteacher responsibilities, major difficulties of the job, and so on. It is well documented that high reliability can be achieved for simple forms of content analysis in which coding is essentially a mechanical task (Holsti, 1969; Miles and Huberman, 1994; Van Maanen, 1979) and independent judges, therefore, were not considered necessary. Conversely, however, as codes and categories of analysis become more detailed and inferential judgements are required, then the whole content analysis procedure becomes increasingly complex and poses potential reliability problems (Green, 1995). Nonetheless, it is also well-documented that the more complex content analyses usually yield results that are more likely to lead to serendipitous findings and new theoretical integrations, allowing researchers to go beyond initial preconceptions and frameworks (Miles and Huberman, 1994). It is to the more complex, detailed qualitative data analyses undertaken in this study that discussion now turns.

6.2   Qualitative data preparation

The detailed qualitative data analysis of the interview schedules involved coding the schedules and using those codes in various statistical analyses to be described later in this chapter. The qualitative data analysis procedure used was closely aligned to the basic steps outlined above as illustrated in Figure 6.1.

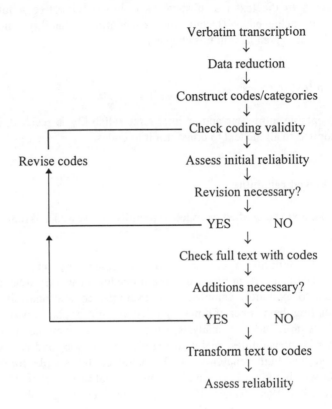

Verbatim transcription
↓
Data reduction
↓
Construct codes/categories
↓
Check coding validity
↓
Revise codes   Assess initial reliability
↓
Revision necessary?
↓
YES   NO
↓
Check full text with codes
↓
Additions necessary?
↓
YES   NO
↓
Transform text to codes
↓
Assess reliability

Figure 6.1   Qualitative data analysis procedure

Immediately following each interview, a single summary sheet was completed containing information about main themes or points which arose during the interview, plus any additional pertinent issues or observational data which were considered useful for the content analysis of the scripts, but which could not be committed to memory (Van Maanen, 1979).

Verbatim transcription

The eighty interview tapes were transcribed verbatim into the semi-structured interview schedule booklet detailed in Appendix A. One disadvantage of verbatim transcription is that it is a labour intensive and very time-consuming procedure (Green, 1995). Indeed, some researchers advocate either not taping interviews at all, or taking copious notes whilst conducting the interview (Kahn, 1957). Nevertheless, for the purposes of this study, the advantages of verbatim transcription were considered to far outweigh this disadvantage for a number of reasons. As Miles and Huberman (1994) point out, listening to and transcribing each tape constitutes an important stage of the content analysis procedure. Further, transcription gives the researcher a complete data base of not only what was said, but also how it was said. For example, if a respondent replies loudly and emphatically, this can be noted in the transcription. Furthermore, transcription permits the researcher to decide at leisure what themes, issues and data are of the greatest importance, thus guarding against what Miles and Huberman call 'premature closure'. In other words, transcription guards against deciding prematurely what main issues are worthy of pursuing in the data.

Data reduction

Having transcribed the interview tapes, the bulk of the data then had to be reduced into manageable analysable units (Miles and Huberman, 1994). For this, a data reduction proforma was designed (see Appendix C) which enabled the raw data from the interview transcriptions to be selected, simplified, abstracted and transferred into a manageable form, but which still allowed focus on the issues of pivotal interest to the research.

Like transcription, data reduction is a time-consuming task but as some researchers recognize (Huberman and Miles, 1983; Van Maanen, 1979), data reduction is not separate from analysis but is, rather, an important part of the content analysis. Thus, during data reduction, analytical choices were made about which data chunks to code, which data to temporarily discard and in this way the data were sorted, organized and reduced in preparation for coding.

In the original report of this study (Oakland, 1991), the qualitative data analysis procedures outlined above and subsequent coding of the scripts pertained to four areas: absoluteness, attributional style, external resource adequacy and effective handling of emotions. The coding and results relating to effective handling of emotions are not described here, however, because, following the study

- it was difficult to specify whether this variable should be treated as an independent or dependent variable

- it was recognized that the way in which handling emotions was measured was somewhat limited.

Nonetheless, interested readers can consult Oakland (1991) for a detailed discussion of the variable relating to the ability to handle emotions effectively in a problem situation.

6.3   Coding absoluteness

One of the major objectives of this study was to attempt to identify and describe the private dialogues which individuals engage in when appraising and attempting to deal with problematic situations. Of special interest were the private dialogues arising from situations in which an individual's absolutist beliefs are violated (as discussed in chapter 3).

The procedure for coding the interview schedules for absoluteness involved the author and an independent judge, both of whom were familiar with the underlying theory of absolutist thinking and the ways in which it is usually expressed in terms of emotional reactions and behaviours. For the content analysis procedure, the following working definition and coding criteria were agreed upon and used by both judges.

Working definition of absoluteness

Absoluteness is a mode of thinking which is essentially insisting upon or demanding conformity to certain standards of belief and/or behaviour - such demands being made either:

- of themselves

- of others

- of the environment

- of cosmic forces, God, fate, etc.

Coding criteria 1

Absolutist thinking is characterized by one or more (or a combination of) the following themes:

- Victimization/persecution complex

- Demands for perfectionism or infallibility

- A sense of injustice/unfairness

- Inability/unwillingness to be flexible or change

Coding criteria 2

- Judgements should be made after reading the complete interview transcript

- Subject's responses relating to situations or life generally (as opposed to the specific situation in question) should not, by themselves, be judged as indicative of absoluteness. Rather, category judgements should be made on the basis of situation-specific responses. However, generalized responses may be evaluated **in conjunction with** situation-specific responses when making a judgement.

- Working with the complete interview scripts will entail the unavoidable reading of data relating to emotional arousal and/or physical symptoms - this data should not influence the category judgements.

- If category assignation proves difficult or decisions marginal, the interview tapes should be consulted.

Coding criteria 3

The interview scripts are to be assigned to one of the following four categories:

Category A -   No sign of absoluteness

Category B -   Elements of absolutist thinking but no real negative impact on the situation*

Category C -   Indications of absoluteness and some degree of negative impact on the situation*

Category D -   Highly absolutist with negative impact on the situation*

*where 'negative impact on the situation' refers to absoluteness having deleterious effects on the individuals attempts at coping with the situation.

In assigning the scripts to one of the above four categories, it was assumed that categories A and B were indicative of 'Non absolutist' behaviour, whilst C and D were indicative of 'absolutist' behaviour. In other words, coding was on a continuum which could be collapsed into two groups if judgements proved to be too difficult because of the complexity of the data (Holsti, 1969).

Coding and reliability for absoluteness

Using the working definition of absoluteness and the coding criteria detailed above, both judges independently assigned 10 scripts to one of the four categories and these were used as training scripts (Green, 1995). Initial agreement between the judges was, as expected, not very high with agreement being reached on only five of the scripts on the four-point scale and seven on the two-point scale. This was not considered unusual for a training phase since lack of experience with any scoring procedure can produce low percentage agreement (Holsti, 1969). A further forty scripts were then independently coded and results were compared. Agreement was reached on twenty-one of the scripts on a four point scale and thirty on a dichotomous scale.

Cohen's Kappa was calculated to establish inter-rater reliability. Cohen's Kappa is a stringent statistic designed to correct for chance agreement (Cohen, 1960). Thus, values can be compared across studies and, since Kappa does not variously inflate the actual level of agreement, it is almost always preferable to simple agreement percentages or reliability coefficients which are widely used in qualitative studies (Bakeman and Gottman, 1987). Substituting the results from the two judges into the formula for calculating Cohen's Kappa (Leach, 1979) gave a Kappa value of .30 on a four-point scale and a Kappa value of .46 on a two-point scale.

According to Fleiss (1981) and Cicchetti and Sparrow (1981) an informal rule of thumb characterizes Kappas as follows:

- .40 - .60 as fair,

- .60 - .75 as good,

- and over .75 as excellent.

Consequently, the Kappa value of .30 was considered to be unacceptably low to warrant coding the remaining scripts on a four-point scale. This was disappointing but understandable given the complexity of the data and the inherent difficulties of defining mutually exclusive categories for degrees of absolutist thinking. (A number of other factors may also have contributed to this disappointing result and these are addressed as limitations of the study in chapter 10). Nevertheless, the

Kappa value of .46 was considered to be reasonably acceptable given these problems and the fact that Kappa is a stringent statistic for inter-rater reliability.

The remaining thirty scripts were coded dichotomously by the first judge. Decisions were then made about the fifteen disagreements (ten scripts and five training scripts). For this, each script was re-read and coded dichotomously except for two of the respondents about whom there had been a fundamental disagreement - namely, disagreement about a coding of A as opposed to D. In these two cases the interview scripts were re-read and the interview tapes replayed before final decisions were made. Eight weeks later, the first judge re-coded all eighty scripts dichotomously (Miles and Huberman, 1994) and intra-rater agreement was reached on seventy-four scripts (93%).

Forty-nine headteachers (61%) were coded as 'Absolutist' and thirty-one (39%) as 'Non-absolutist'. Phi correlation coefficients were calculated as appropriate measures of association between truly dichotomous variables (e.g., sex, school type) and the dichotomized variable, absoluteness (Marascuilo and Sweeney, 1977). Significantly more absolutist respondents had visited their general practitioner ($\emptyset$ = .326, X^2 = 8.28, [d.f.l.] p = >.01) and significantly more of the First school heads were absolutist ($\emptyset$ = .291, X^2 = 6.80, [d.f.l.] p = >.01.

6.4   Coding attributional style

The interview schedule was designed to give data about two problem situations per respondent; a problem with a successful outcome and a problem with an unsuccessful outcome. A major objective of the study was to explore the dialogues individuals engage in when making attributions about the outcomes of the two problems they described. For this, the scripts had to be coded according to attributional style.

Coding and reliability for attributional style

Causal attribution theory and empirical research (as detailed in chapter 3) were used as the framework from which to develop a coding scheme for the respondents' attributional tendencies. A pilot study was carried out in which forty problem situations (twenty interview scripts) were coded by the author and assigned to one of the three following categories:

Category A   When attributions were **external, stable, uncontrollable** and referred to situational factors, material resources, other people, fate, luck, God and so on.

Category B	Scripts were assigned to this category when attributions were **internal-behavioural** and referred to some transient and potentially **controllable** action(s) or behaviour by the subject.
Category C	When **internal-characterological** attributions were made referring to stable, **uncontrollable** factors such as personality or character.

Consistent with the underlying attribution theory, scripts coded either A or B were considered to be evidence of the **self-serving attributional style**. Scripts coded C were taken as evidence of a **non-self-serving attributional style**.

The pilot study revealed that two major changes were required before coding could proceed further. First, in problem A, relating to a successful outcome, all the respondents attributed the outcome to their personal skills, abilities and/or their behaviours at the time in question. In other words, the attributions they made were internal and self-serving. Thus, the separate categories for internal-behavioural (self-serving) and internal-characterological (non-self-serving) were not appropriate when coding attributions for successful outcome situations. This is congruent with other studies on attribution (Arkin et al., 1976; Baumgardner et al., 1986) where individuals, irrespective of health, make only self-serving attributions and give themselves credit for successful outcomes.

The second major change required concerned the coding of attributions for the unsuccessful outcome. The pilot study made it apparent that assuming external attributions are always self-serving is not adequate. For example, one respondent, when asked about the unsuccessful outcome replied, 'The situation has worsened.... and we're not talking about personal skills here - we're talking about lack of resources.... it makes me **very** angry... I never get **any** help and yet **I'm supposed** to sort it out... it's **ludicrous!**' This, along with many other similar replies, indicated a need for sub-dividing the external category into two parts:

1. **External** and essentially self-serving in the sense that external factors (resources, other people, etc.) are blamed for the outcome and the individual thereby **exonerates** themselves from blame for the unsuccessful outcome (e.g., I don't blame myself for the outcome, the finances are just not available).

2. **External** but essentially non-self-serving whereby the individual acknowledges external constraints and yet still feels **implicated** in, responsible for, or 'owns' the failed outcome (e.g., The outcome is determined by resourcing, yet I feel I am responsible).

Accordingly, these changes were made and Section A, the attributions for successful outcomes, were coded dichotomously as either:

116

1. **External** (non-self-serving) - Success due to external factors such as resources, other people, fate, luck, God, and so on.

2. **Internal** (self-serving) - Success due to own skills, abilities, behaviours, personality, etc.

Attributions in Section B of the interview relating to an unsuccessful outcome were coded using the following four categories:

1. **External-exonerated**
   When attributions were to external, stable and uncontrollable factors such as resourcing constraints, legislation or other people, and the individual thereby 'disowned', exonerated themselves from, or did not feel responsible for the unsuccessful outcome.

2. **External-implicated**
   When the individual acknowledged external situational constraints but nevertheless felt implicated in or responsible for, or 'owned' the unsuccessful outcome.

3. **Internal-changeable**
   Attributions to internal, transient and potentially controllable factors such as behaviours at the time, or amount of effort exerted in the situation (e.g., I've learnt from my mistake and I won't do that again).

4. **Internal-unchangeable**
   Unsuccessful outcome due to internal, stable and uncontrollable factors such as personality, disposition, character, personal skills or ability (e.g., I blame myself - I need to be more forceful).

Coding and initial reliability

Content analyses of the scripts were carried out by the author and an independent judge. Prior to the study, the independent judge was not familiar with attribution theory and research. Consequently, a training script had to be prepared to familiarize him with the underlying basic concepts of attribution theory and the rationale of the coding scheme. The training script can be seen in Appendix D.

Sixteen randomly selected scripts were used as training scripts and independently coded. Simple agreement between the two judges was reached on twelve scripts coded on a four-point scale (75%) and fifteen scripts coded dichotomously (94%). Following discussions, three modifications were made to the coding procedure. First, both judges agreed it would be useful to code and then re-code the first two or three scripts at the end of each coding session. Second, because of the volume and complexity of the data, decisions were made to make a two-stage judgement for each respondent: namely, first make a judgement as to whether the person is essentially making self-serving attributions or not, and second, (on re-reading if necessary) make a judgement as to whether those attributions are internal or external. This two-stage decision procedure has been shown to improve reliability in content analysis (Schutz, 1958). Finally, the judges agreed that coding the interview scripts presented an inescapable methodological difficulty. As Schank and Abelson (1977) note, when making causal statements, people attempt to be concise and consistently omit information that they feel could easily be inferred by the listener or reader. It was agreed as necessary, therefore, to use whatever contextual clues the transcripts provided in order to arrive at assumptions and ultimately, coding judgements.

Coding and assessing reliability

Forty randomly selected scripts were independently coded (eighty problem situations) and results compared. For Section A, the successful outcome situation, the two judges were in complete agreement that all respondents had made self-serving attributions and attributed the outcome to their personal skills, behaviours and/or abilities, thereby taking credit for the success. For Section B, relating to an unsuccessful outcome, attributions were diverse and yet, on a four-point scale the judges agreed on thirty-six codes, yielding an encouraging Kappa value of .73. On a dichotomous scale, agreement was reached on thirty-nine codes giving an excellent Kappa value of .94.

Given the nature, volume and complexity of the data, the Kappa values were considered to be pleasingly high and indicated that the coding scheme was acceptably reliable to warrant coding the remaining scripts on both a four-point and two-point scale for analysis purposes. Although it is well-documented that very high coding reliabilities can be achieved by coding attributions in isolation after they have been extracted from the text (e.g., Stratton, Heard, Hanks, Munton, Brewin and Davidson, 1986), to extract text or statements relating to attributions in this study and examine them in isolation would have ignored other important contextual clues and reduced validity. The remaining scripts were coded by the first judge on both a four-point and a two-point scale. Six weeks later, all eighty scripts were coded again dichotomously and intra-rater agreement was reached on seventy-seven of the scripts (97%). The frequencies are given in Table 6.1.

Table 6.1
Frequencies of headteachers and attributional style categories

No. of heads	Attributional category	Total no./percentage
24	External-exonerated	39/49% = Self-serving
15	Internal-changeable	
24	External-implicated	41/51% = Non-self-serving
17	Internal-unchangeable	

Relationships between attributional style and other dichotomous variables were examined and phi coefficients indicated that significantly more respondents evidencing a non-self-serving attributional bias had visited their GP ($\phi = .299$, $X^2 = 7.01$, [d.f.1.] $p = >.01$). In addition, tetrachoric correlation coefficients (r_t) were calculated as an appropriate measure of association between the dichotomized variables, absoluteness (ABSOL) and attributional style (ATTRIB). Substituting the data into the cosine-pi formula used for estimating r_t (Guilford and Fruchter, 1978) and entering the values into the table of natural cosines gave the following results for the degree of association between ABSOL and ATTRIB:

$r_t = .78$

Since r_t is subject to exactly the same type of interpretation that applies to Pearson's r, absoluteness and attributional style were highly and positively correlated, indicating that absolutist thinking is strongly associated with a non-self-serving attributional style.

For heuristic purposes, tetrachoric coefficients were also calculated to explore the relationship between absoluteness and the four facets of attributional style: external-exonerated, external-implicated, internal-unchangeable and internal-changeable. The results are shown in Table 6.2.

Table 6.2
Tetrachoric correlations between absolutist thinking and attributional style

ABSOL and External exonerated	$r_t = -.84$
ABSOL and External implicated	$r_t = .87$
ABSOL and Internal unchangeable	$r_t = .81$
ABSOL and Internal changeable	$r_t = -.51$

The results show absoluteness to be associated with every facet of attributional style but most strongly associated with the attributional tendency to feel implicated in or responsible for situations in which external resources are constrained. Absoluteness was also strongly but inversely related to both the self-serving attributional styles whereby the individual either exonerates themselves from blame, or blames unsuccessful outcomes on potentially changeable factors.

6.5 Coding external resource adequacy

The final stage of the detailed content analysis involved coding the interview scripts according to the adequacy of external resources in each problem situation. In each situation described by the respondents, different permutations of external resources were required, making it impossible to meaningfully compare one individual with another in terms of external resource adequacy. A coding scheme was devised, therefore, which would enable such a comparison but which accounted for the intra-person differences in external resource requirements.

The coding scheme related only to external resources (advice, emotional support, information, financial and practical assistance) and did not include what the respondent had said about the adequacy of their personal skills. In the interview, external resource adequacy was measured on a seven-point scale of adequacy where 1 = Not at all, 7 = Very much so, and 4 = Moderately. Each problem situation was examined and the scripts were assigned to one of three categories as follows:

Category 1 - Adequate

When the scores for every external resource required were more than moderately adequate (i.e., scores were 5, 6, 7, or any combination of these scores).

Category 2 - Moderately adequate

When, irrespective of higher or lower scores, any one (or more) of the resources were rated as moderately adequate (i.e., 4). For example, the following case would be counted as belonging to category 2:

Advice = 3, emotional support = 4, financial = 1, information = 7, practical assistance = 7.

Category 3- Inadequate

When every one of the external resources required were rated as less than moderately adequate (i.e., 1, 2, or 3).

The scripts were duly coded using this scheme. An independent judge was not considered necessary because the data were unambiguous and the coding essentially a mechanical task. The resulting frequencies are shown in Table 6.3.

Table 6.3
Frequencies of external resource adequacy in problems A and B

External resources	Successful Outcome Problem A	Unsuccessful Outcome Problem B
Adequate	50 (63%)	19 (24%)
Moderately	28 (35%)	46 (58%)
Inadequate	0	9 (11%)
	78* (98%)	74* (93%)

(*variable n sizes because not everyone required external resources.)

So far, the analyses in this chapter have been concerned with identifying and quantifying certain interview variables relating to absoluteness, attributional style and external resource adequacy. These quantified data from the content analyses are now merged with the quantitative data from both the questionnaire and the interview for statistical analysis.

6.6   Quantitative data analysis: objectives and methodological issues

The quantitative data analysis, involving all the variables in the study was focused on the major objectives of this research - to explore and identify those variables which best explain both situational and health outcomes. More specifically, correlational and regression analyses were used to explore and identify those variables which best predicted

- the successful outcome in problem A (A.OUTCOME)

- the unsuccessful outcome in problem B (B. OUTCOME)

- psychological well-being (GHQ)

- physical symptoms (SYMP).

Before describing these analyses, a number of methodological issues are addressed concerning the procedures which were used.

Pearson product moment correlation

Pearson product moment correlation coefficients (r) were computed as appropriate measures of the degree of association between variables measured at the interval level (Leach, 1979). Further, in order to ease interpretation, the dichotomously measured variables were also included in the Pearson correlation procedures, for whilst it is technically correct to use the point-biserial as a measure of association between dichotomous and interval level variables, Pearson's r is sufficiently robust to withstand certain measurement deviations (Guilford and Fruchter, 1978). Indeed, when point-biserial values were calculated between such variables as absoluteness and GHQ, the results were the same as or very closely approximated the Pearson's r values reported in the following pages. (See Oakland, 1991 for rpbi values and comparisons).

When Pearson's r is used for inferential purposes, the two assumptions underlying the coefficient are:

- Homoscedacity - that is to say, the variance in one of the variables is comparable to the variance in the other variable.

- Normality - the distribution of all values on the two variables must be approximately normal (Cohen and Holliday, 1982).

After checking that the data complied with the above assumptions, Pearson's r coefficients were computed and, since the direction of the relationship between the pairs of variables could not be specified in advance, two-tailed significance tests were requested.

Treatment of missing data

A number of the quantitative interview variables had to be coded as missing values, because respondents sometimes found it impossible to give a single numerical reply concerning variables such as confidence and control. Because respondents were describing dynamic situations, they insisted on giving dynamic answers to questions about confidence and control. For example, one headteacher when asked to quantify control, replied

At first I had no control at all - it was in the governors' hands to make the appointment. But then, the ball was in my court and events were more or less up to me.

(30A-F-FS)[*]

(*where 30A-F-FS = Interview number 30, section A, female, First School).

This head gave a quantitative answer of $1 \rightarrow 7$ which represented her changing perceptions regarding confidence as the problem situation unfolded. The difficulty some respondents had in giving static, quantitative answers, not only reinforces the dynamic nature of coping in stressful situations but also highlights the limitations of using **only** questionnaire measures in coping research (Oakland, 1991; Oakland and Ostell, 1995). Nevertheless, for analysis, such replies had to be treated as missing values but were excluded on an analysis-by-analysis basis thereby using the maximum information available for every calculation (Norusis, 1983).

Regression analysis

Whereas correlation coefficients give a measure of the general relationship between two variables, regression analysis is a means of predicting the specific values of one variable when values of the other variable(s) are known. This is useful in two ways. First, it almost inevitably offers a fuller explanation of the dependent variable, since few phenomena are products of a single cause. Second, the effect of a particular independent variable is made more certain because the possibility of distorting influences from other independent variables are removed (Lewis-Beck, 1980).

The attributes of good predictor variables are twofold: they must be related to the dependent variable but not highly related to any other independent variable (Hanke and Reitsch, 1940). However, some of the variables in this study proved to be highly intercorrelated, which in regression leads to a situation known as multicollinearity. This can cause problems whereby the highly correlated independent variables explain the same variation in the dependent criterion and thus, using the variables together does not improve the prediction.

Multicollinearity is commonly present in social science data (Lewis-Beck, 1980), but a solution which is widely used and accepted is to use multiple linear regression techniques which select independent variables and discard other related or offending variables.

In the original report of this study (Oakland, 1991) stepwise multiple linear regression equations were computed where the independent variable that explains the greatest amount of variance in the dependent variable enters the equation first. Subsequently, however, more sophisticated analyses have been conducted using hierarchical multiple regression and incorporating additional variables.

Hierarchical multiple regression differs from stepwise regression in that the order in which the predictor variables are to be used can be specified in advance by the researcher (Achen, 1982). Here, the choice of variables is guided by two main considerations:

- the theoretical model or conceptual framework which relates to the chosen variables;

- the strength of the relationships or intercorrelations between the variables.

These later analyses, to determine the best predictors of situational and health outcomes, are described below.

6.7 Critical variables in the hierarchical regression analyses

The aim of the analyses was to identify those combinations of variables which best predicted the outcomes of headteachers' problem solving efforts for problem A (successful outcome) and problem B (unsuccessful outcome), and the headteachers' psychological health and physical symptoms. Variables critical to these analyses are identified in the models of stress processes and problem solving offered in chapter 1 (figures 1.1 to 1.4 - see also Oakland, 1991, and Ostell 1991) as well as in the literature review.

The initial stage of the analyses was concerned with eliminating from consideration any variables believed on theoretical grounds to be relevant to the study but which empirically proved unusable. First questionnaire and interview variables (including biographical data) were intercorrelated. Because some interview variables were related to problem A and some to problem B two separate correlation matrices were generated. Only selected portions of these matrices are discussed here but the complete matrices are reported in Oakland (1991).

Altogether nine variables were excluded from the hierarchical analyses. First, the number of years' teaching experience was excluded because it was significantly associated only with the age of the headteacher ($r = .68$). Second, although a strong association was found between the number of pupils on the roll and the number of teaching staff ($r = .89$), neither of these variables were significantly related to the variables of pivotal interest to the study, namely outcome A, outcome B, psychological health and physical symptoms. Third, although it was hypothesized that an event would be appraised as more unpleasant if it was both unfamiliar and unexpected, significant associations were only found in section A of the interview. Fourth, the variables which measured perceptions of control, confidence, personal skills and how well the problem situation was handled were excluded because the way in which these variables were measured made it difficult to specify whether they should be treated as independent or dependent variables. Again, interested readers can refer to Oakland (1991) for a description of the analyses and results relating to perceptions of control, confidence, personal skills and how well the problem was handled.

The remaining variables which were used in the hierarchical analyses are summarized in Table 6.4 and intercorrelations between these variables are reported in Table 6.5.

Table 6.4
Guide to variable interpretation and scoring

Variable	Interpretation	Scoring	High score associated with
AGE	Age		
SEX	Sex	0 or 1	0=Male, 1=Female
YRSHEAD	No. of years in headship		
SCHOOL	First or Middle school	0 or 1	0=First, 1=Middle
DISADV	School receives/does not receive 'disadvantaged area' funding	0 or 1	0=Funding, 1=no funding
NEM	Negative emotionality	0-11	Elevated neuroticism
AJE	Affective job experience	17-102	Unpleasant job demands
GHQ	General Health Questionnaire	0-36	Poor psychological health
SYMP	Physical symptoms	17-102	Poor physical symptoms
ABSOL	Absoluteness	0 or 1	Absolutist thinking style
ATTRIB	Attributional style	0 or 1	Non-self-serving attributional style
A/B.RESOURCES	External resource adequacy in section A or B	1-3*	Inadequate external resource
A/B.OUTCOME	Situational outcome in section A or B	1-4*	Outcome worsened

*
Interview coding scores reversed for ease of interpretation in correlation procedures.

Table 6.5

Intercorrelations between main questionnaire and interview variables

		1	2	3	4	5	6	7	8	9	10	11	12	13	14	15
1	AGE		.32	.53**	-.02	-.06	-.08	-.05	.12	.11	-.24	.14	-.09	.19	-.19	.15
2	SEX			-.21	-.41**	.30	.08	.02	.12	.20	-.27	.20	-.08	.13	.03	.06
3	YRSHEAD				-.04	-.02	-.18	-.09	.02	.04	-.07	.04	-.09	.08	-.13	.07
4	SCHOOL					.35*	-.16	-.13	-.20	-.20	-.29*	.25	.12	-.34*	.14	.12
5	DISADV						-.22	-.04	-.22	-.08	.25	-.30	.211	-.22	.06	.03
6	NEM							.54**	.67**	.55**	.39**	.49**	.39**	.13	-.13	.05
7	AJE								.65**	.46**	.33*	.31*	.21	.21	-.11	.31*
8	GHQ									.72**	.60**	.67**	.32*	.25	-.27*	.18
9	SYMP										.61**	.61**	.28	.22	-.23	.15
10	ABSOL											.76**	.33	.40**	.23	-.12
11	ATTRIB												.36*	.38**	-.27**	.12
12	A.RESOURCES													.46**	.38**	-.01
13	A.OUTCOME														.07	.07
14	B.RESOURCES															-.11
15	B.OUTCOME															

* p<.01   ** p<.001

126

Two principles, used in conjunction, determined the order in which these variables were input into the hierarchical analyses. First, variables were input according to the degree to which headteachers could manage the impact of them upon problem solving and stress processes. Thus personal characteristics and situational factors over which heads had no control regarding impact (e.g., biological factors such as sex and age, and school type - whether 'first' or 'middle' schools) were input before those variables for which some self-management was possible. The second principle was that variables were input, as far as possible, in the order in which they contribute to stress processes (e.g., beliefs and values which influence primary appraisal would be input prior to external resources which influence secondary appraisal processes). This is not meant to imply that these variables operate in an invariant sequence, rather that the final equations for the analyses should model typical influences of these variables on stress processes and problem solving.

The overall sequence determined by these two principles was as follows:

- Step 1: Age, sex, and years in headship

- Step 2: School type, whether first or middle

- Step 3: Whether or not a school received funding for being in a 'disadvantaged' area

All these variables are ones over which heads have no direct control regarding their impact upon problem solving and stress processes.

- Step 4: NEM was introduced at this stage to remove any confounding measurement effects (as discussed previously) and, because it is believed to have a strong genetic basis, its substantive influence on stress processes is only partly under the control of a headteacher.

- Step 5: Absoluteness or Attributional style. As these two variables are very highly correlated only one could be used in each operation.

- Step 6: External resource availability, although this is a situational variable it could be considerably influenced by a headteacher's behaviour.

- Step 7: Affective Job Experience (AJE)

Although variables were input in the above sequence, not all variables were used for each analysis as some were not correlated to the criterion variables (problem outcomes A and B, psychological health and physical symptoms). Further, interactions between variables are not reported in the main analyses (i.e., tables 6.6

- 6.11), as preliminary investigations indicated that no interactions achieved significant effects. Certain near significant interactions are mentioned when relevant.

Finally, because the predictor variables were measured using different kinds of scales (e.g., dichotomous, interval, etc.) the headteachers' scores were converted to Z scores thus standardizing the distributions of scores for each predictor variable.

6.8   Predictors of successful outcomes (A. OUTCOME)

Only six of the seven steps outlined above were used in this hierarchical analysis; NEM was not included. It was excluded because there is no confounding measurement effect between NEM and problem outcome (see chapter 3 section 2) and because NEM had a very low correlation (-.13) with outcome A.

The results of the analysis are reported in table 6.6. The upper part of the table details the amount of variance (R^2) in the dependent variable explained by the independent or predictor variable(s) entered at each step of the analysis and the change in R^2 (ΔR^2) from one step to the next. The lower part of the table reports the final model or equation obtained at the last step of the hierarchical analysis. That is it reports: the standardized regression coefficients (Betas) for each variable, the overall variance explained (R^2 (Model)) in the dependent variable, and the statistical significance of the final model as a predictor of the dependent variable for the last step in the analysis.

Three variables accounted for significant increases in variance explained at different steps in the hierarchical analysis. The type of school (first or middle) accounted for 9.8% of the variance, absolutist thinking added a further 6.3% and resources explained 9.7% of the variance.

The final model indicates, however, that only the regression coefficients for type of school and resources are significant. Thus the perceived adequacy of the resources available was high for problems with a successful outcome and headteachers in middle schools reported higher levels of perceived success at problem solving than heads in first schools.

The funding for resources is predictable but also encouraging as it reinforces the view expressed earlier that it is important to measure external resource adequacy as a factor in coping as well as that of internal resource adequacy. Possible reasons for the finding concerning nature of school are discussed in chapter 7. The fact that absolutist thinking is significant as a step in the hierarchical analysis but not in the final model indicates either that its contribution to problem solving is relatively weak or perhaps that more reliable measurement of this variable would have resulted in a stronger effect. The direction of the effect is in line with predictions, namely, that the more absolutist a headteacher the less successful they were at handling the problem with a successful outcome.

Table 6.6

Hierarchical regression analysis predicting successful outcomes

	Independent variable	Cumulative R^2	ΔR^2	F	p
Step 1	AGE, SEX, YRSHEAD	.049	.049	1.29	.283
Step 2	SCHOOL	.147	.098	8.68	.004**
Step 3	DISADV	.161	.013	1.17	.282
Step 4	ABSOL	.224	.063	5.95	.017*
Step 5	A.RESOURCES	.316	.092	9.70	.003**
Step 6	AJE	.318	.002	.17	.677

*p<.05   **p<.01   ***p<.001

Final Model

Variables	Beta	T	p
AGE	.153570	1.264	.2104
SEX	.083534	.724	.4713
YRSHEAD	-.065744	-.541	.5901
SCHOOL	-.261016	-2.275	.0259
DISADV	-.043340	-.398	.6918
ABSOL	-.163189	-1.380	.1719
A.RESOURCES	-.320445	-3.017	.0035
AJE	.044483	.418	.6774

Overall R^2 (Model) = .318, F (Model) = 4.131, p = .000

Note:

R^2 *denotes the amount of variance in the dependent variable which can be explained by the independent variable(s) entered at each step of the equation.*

ΔR^2 *denotes the change in R^2 from one step to another in the equation.*

F   *= statistic for the change in R^2*
R^2 *(Model)*   *= overall value of R^2 for the final equation*
F *(Model)*   *= statistic for the final equation*

Beta values are the standardized regression coefficients for each variable in the equation.

T   *= value of regression coefficients*
p   *= value of regression coefficients*

6.9   Predictors of unsuccessful outcomes (B. OUTCOME)

The same hierarchical analysis was used for problem B as for problem A, that is, excluding the NEM variable. The stepwise analysis and the final model shows that a much smaller amount of variance in the dependent variable is accounted for (16.3%) in this analysis and that only the Affective Job Experience scale (AJE), which accounts for 9.7% of the variance, is a significant predictor of the unsuccessful outcome (see table 6.7). This indicates that the more unpleasant the experience of heads with the job demands they faced the more unsuccessful they were at handling problem B. Whether high scores for this variable reflect a lack of motivation regarding problem solving, or a lack of ability, or both, is unclear. What is clear is that the analysis provides little insight into the variables which explain the unsuccessful outcomes for problem B.

The analyses for problem solving are useful in that they identify variables which do not contribute to problem outcomes, namely: biographical variables regarding age, sex and years of headship; NEM; and the status of a school as disadvantaged or not. The analyses are less useful in identifying comprehensible factors leading to particular outcomes. External resource adequacy results, predictably, in greater success at problem solving and perceiving job demands as unpleasant predicts lack of success with problems. In chapter 7, however, qualitative data provide ideas which suggest why particular outcomes result from certain problems.

6.10   Predictors of psychological health (GHQ)

Six steps were used in the hierarchical analyses for psychological health (GHQ). NEM was included because it proved highly correlated ($r = 0.67$, $p<0.001$) with GHQ scores reflecting the confounding measurement error discussed previously (chapter 3 section 2) and, no doubt, a substantive effect of negative emotionality contributing to the distress processes which are measured by GHQ.

The resources variables (A.RES and B.RES), however, were not included. It obviously did not make sense to combine the perceived adequacy of resources for problems with successful and unsuccessful outcomes into one variable. Explanatory analyses with each variable in different models (equations), in which they were entered at the sixth or seventh step, also indicated that they accounted for very little variance (see also Oakland, 1991).

The cognitive variables, absolutist thinking (ABSOL) and attributional style (ATTRIB), were also highly correlated ($r = 0.79$, $p<0.0001$) indicating considerable overlap in terms of the basic cognitive construct they assess and that each also taps unique aspects of this construct. Thus two separate analyses were performed for psychological health, one incorporating ABSOL at step 5, the other incorporating ATTRIB. The results of the analyses are reported in tables 6.8 and 6.9 respectively.

Table 6.7
Hierarchical regression analyses predicting unsuccessful outcomes

	Independent variable	Cumulative R^2	ΔR^2	F	p
Step 1	AGE, SEX, YRSHEAD	.031	.031	.82	.489
Step 2	SCHOOL	.041	.010	.78	.379
Step 3	DISADV	.041	.000	.00	.990
Step 4	ABSOL	.061	.020	1.52	.221
Step 5	B.RESOURCES	.066	.006	.44	.509
Step 6	AJE	.163	.096	8.15	.006**

*$p <.05$ **$p <.01$ ***$p <.001$

Final Model

Variables	Beta	T	p
AGE	.146916	1.084	.2821
SEX	.008081	.063	.9498
YRSHEAD	.029495	.220	.8268
SCHOOL	.178191	1.394	.1676
DISADV	.005310	.045	.9646
ABSOL	-.021087	-.164	.8705
B.RESOURCES	-.062714	-.550	.5843
AJE	.334462	2.855	.0056

Overall R^2 (Model) = .163, F (Model) = 1.725, p = .107

Note:

R^2 denotes the amount of variance in the dependent variable which can be explained by the independent variable(s) entered at each step of the equation.

ΔR^2 denotes the change in R^2 from one step to another in the equation.

F	= statistic for the change in R^2
R^2 (Model)	= overall value of R^2 for the final equation
F (Model)	= statistic for the final equation

Beta values are the standardized regression coefficients for each variable in the equation.

T	= value of regression coefficients
p	= value of regression coefficients

Table 6.8
Hierarchical regression analysis predicting psychological health (GHQ)
(Stage 1 - including ABSOL)

	Independent Variable	Cumulative R^2	ΔR^2	F	p
Step 1	AGE, SEX, YRSHEAD	.026	.026	.68	.568
Step 2	SCHOOL	.053	.027	2.10	.151
Step 3	DISADV	.077	.024	1.19	.171
Step 4	NEM	.496	.419	60.70	.000***
Step 5	ABSOL	.591	.095	16.74	.000***
Step 6	AJE	.674	.084	18.31	.000***

*p<.05   **p<.01   ***p<.001

Final Model

Variables	Beta	T	p
AGE	.037024	.441	.6606
SEX	-.044487	-.006	.9955
YRSHEAD	.104633	1.238	.2197
SCHOOL	.023222	.293	.7702
DISADV	-.049909	-.660	.5115
NEM	.374552	4.326	.0000
ABSOL	-.307946	-3.760	.0003
AJE	.352906	4.279	.0001

Overall R^2 (Model) = .674, F (Model) = 18.41, p = .000

Note:

R^2 *denotes the amount of variance in the dependent variable which can be explained by the independent variable(s) entered at each step of the equation.*

ΔR^2 *denotes the change in R^2 from one step to another in the equation.*

F   *= statistic for the change in R^2*
R^2 *(Model)*   *= overall value of R^2 for the final equation*
F *(Model)*   *= statistic for the final equation*

Beta values are the standardized regression coefficients for each variable in the equation.

T   *= value of regression coefficients*
p   *= value of regression coefficients*

Table 6.9
Hierarchical regression analysis predicting psychological health (GHQ)
(Stage 2 - including ATTRIB)

	Independent Variable	Cumulative R^2	ΔR^2	F	p
Step 1	AGE, SEX, YRSHEAD	.026	.026	.68	.568
Step 2	SCHOOL	.053	.027	2.10	.151
Step 3	DISADV	.077	.024	1.19	.171
Step 4	NEM	.496	.419	60.70	.000***
Step 5	ATTRIB	.612	.116	21.52	.000***
Step 6	AJE	.710	.098	24.12	.000***

*p<.05   **p<.01   ***p<.001

Final Model

Variables	Beta	T	p
AGE	.061345	.790	.4321
SEX	-.014856	-.199	.8428
YRSHEAD	.087987	1.102	.2743
SCHOOL	.015217	.205	.8384
DISADV	-.019627	-.273	.7859
NEM	.296819	3.477	.0009
ATTRIB	.384786	4.956	.0000
AJE	.377793	4.912	.0000

Overall R^2 (Model) = .710, F (Model) = 21.75, p = .000

Note:

R^2 denotes the amount of variance in the dependent variable which can be explained by the independent variable(s) entered at each step of the equation.

ΔR^2 denotes the change in R^2 from one step to another in the equation.

F	= statistics for the change in R^2
R^2 (Model)	= overall value of R^2 for the final equation
F (Model)	= statistic for the final equation

Beta values are the standardized regression coefficients for each variable in the equation.

T	= value of regression coefficients
p	= value of regression coefficients

In these analyses the biographical variables (age, sex, years of headship) and the school variables (first/middle, disadvantaged/not disadvantaged) were not significant predictors of psychological health and between them only accounted for 7.7% of the variance in GHQ scores.

NEM is a highly significant predictor of psychological health contributing 41.9% to the variance in GHQ scores at step 4 indicating that high negative emotionality scores are associated with poorer psychological health. Part of this explained variance is due to confounding measurement error and part due to a genuine distress effect. As pointed out previously, however, the relative contribution of each effect to the increase in explained variance cannot be determined.

At step 5 in the first analysis absolutist thinking added a further 9.5% to the explained variance (table 6.8) and in the second analysis attributional style added 11.6% to the explained variance (table 6.9). Thus absolutist thinking was associated with poorer psychological health whereas non-absolutist thinking was associated with better psychological health. Similarly, heads with a self-serving attributional style had better psychological health than those with a non-self-serving attributional style. Neither of these cognitive variables has been measured previously in studies of stress and each clearly accounts for unique and highly significant additional variance in health scores above that explained by NEM.

The AJE variable also explained a further 8.4% of variance in the first analysis (table 6.8) and 9.8% of variance in the second analysis (table 6.9). The higher the perceived unpleasantness of headteachers' job demands the poorer their psychological health.

Comparing the final models for each analysis these variables (NEM, ABSOL/ATTRIB and AJE) remain highly significant predictors. It is also clear that while NEM accounts for a large percentage of the variance in health scores in both analyses and has the highest beta in the first analysis (table 6.8), it is ATTRIB and AJE which have higher betas than NEM in the second analysis (table 6.9). These results are discussed further in chapter 8.

6.11   Predictors of physical symptoms (SYMP)

The final phase of the quantitative analyses was to determine those predictors which best predicted the physical symptoms of headteachers as measured by the SYMP scale. As before, two analyses were conducted using absolutist thinking and attributional style in step 5. The results are reported in tables 6.10 and 6.11 respectively. Once again the biographical and school variables did not predict the symptom scores whereas NEM accounted for a considerable amount of variance in SYMP scores (30.9%) but much less than for GHQ scores (41.9%). High negative emotionality was associated with high physical symptoms score. This reduction in the amount of variance explained can be attributed in part to the fact that NEM has

Table 6.10
Hierarchical regression analysis predicting physical symptoms (SYMP)
(Stage 1 - including ABSOL)

	Independent Variable	Cumulative R^2	ΔR^2	F	p
Step 1	AGE, SEX, YRSHEAD	.049	.049	1.29	.283
Step 2	SCHOOL	.067	.018	1.47	.229
Step 3	DISADV	.067	.000	0.02	.881
Step 4	NEM	.376	.309	36.22	.000***
Step 5	ABSOL	.517	.141	20.94	.000***
Step 6	AJE	.530	.013	1.98	.164

*$p < .05$ **$p .01$ ***$p < .001$

Final Model

Variables	Beta	T	p
AGE	-.009503	-.094	.9252
SEX	-.104588	-1.090	.2793
YRSHEAD	.109979	1.083	.2825
SCHOOL	-.009580	-.101	.9201
DISADV	.145581	1.601	.1138
NEM	.355447	3.416	.0011
ABSOL	-.423271	-4.299	.0001
AJE	.139573	1.408	.1636

Overall R^2 (Model) = .530, F (Model) = 10.01, p = .000

Note:

R^2 denotes the amount of variance in the dependent variable which can be explained by the independent variable(s) entered at each step of the equation.

ΔR^2 denotes the change in R^2 from one step to another in the equation.

F	= statistic for the change in R^2
R^2 (Model)	= overall value of R^2 for the final equation
F (Model)	= statistic for the final equation

Beta values are the standardized regression coefficients for each variable in the equation.

T	= value of regression coefficients
p	= value of regression coefficients

Table 6.11
Hierarchical regression analysis predicting physical symptoms (SYMP)
(Stage 2 - including ATTRIB)

	Independent Variable	Cumulative R^2	ΔR^2	F	p
Step 1	AGE, SEX, YRSHEAD	.049	.049	1.29	.283
Step 2	SCHOOL	.067	.018	1.47	.229
Step 3	DISADV	.067	.000	.023	.881
Step 4	NEM	.376	.309	36.22	.000***
Step 5	ATTRIB	.499	.123	17.67	.000***
Step 6	AJE	.522	.023	3.41	.069

*$p < .05$ **$p < .01$ ***$p < .001$

Final model

Variables	Beta	T	p
AGE	.039532	.397	.6929
SEX	-.135215	-1.411	.1625
YRSHEAD	.093575	.913	.3646
SCHOOL	-.030503	-.319	.7503
DISADV	.170610	1.846	.0691
NEM	.296934	2.709	.0085
ATTRIB	.411275	4.125	.0001
AJE	.182360	1.846	.0690

Overall R^2 (Model) = .522, F (Model) = 9.70, p = .000

Note:

R^2 *denotes the amount of variance in the dependent variable which can be explained by the independent variable(s) entered at each step of the equation.*

ΔR^2 *denotes the change in R^2 from one step to another in the equation.*

F	= statistic for the change in R^2
R^2 (Model)	= overall value of R^2 for the final equation
F (Model)	= statistic for the final equation

Beta values are the standardized regression coefficients for each variable in the equation.

T	= value of regression coefficients
p	= value of regression coefficients

a more direct impact upon psychological states (as measured by the GHQ) than upon physical symptoms which are subject to influence by many other factors. These results are explored further in chapter 8.

Absolutist thinking was a highly significant predictor of physical symptoms in analysis one, increasing the explained variance by 14.1% (table 6.10), as was attributional style in the second analysis, which accounted for 12.3% of the variance (table 6.11). Absolutist thinkers and those with a non-self-serving attributional style had high physical symptoms scores. In the final model for both analyses NEM had smaller betas than absolutist thinking and attributional style.

AJE scores failed to predict physical symptoms in analysis one which included absolutist thinking, but approached significance in the second analysis including attributional style (p = 0.069).

The analyses of health outcomes proved more illuminating than those concerning problem outcomes. In particular, two variables which play a key role in appraisal processes (absolutist thinking and attributional style) have emerged as predictors of psychological and physical health.

6.12   Chapter summary

This chapter has detailed the quantitative and qualitative data analyses, including the coding and quantification of some of the qualitative interview data. The statistical analyses have indicated the magnitude of the associations between certain variables in the theoretical process model of stress, coping and health and highlighted the quantitative findings of pivotal interest to the study.

The main objectives of this study were to determine the factors which can influence the outcome of problem situations headteachers have to deal with at work and explore the impact on their psychological and physical health. In all the analyses, neither the age of the headteachers, nor the sex, nor the number of years experience in headship was significantly related to situational or health outcomes. The best predictors of successful outcomes were school type (i.e., First or Middle) and external resources. Only perceived job demands (AJE) proved to be a significant predictor of unsuccessful outcomes, but the qualitative interview data are used to throw some light on this result in chapter 7. Negative emotionality, absolutist thinking and attributional style accounted for varying and substantial amounts of the variance in both psychological health (GHQ) and physical symptoms (SYMP). In the case of GHQ, perceived work demands also made significant contributions to the dependent criterion, even when the main cognitive variables ABSOL and ATTRIB were included in the same equation.

To some extent, the relationships between NEM, GHQ and SYMP were expected since other studies have found NEM to be strongly associated with self-report health measures. However, the real value of these analyses is in identifying absolutist thinking, attributional style and external resource adequacy as vital components of the stress process and as powerful predictors of situational and/or health outcomes. The former two variables illustrate the key role of appraisal processes in determining individuals health outcomes.

These quantitative data now need to be supplemented by qualitative data in order that a better understanding can be gained, for example, of how individuals high in NEM appraise situations differently to those low in NEM and of why headteachers who appraise situations in an absolutist way or with a non-self-serving attributional style had poorer psychological and somatic health. Chapter 8 explores these and other health-related issues through an examination of the qualitative data collected during the interviews with headteachers.

7 Work problems, coping and outcomes

In this chapter, attention turns to the results of the data analyses relating to how headteachers attempt to cope with difficult situations at work and the factors which can influence situational outcomes.

The main purpose of the semi-structured interviews with the headteachers was to explore how they perceived, felt about and attempted to cope with two difficult work situations. Each interview comprised two sections - the first relating to problem A, described by the headteacher as having a 'successful' outcome. The second section related to problem B, a situation described as having an 'unsuccessful' outcome.

7.1　Main determinants of successful outcomes

Of the seven variables used in the hierarchical regression analyses (detailed in chapter 6), three variables were statistically significant predictors of successful outcomes, namely: school type, absolutist thinking and external resources.

School type

The results indicated that the headteachers from middle schools described the problem with a successful outcome as more successful than did first school heads. That is, the middle school heads tended to describe the outcome as 'resolved' rather than 'improved' whereas the reverse was true for first school heads.

The data do not point to an obvious, straightforward explanation for this difference between school types. The finding may be related to differences in the roles of first and middle school headteachers. For example, from the qualitative interview data it was apparent that middle school heads tend to have lower involvement in day-to-day teaching and concentrate more on administrative and related problems and, particularly in the larger schools, often have several support staff (e.g., a middle management team) to assist them. The reverse tends to be true for first school heads who might therefore be more involved in less successful situations because of the wide range of activities they regularly undertake and the fact that they have fewer colleagues to assist them.

Absolutist thinking

In the regression analyses, absolutist thinking also added 6% to the explained variance of the dependent criterion - successful outcome. It was a marginally significant factor indicating that headteachers with an absolutist thinking style tended to describe the outcome as 'improved' rather than 'resolved' whereas the reverse was true for those with a non-absolutist style. One explanation for this finding may be that, as discussed in earlier chapters, the absolutist-type dialogues people engage in during appraisal and coping can deflect the person from problem-solving and thereby influence actual coping behaviour and ultimately, situational outcomes. Of course it is equally feasible that an unsuccessful situational outcome could **result in** absolutist dialogues (e.g., It's so unfair..... etc.). As coping is an ongoing, cyclical process (Oakland, 1991; Ostell, 1991) absolutist thinking probably figures as both a cause and a reaction in this cycle.

External resources

In chapter 5, details were given of paired T-tests which showed highly significant differences in the adequacy of advice, information and emotional support in sections A and B of the interview. These results indicated therefore that in line with the model of stress posited in chapter 1, the outcome of a situation can be influenced by the adequacy of external resources which are available to the individual. The results of the hierarchical regression analysis added further credence to this idea by showing adequate external resources to be a very significant predictor of successful outcomes.

This result is important because as the literature review in earlier chapters showed, relatively few studies of stress and coping have attempted to assess external resource adequacy empirically, even though the importance of external resources has been emphasized theoretically for decades. Furthermore even studies which have considered external resources have tended to limit their enquiries to social support rather than finances, advice, information and so on. Thus, this result demonstrates empirically that external resources are an integral part of the coping process and that their adequacy can affect coping outcomes. Just how external resources might affect situational outcomes can be best explored using the qualitative data.

According to the stress model, if external resources are required in a problem situation, the availability and adequacy of those resources not only influences primary and secondary appraisal but also shapes coping activity. In other words, the resources a person believes are available affects both primary appraisals of potential costs and secondary appraisals of coping options and viable coping responses. By presenting the qualitative data in tabular form, the intention is to illustrate and highlight the contrasting effects on appraisal and coping outcomes when external resources are adequate and when they are inadequate. Consider first the effects on appraisal and coping of adequate external resources in Table 7.1.

Adequate resources, appraisal and coping outcomes

A general observation from looking at Table 7.1 is that when external resources are required in a problem situation and are both available and adequate, this has positive effects on appraisal, coping options and responses. It can be seen, for example, that adequate advice from others can generate alternative ideas for coping and thus increase the individual's coping choices. In other examples, the advice is functional because it reassures the individual or reinforces the strategies they have already considered, thus enhancing confidence. It is also evident that perceived adequate emotional support has positive, comforting effects on the individuals, again boosting perceptions of confidence about dealing with the problem. Practical assistance or help in these examples facilitates the situation because the actual task of coping is shared between the headteacher and the helper(s), reminiscent of the proverb, 'A trouble shared is a trouble halved'. These facilitative effects on appraisal and coping are not evident however when external resources are rated as inadequate as the examples in Table 7.2 illustrate.

Inadequate resources, appraisal and coping outcomes

The data in Table 7.2 illustrate the negative and potentially dysfunctional effects which inadequate resourcing can have on appraisal, coping options and responses. The examples show how lack of adequate help and/or advice can affect persistence and motivation and sometimes thwart coping attempts altogether leading to frustration, anxieties and feelings of hopelessness and helplessness. Other distressing reactions such as anger and sadness are aroused when financial resources, which would help to solve the situation, are inadequate or not available at all. Hence, the general negative tone apparent in appraisals when external resources are inadequate, contrasts sharply with appraisals when resources are adequate.

In summary, these data highlight the complexity of coping and the fact that a problem situation is often dealt with by more than one individual be it through delegation or collaborative coping efforts. Above all, these data show that external

Table 7.1   Effects on appraisal and coping of adequate* external resources

Reference	Advice	Emotional support	Inform-ation	Help/ assistance	Financial	Effects on appraisal and coping
1A-M-FS	N/A	7	N/A	7	N/A	I asked a colleague for help and we dealt with a parent each. Practically it facilitated things and I was confident we'd sort it out because he was so supportive.
9A-M-FS	N/A	5	5	6	N/A	I got lots of information which meant I could consider different strategies. This made me feel confident because I knew I'd got a good case against her. I also talked it through with my wife and the deputy which helped because it's supportive.
27B-F-FS	5	6	N/A	5	N/A	I used my colleagues as sounding boards for advice and support which helped my confidence. The advisor helped by actually setting the probationer's targets, which was a job less for me.
35A-F-FS	6	7	7	6	N/A	The Education Welfare Officer and the Social Services were very supportive and informed me of the laid down procedure for cases like this - it was so helpful - you can't go wrong when there is a set procedure.
39B-M-MS	7	N/A	N/A	N/A	N/A	I talked with the deputy and asked her advice which helped because it reinforced what I'd done and confirmed my first thoughts.

*where 'adequate' = score 5, 6 or 7
N/A = not applicable

Table 7.2   Effects on appraisal and coping of inadequate* external resources

Reference	Advice	Emotional support	Information	Help/ assistance	Financial	Effects on appraisal and coping
11B-F-FS	N/A	N/A	N/A	1	N/A	I've had no help at all from external agencies and without help I can't diffuse the situation - it's so frustrating.
13B-F-FS	3	N/A	N/A	3	3	We need more finances and, there were great time lags before the Educational Psychologists did anything, and then they didn't know what to do. We've drawn a blank wall, I feel lost and not sure what to do next.
21B-F-FS	3	N/A	3	2	1	Those giving the advice are also in the dark - it makes me apprehensive. And it's frustrating because the information is only available in bursts. We can't get any more help and there's no money available to buy the equipment needed - so there's little chance that I'll sort it out anyway.
33A-F-FS	N/A	N/A	N/A	1	N/A	No help at all is offered from the LEA and yet training would help enormously - instead I just carry on trying to deal with it and worrying about my skills.
63B-M-MS	1	3	N/A	N/A	1	The financial situation is pathetic. In spite of all my efforts the facilities here get more and more archaic. I asked the Health and Safety representatives for advice - they came along, but nothing's changed. The staff try to understand but they still give me earache. I'm resigned to the fact that nothing will happen now - it makes me so angry and sad for the kids.

*where 'inadequate' = score 1, 2 or 3
N/A = not applicable

143

resources are an integral part of the appraisal and coping process and how their adequacy can have profound effects on coping options, coping action effectiveness, psychological distress and ultimately, situational outcomes (Oakland and Ostell, 1995). These results suggest that situational rather than individual factors contributed most to successful problem solving at work for the headteachers.

7.2   Main determinants of unsuccessful outcomes

Only one of the variables used in the hierarchical analyses for the successful outcomes was a significant predictor for the problems with unsuccessful outcomes, namely, job demands which accounted for 10% of the variance. Headteachers who had high 'pleasantness' ratings for their job demands described the unsuccessful outcome as 'unchanged' rather than 'worsened'. The reverse was true for headteachers with low 'pleasantness' or 'unpleasantness' ratings for their job demands. This finding is hardly an explanation for unsuccessful outcomes as it could be that heads who perceived the greatest lack of success with handling these work problems tended to view their work demands as less pleasant.

Thus the quantitative analyses did not throw much light upon the question of why certain problems were not managed successfully. Qualitative analysis, however, suggested that the differences in outcome most probably reflected differences in the nature of the problems concerned. These differences were by no means completely clear-cut, but problems with successful outcomes tended to be ones which were more discrete and structured. Procedures or guidelines about how to handle these situations frequently existed and the heads had often encountered similar situations before. In contrast problems with unsuccessful outcomes could be characterized as ones which tended to become protracted because adequate resources were not available and because the headteachers were only partly responsible for sorting out the situations as other agencies were responsible for some facet of the problems (e.g., involvement of the Social Services for a child with difficult behavioural problems). Over time some heads became more emotionally involved with these problems and their lack of success was often de-motivating resulting in them experiencing strong anger and despair about the situations (see, for example, quotations 63B-M-MS and 21-B-FS in table 7.2.

7.3   Work problems and coping strategies

This section focuses on the results of the data analyses relating to the ways in which the headteachers attempted to cope with difficult work situations. As detailed in chapter 4, open-ended questions were asked about the coping strategies the headteachers used in response to stressful work situations and a coping response prompt list (see Table 4.4) was used to assist memorial recall and encourage elaboration. Questions were also asked about the effectiveness of the responses in an attempt to circumvent a weakness of many other studies which ignore whether or not a strategy worked and to explore and better understand the impact of in/effective actions on stress reactions and situational outcomes.

The number, nature and combinations of problem focused strategies varied tremendously and involved a multiplicity of factors including situational requirements, time constraints, personal skills, judgements and choices, access to external resources and so on. But broadly speaking, when their statements about coping were considered in purely semantic terms and in isolation from other contextual data, it was clear that the headteachers' responses fell into the familiar problem focused categories evident in most coping studies (e.g., Folkman et al., 1986a). For example, consider how the headteachers' open-ended responses reflect the problem focused strategies typically included in checklists such as the Ways of Coping Checklist (WCCL):

> I went home and formulated a plan for how to deal with her.
>
> (21B-F-FS)
>
> *I made a plan of action and followed it.*
>
> (WCCL item 26)

> I contacted the Schools Adviser for advice on what to do.
>
> (5A-F-FS)
>
> *I asked a friend/colleague I respected for advice.*
>
> (WCCL item 42)

> I contacted the Social Services to get more information about the boy.
>
> (32B-M-FS)
>
> *Talked to someone to find out more about the situation.*
>
> (WCCL item 8)

> I thought it through carefully all the night before, rehearsing in my mind what I would say.
>
> (51A-M-MS)
>
> *I went over in my mind what I would do or say.*
>
> (WCCL item 62)

The above examples illustrate how the headteachers' problem focused strategies, when considered as isolated statements, closely mirror the responses usually included in coping checklists (Oakland and Ostell, 1995). An original intention of this study was to categorize the open-ended responses and create a quantitative measure of coping to use as a potential predictor of situational and health outcomes. However, numerous attempts to content analyze the qualitative coping data and construct meaningful and reliable quantitative categories for the coping strategies proved impossible for two main reasons:

1. Classifying the strategies according to whether and/or how often the respondents sought resources such as advice or more information was of little value when data about the **external resource adequacy** were considered.

2. Classifying the strategies according to the type and/or how often they were used was meaningless when data about their **effectiveness** was considered.

Nevertheless, through an examination of the qualitative coping data it is possible to

- describe some of the strategies used by the headteachers

- illustrate the impact the strategies had on situational outcomes and/or psychological stress reactions

- demonstrate that the two reasons why a quantitative measure of overt problem focused coping could not be derived from the data draw attention to certain weaknesses in current methods of assessing coping behaviours.

Coping, external resource adequacy and outcomes

One reason why it proved impossible to quantify the problem focused strategies is related to external resource adequacy. Most of the problem situations described involved other people than the head who were required to give help, advice, information, emotional support and so on, to the headteacher. Hence, as the above quotes indicate, on describing coping responses they indicated they had 'Contacted the Schools Adviser for advice on what to do' (5A-F-FS) or 'Contacted the Social Services, to get more information' (32B-M-FS). It proved futile however to try and code such responses in terms of whether or how often they had sought advice or information since what was more important regarding situational and/or health outcomes was the adequacy of the advice and information. For instance, the first head who 'contacted the Schools Adviser for advice on what to do' qualified this by adding 'but the Adviser did not know what to do either.' (5A-F-FS). Similarly, the headteacher who 'contacted the Social Services to get more information' had his efforts thwarted when he was told that the information regarding the boy was 'highly confidential' (32B-M-FS). Thus, the important factor here in terms of outcomes is not that the heads sought advice or information but rather, the adequacy of that advice and information.

This raises questions about the utility of coping checklists which focus on whether and how often advice, information, emotional support etc., were sought and try to determine relationships between these behaviours and various situational and health outcome measures. The data here indicate that coping items which focus on resource adequacy would be of greater value as potential predictors of outcomes.

Coping, effectiveness and outcomes

The second reason it proved impossible to quantify the coping behaviours concerns coping effectiveness and also highlights a limitation in existing coping measures. In chapter 2, details were given of the extensively-used method of assessing coping behaviours which comprises lists of cognitive/behavioural strategies people might use to manage the problem and/or their emotional reactions. Respondents report how frequently they used a strategy and the frequency is then correlated with various situational/personal outcome measures. The qualitative data in this study, however, indicated that knowledge of the frequency with which a strategy is used is far less important (in terms of situational and personal outcomes) than knowledge about the effectiveness of the strategy.

Congruent with Pearlin and Schooler (1978) it was evident in this study that the number of coping strategies respondents used varied tremendously. But extending previous research, the qualitative data showed that the effectiveness of coping actions also varied greatly from one problem to another. More specifically, some headteachers used a single action such as talking with a parent to diffuse a situation or devising a work schedule plan for a probationary teacher and this resolved the problem satisfactorily, whilst another headteacher makes a plan of action to deal with a situation, executes the plan, the plan is not effective and the situation remains unchanged. Consider, for example, the impact on situational and personal outcomes of this headteacher's planful problem focused strategy:

> I sat down with the caretaker and together we drew up a work schedule for him so that he would have a structure or routine to work to. But nothing has changed - he still doesn't do his job properly and still has no initiative. I can do without this, it's a pain in the head. I've no time - I'm so busy - administration like this is a real headache.

> (1B-M-FS)

Or consider the effects on situational and personal outcomes when, over a period of weeks, a number of plans are executed, none of which change the situation.

> I devised a Star Chart reward system for good behaviour and to give them some responsibility but there has been no change in the boys' behaviour - they weren't bothered if they didn't get stars. So I talked to their parents to make them aware - but the parents are neither concerned nor supportive. Next I withdrew some of the boys' privileges and kept them in at break times, but it didn't bother them - they just misbehaved inside. So now I've contacted the Educational Psychologist for advice and he doesn't know what to do either. I feel lost - I've drawn a blank wall - all my

actions have been to no avail and I feel I've exhausted all the strategies and nothing works.

(13B-F-FS)

Worse still are the effects on situational and personal outcomes when numerous different strategies had been utilized over a period of years, yet the situation remained unchanged.

> Over the last three years I have tried to manage the caretaker's marginal performance with practically total failure. I've talked to the caretaker, discussed it with another head and my two deputies and nothing's changed. I spoke with his line manager and nothing changed. I've negotiated tasks for him with the Union but the talks broke down and still his performance is unacceptable. The school is still dirty. It's a health risk and embarrassing when visitors come and there's nothing I can do about it. I don't feel I will be able to sort it out - I'm not confident of success in the future. It makes me frustrated and angry that somebody is able to get away with not doing the job they're paid for. I feel dejected when I walk around the building and think it's disgusting. I've been totally ineffectual.

(77B-F-MS)

In line with the coping model in chapter 1, it is clear that problem focused strategies typically involve direct actions to change the situation itself, utilizing available resources such as relevant information or advice, negotiating, planning and so on. But the above quotations not only illustrate the type of problem focused strategies used but also show that the frequency with which planful problem solving responses are made is not necessarily associated with better psychological or situational outcomes. On the contrary, the data show the frustration and anxieties which can result when repeated 'plans of action' result in the situation remaining unchanged. Given this, it is hardly surprising that many studies which have looked at the relationship between coping frequency and various situational and health outcome measures have yielded inconsistent, contradictory results (see literature review in chapter 2 for details). The data here clearly indicate that action effectiveness, not frequency, is the important factor regarding outcomes (Oakland and Ostell, 1995).

Elaborating further on the importance of knowing about coping effectiveness in relation to outcomes, the qualitative data give insights into the dynamic nature and multidimensionality of problem situations to show how coping attempts often exacerbated or worsened the original situation, sometimes causing additional problems which had to be dealt with. Consider how this head's coping efforts generate additional problems:

> I talked in a reasoned way with her about the problem and offered
> to help but she got very upset and contacted the Director of
> Education which I then also had to deal with. I asked the schools
> Adviser, who suggested I "leave things to settle down" which I
> did. But things just got worse. There was a dreadful atmosphere
> in school - it affected everybody. Then I contacted my Union and
> they said they backed me but couldn't do anything to help, and
> things just went from bad to worse. I blamed myself for
> everything and questioned whether I was right for the job.

(5B-F-FS)

Similarly, the following head pursues many courses of action, most to no avail, others only effective for a while and the situation deteriorates creating further problems to be handled.

> I had meetings, interviews and case conferences with the Police,
> Schools Advisers, and Social Services but his behaviour
> continued and the staff got more and more upset. So I had to
> have discussions and counselling sessions with the bruised staff to
> restore their confidence. Meanwhile, I developed plans to modify
> his behaviour - they worked for a while but then he reverted back
> to his ways. Then last week he assaulted another child and had to
> be suspended. In a way things have worsened because I've heard
> he's now wandering the streets. But in another way, it's
> improved because he's gone and the staff are happier. Now I feel
> dreadful, dreadful - but I don't know what else I could have done.

(49B-M-MS)

To summarize these findings on headteacher coping and outcomes, the qualitative responses in this study are of value for two main reasons. Firstly, the data are valuable for better understanding the coping process. Whereas quantitative data can only yield a snapshot of coping, the qualitative data illustrate the tremendous diversity and complexity of coping behaviours. The data also show its dynamic nature and that coping actions are often used reiteratively or on a trial-and-error basis according to a complicated and ever-changing interaction of personal and situational variants. In some cases, actions are immediately effective, in others, strategies are initially effective but then cease to be so. Sometimes, wide varieties of strategies employed over long periods of time prove totally ineffectual leaving the problem unchanged or worsened. At no time is coping a static, unitary event.

The second reason the qualitative data in this study are valuable is because they highlight important weaknesses in the quantitative measures of coping which are widely-used in coping research. Quantitative coping checklists assess coping with items which are targeted at whether and how often external resources such as advice, finances, information and so on were sought. Yet the qualitative data show it is external resource **adequacy** which is the most important determinant of situational and personal outcomes. Further, current methods of assessing coping are preoccupied with the type of strategy and/or how often it is used and how these factors relate to personal and situational outcomes. As the qualitative data show, however, a much more important factor concerns the **effectiveness** of the strategies employed. If we are to improve our understanding of the relationship between coping behaviours and outcomes, future measures of coping need to incorporate assessments of external resource adequacy and the effectiveness of any coping actions taken (cf., Oakland and Ostell, 1995).

8 Main influences on headteacher health

The results of the quantitative and qualitative analyses relating to the psychological and physical symptoms of the headteachers are discussed in this chapter. Where appropriate, the qualitative data are used to amplify the quantitative findings and to demonstrate how headteachers who have poor health differ markedly from their counterparts in how they think about, react emotionally to and attempt to cope with stressful situations in the workplace.

8.1 Biographical details and headteacher health

In all the analyses, the biographical variables relating to the age and sex of the headteachers and the number of years experience they have had in headship were not significantly related to the psychological well-being or physical symptoms scores as measured by the GHQ and SYMP scales. This result is somewhat surprising as one might expect that years of experience in coping with problem situations which arise in headship would have positive implications for headteacher health and well-being. Nonetheless, perhaps this result is indicative, in part, of the unprecedented **changes** in the types of problem headteachers now have to deal with (as discussed in chapter 4). In other words, irrespective of age, sex and experience, most headteachers experienced difficulties coping with the demands of changing work practices, the sheer volume and the nature of the problems they faced.

8.2 Negative emotionality and headteacher health

A measure of negative emotionality (NEM) was included in this study because it was hypothesized that it would influence not only the headteacher's reactions to their problems at work but also their reporting of psychological and somatic health.

In line with these predictions the statistical analyses showed NEM to be highly and significantly correlated with reported work demands (AJE) as well as with both health measures, GHQ and SYMP, thus providing some support for findings in other studies (e.g. Brief et al, 1988; Burke, Brief and George, 1993; Janman, Jones, Payne and Rick, 1988; Parkes, 1990; Payne and Hartley, 1987). For instance, the strong correlation found here between NEM and the psychological health measure GHQ (.67) is similar to the relationship Payne and Hartley found (.63) between the Eysenck measure of trait neuroticism (Eysenck and Eysenck, 1964) and Goldberg's GHQ as well as a correlation of .57 found by Janman et al using the same measures. Further, in the current study, NEM correlated strongly (.55) with the physical symptoms measure (SYMP) which is congruent with Watson (1988) who found negative affectivity to be moderately correlated with two physical complaints measures which were used (.39 and .41). Furthermore, the strong relationship (.54) found between NEM and the job stressor measure (AJE) is similar to findings of other studies which have indicated that perceptions of occupational stressors are strongly related to personality variables like negative affectivity (Parkes, 1990; Payne, 1988).

The nature of the relationship between NEM and these other variables has generated considerable debate and several proposals have been offered to explain the findings.

NEM: Predisposition or vulnerability / reactivity?

One explanation for the high correlation between NEM and outcomes such as psychological health is that high NEM individuals are **predisposed** to interpret things negatively and are more likely to report distress, discomfort and dissatisfaction over time than low NEM individuals regardless of the situation, 'even in the absence of any overt or objective source of stress' (Watson and Clark, 1984, p.483). This view is based on findings from laboratory experiments and would help explain a significant main effect in regression analysis.

An alternative explanation is that high NEM individuals are vulnerable or react adversely to stress. The concept of NEM as an index of **vulnerability** or **reactivity** to stress was originally developed by Spielberger, Gorsuch and Lushene (1970), but has been alluded to more recently by Parkes (1990) in her study of coping, negativity and work stress. If this explanation is correct it indicates that NEM plays a moderating role in the relationship between work demands and psychological health. The explanation can be tested by creating a variable in a regression analysis which represents the interaction of work demands and NEM (i.e., Work demands X NEM) and using this variable as a predictor of psychological health. Parkes assessed negativity in her study by using Eysenck's Neuroticism scale (Eysenck and Eysenck, 1975). It was not strongly associated with perceptions of high work demand but, when highly neurotic individuals perceived high levels of demand, they responded with high levels of affective distress. Individuals low on neuroticism did not evidence this reactivity. The interaction between neuroticism and work demands was significant.

In the current study, NEM was shown to have a highly significant main effect in the regression analyses and an interaction with perceived work demands (i.e. NEM X AJE) which approached significance (p = 0.07) and accounted for 3% of the variance in GHQ scores. As sixty-seven per cent (67%) of the variance had already been accounted for by the biographical variables, NEM, ABSOL and AJE it is not altogether surprising that the NEM X AJE interaction was relatively small. Thus the quantitative analyses support the interpretation of NEM as a dispositional variable and indicate a possible vulnerability / reactivity effect as well.

It is possible to explore further these alternative explanations of the role of NEM within this study by drawing on the **qualitative** interview data to examine if and/or how high and low NEM headteachers differ in their appraisals of and reactions to everyday-type problem situations at work.

To obtain data about appraisal of and emotional reactions to problem situations, the headteachers were asked:

- whether the situation was expected or unexpected, familiar or unfamiliar and pleasant or unpleasant;

- to what extent they felt they had control over being able to deal with the problem;

- how confident they felt about being able to deal with the problem satisfactorily;

- what emotional reactions they experienced and why;

- how (if at all) they attempted to manage their emotional reactions.

Consider the replies of two headteachers with vastly different NEM scores (i.e. 2 and 13) but who described **the same problem situation** - finding teaching cover for an absent member of staff. To facilitate comparison, the headteachers' responses are presented in Table 8.1.

Comparing the quotations in Table 8.1 a number of interesting differences are apparent between the low NEM headteacher and the high NEM headteacher. First, although the problem of finding cover for absent teachers is a familiar one to both heads, the low NEM head's replies generally indicate a more positive and matter-of-fact appraisal of the situation than the high NEM head, who describes it as 'irritatingly familiar'. Second, perceptions of control and confidence are different. Though both headteachers say they 'know exactly' what they want to do - the head low in negativity reacts determinedly and confidently, whilst the head high in negativity expresses doubts about situational constraints and uncertainties about dealing with the problem satisfactorily. Third, there are differences in emotional

Table 8.1
Comparison of reactions between a high and a low NEM headteacher

Question	Reactions of low NEM headteacher Reference (6A-F-FS)* NEM Score = 2	Reactions of high NEM headteacher Reference (13A-F-FS) NEM Score = 13
Un/expected	You get to expect this sort of situation because in a school you're bound to get illness	This is the problem, it's always unexpected because you can't know who will be ill
Un/familiar	It's a familiar occurrence which I've learned to accommodate	It's irritatingly familiar - it happens a lot
Un/pleasant	I used to panic but now I think of it as 'part of the job' - it doesn't disturb me - I just act and move	...... Oh no! Not again?
Control	I felt I had a great deal of control because I knew exactly what I was going to do	I knew exactly what I wanted to do but you can't always get supply cover and the constraints therefore made my control moderate
Confidence	I had every confidence that I would be able to deal with this problem because I have a plan for this eventuality	I knew I would get something worked out but there was still some uncertainty
Emotional reactions	Frustrated because I had to change my plans and things were not going like clockwork, but I felt determined and confident because I knew how I was going to sort it out	Anger and frustration because you ring the office and they don't help which puts me in an inner turmoil - I'm a pessimist and think, 'Here we go again' - and it makes me angry because of the time factor and it reflects on the system - you leave messages and no-one replies - I feel agitated because I think of what I could be doing whilst I'm telephoning.
Handling emotions	I just go 'Ugh' and then get on with sorting the situation out	I smoke more at times like these - I won't say it helps.... I get short-tempered - you feel you could scream but you bite your tongue because of professional considerations

*Where 6 relates to sixth interview, A = part A of the interview, F = Female, FS = First School

154

reactions. Whilst both heads reported feeling 'frustrated', the low NEM head indicated self-assuredness and resolve to sort the problem out. In contrast, the high NEM head felt frustrated, reported being in an 'inner turmoil' and related pessimistic tendencies and thoughts which seemingly exacerbated her anger and frustration. Further, when handling their emotional reactions, the replies of the head low in NEM suggest minimal emotional arousal which did not interfere with problem-focused behaviours. In contrast, the head high in NEM reacted by smoking more, being short-tempered and suppressing her desire to 'scream' indicative of the arousal of strong, negative, distressing emotions.

It is worth noting that not only were the heads describing the same problem situation but also, they were both describing a situation which had a 'successful' outcome, i.e. was resolved. However, when asked about how they felt about the outcome, again, differences were apparent. The head low in NEM reported feeling 'relieved and happy that the plan had worked effectively'. The head high in negativity said she felt 'relieved when the plans started to materialize' but then, expressed her anger 'with the system in the first place' and complained about the general lack of financial support for supply teachers. So, even though these heads were dealing with the same situation and in both cases the situation was resolved successfully, for the head high in negativity there were residual negative cognitions and frustrations which remained, even though the problem had been resolved.

The qualitative data detailed above have made it possible to compare a head low in negativity with a head high in negativity to show quite marked differences in both appraisals of and reactions to a problem situation and, although this example draws on data from only two respondents, similar differences were apparent when the remaining interview scripts were sorted into high NEM and low NEM categories (i.e. 1 SD above/below the mean respectively) and compared.

To summarize, the data here appear to give some support to both the predispositional and the reactivity explanations as to how NEM affects appraisals and reported health complaints. On the one hand, the data show congruence with Watson and Clark's (1984) thesis, in that the high NEM individual displayed a tendency to report distress, discomfort and dissatisfaction and tended to focus on negative aspects of the environment in general. The data also give support to Watson and Clark's assertion that low NEM subjects appear more resilient to and dwell less on everyday hassles and frustrations and display a tendency to be more satisfied, self-secure and calm. More generally, the data support the three bipolar sub-divisions of NEM which were posited by Watson and Clark (1984):

- nervousness/calmness

- dissatisfaction/satisfaction with one's self

- pessimism/optimism.

On the other hand, the calm, self-assured replies of the low NEM individual as compared to the agitated, highly emotional replies of her counterpart when faced with a similar situation, go some way to supporting the idea that high NEM individuals respond to high demand situations with higher levels of reactivity or affective distress. Certainly, the high NEM head's responses indicate a vulnerability regarding situational control and confidence which is expressed as elevated levels of negative emotional arousal both during and after problem-solving. In other words, the qualitative data indicate that NEM may influence reported health as a dispositional factor. They also indicate that NEM probably moderates the relationship between job demands and mental health **and** thus acts as a vulnerability / reactivity factor as well.

NEM: A confounding factor?

There is, however, a third way in which NEM might inflate measures of work demands and health outcomes which is seldom addressed in the literature and concerns a methodological issue mentioned in chapter 6. Arguably, there is overlap in the content of certain items in the NEM scale and items in typical job demand scales or health measures such as the GHQ used in this study. Indeed, there is overlap of two kinds. First, there are similar questions about loss of sleep, anxiety, tension, etc., in both the GHQ scale and the NEM measure. To take just one example, the NEM item 'I often lose sleep over my worries' is almost identical to the GHQ item 'Have you recently been losing sleep over worry?' A second kind of content overlap is related to a more generalized concern that items in the NEM and typical job demand measures contain predominantly negatively-toned topics relating to **lack of** autonomy, **inability** to make decisions, work **overload** and so on. This overlap in both content and negative tone between NEM and AJE and NEM and GHQ could spuriously inflate the correlations between AJE, or other measures of work problems, and GHQ.

It is possible to test for a confounding effect using the regression analyses. The amount of variance in GHQ scores accounted for by the AJE scale is estimated first using AJE as the sole predictor. Next, it is used as a predictor **after** NEM has been added to the equation. Any reduction in explained variance for GHQ scores in the second analysis can be attributed to NEM removing the 'confounded' variance before AJE is introduced. For the headteacher study the variance accounted for by AJE reduces from 40% to 11% if NEM is introduced before AJE in a two predictor equation for GHQ. When the biographical variables are introduced first, then NEM and then AJE, the latter still explains only 11% of the variance which, nevertheless, is highly significant. Thus a very strong confounding effect of NEM upon the relations between AJE and GHQ is evident.

In conclusion, the evidence indicates that NEM acts as a dispositional variable predicting poorer psychological health, as a confounding factor which inflates the relations between GHQ and measures of the perceived work environment, and possibly as a vulnerability or reactivity measure such that those high on NEM have poorer psychological health because they react more strongly and negatively to work demands. Thus, it is important to make allowance for the potential confounding measurement effects between independent (job based) and dependent (health outcome measures) variables in occupational stress research either by redesigning the measures or, when using variables such as NEM, by partialling out statistically any confounding effects.

Although NEM accounts for considerable variance in the regression analyses, it does not provide a deep understanding of the actual processes which underlie headteacher stress reactions because most of the variance explained by NEM is artifactual as far as the study is concerned. Two other cognitive variables which were also found have a significant influence on the headteachers' health scores provide deeper insights into the mental processes associated with stress reactions and are discussed below.

8.3 Absolutist thinking and headteacher health

A major objective of this study was to attempt to identify the private dialogues people engage in when situations threaten or violate beliefs/values which they hold in a absolutist manner. According to theory detailed in chapter 3 (see also Ostell, 1992, 1995a), this violation can result in the arousal of strong, negative emotional reactions, particularly anger. From this, it was hypothesized that highly absolutist headteachers would be more likely than non-absolutist heads to suffer poorer psychological and physical health.

These hypotheses were confirmed by the statistical analyses which showed that absolutist thinking was highly significantly correlated with both the psychological health of the headteachers as measured by the GHQ ($r = .60$) and physical symptoms measured by the SYMP scale ($r = .61$). Analysis also revealed that significantly more absolutist headteachers visited their doctor in connection with their symptoms. Similarly, in the hierarchical regression analyses, absolutist thinking was a highly significant predictor of psychological well-being and headteacher symptoms accounting for substantial amounts of unique variance in the health scores, even after the powerful predictor variable NEM had been entered into the equations. Clearly, these results indicate that absolutist thinking, identified for the first time in a study of stress, plays an important part in the relationship between stress and health and merits further attention. The exact nature of its role can best be understood by examining the qualitative data.

In this study, absoluteness was defined as a mode of thinking whereby a person demands or insists upon conformity to certain absolutist standards of belief and/or behaviour - these demands being made either of themselves, other people or the environment in general. Theoretically, a consequence of holding beliefs in an absolutist way is that the individual often experiences strong, negative emotions when their standards are threatened or violated. These emotions are a product of thoughts or private dialogues which the person engages in and they often reflect one or a number of the following themes:

- victimization / persecution complex

- a sense of injustice

- perfectionism / infallibility

- inability or unwillingness to change

Although the conceptual boundaries of these themes is somewhat indistinct, it is useful to retain these categories for exploring the qualitative data to illustrate the nature of absoluteness, the role it plays in the aetiology of distressing emotions and the implications it has for the outcomes of problem situations and headteacher health.

Victimization / persecution complex

Consider how a headteacher's thoughts reflect feelings of victimization when events and other people's behaviour do not conform to her absolutist standards.

> Our school has not been allocated the same teacher allowance as the other schools involved in the project. We have monthly meetings about it, but we don't agree on anything. It makes me feel really chewed up and very angry - there's a lot of bad feeling - it's been going on for two terms and there's no rapport between us. I feel I'm being put down and undermined deliberately in these meetings - it's a blow to self-esteem. We're all worth something but I don't say anything to them because of professionalism. I feel very alone and sometimes think of resigning. I wonder sometimes how much more can I take?
>
> (8B-F-FS)

Here, events (the allocated teacher allowance) and the behaviour of other people in the meetings contravene what this head demands should be happening. Her angry reactions are further exacerbated by private dialogues about being deliberately 'put down' and 'undermined' which reflects the victimization she feels and leads to thoughts of helplessness and resignation. Amongst other things, this and many of the subsequent quotes in this chapter illustrate how in appraisal, the perceived costs of a situation (as detailed in chapter 1) can give rise to negative emotional reactions. For example, costs for this head include a utilitarian cost of having an inadequate teacher allowance, the cost to her own physical well-being when the constant lack

158

of rapport makes her feel 'chewed up' as well as the perceived costs to her self-esteem. Her private dialogues about being deliberately put down and victimized serve to increase the adverse emotional reactions to the perceived costs of the situation.

A similar theme of victimization is apparent in the thoughts of a headteacher who had been trying, over several months, to deal with bad behaviour in a group of boys.

> I've always prided myself on discipline, but over several months I've tried everything to no avail. These boys just think it's a huge joke, which is demeaning for me - they don't seem to care. It's time-consuming, time-wasting and involves staff and 'innocent' children - it makes me very angry. They (the boys) don't care, they haven't learnt their lesson, they are disruptive and waste everyone's time. They laugh in my face which makes me furious - I could knock their heads off. They are flying in the face of my authority - I get **really** cross because I feel they're deliberately aggravating me.

(13B-F-FS)

Again, the dominant theme here is victimization. Strong feelings of anger are aroused in the headteacher because the boys' behaviour does not conform to the absolutist standards she insists upon. These feelings are compounded further by perceptions of being deliberately victimized. She thinks, for instance, that the boys deliberately misbehave and scoff at her position of authority and this perceived intentionality exacerbates her feelings of anger. This is reminiscent of Ostell (1992) and Woolfolk and Richardson's (1978) theory that actions which are perceived as both unjustified and intentional are particularly likely to arouse strong feelings, usually of anger, whilst actions which are believed to be accidentally caused usually result in a more benign reaction.

A sense of injustice

Closely allied to feelings of victimization were the dialogues which reflected perceptions of injustice or inequity. In accordance with theory (Ellis, 1962; Ostell, 1992), it was evident that these perceptions of injustice stemmed from moralistic ways of thinking whereby the individual demanded or legislated certain standards of belief and/or behaviour of themselves and/or other people. When these standards were not met, the headteacher reacted with frustration, anger, anxiety and so on and ruminated about injustice.

Consider this headteacher's perceptions of inequity, his emotional reactions and how the effects extend beyond the problem situation - having to raise money for educational visits because of a limited budget.

> One of my biggest frustrations is that the nice bread and butter kids in this school are not getting equal opportunities as those in wealthier areas. It's so frustrating, because I'm aware of the need to offer children varied activities, but my expenditure is very limited, so I have to try and raise the money elsewhere. It makes me resent those in ivory towers who are dictating policy to heads and setting the parameters within which we have to work - its ludicrous. It makes me very angry and causes so much work I haven't enough time for my family and they resent it. I'm at the end of my tether. I run out of patience at home and then feel guilty.

> (63A-M-MS)

For this head, the limited budget, school policy, extra workload and absolutistic demands about inequity and injustice combine to arouse feelings of frustration, anger, indignation and guilt which have ramifications beyond the problem situation itself.

Similar themes were apparent in the dialogues of the following two headteachers, both of whom were distressed by the behaviour of a teacher in a particular event. But, in both cases, the dialogues and the concomitant emotions continued weeks after the event had passed.

> I was annoyed with a capital 'A' when I found out she hadn't really been sick but had been to London. She missed the Baker training day and she was the one who most needed the training. I was so frustrated when she didn't turn up. And she drew pay for that day - I was very hurt that someone could be so unthinking towards the staff and children. It was a selfish and immoral thing to do. When she did return to school, I should have asked for more information and tried to 'nail' her, but I was so angry inside, I couldn't think clearly. It's water under the bridge now but I still feel angry when I think of it.

> (16B-M-FS)

And the distressing emotions linger on for this head too:

> I was very, very hurt by what she did - and angry. I'm a selfish person, I work hard and her behaviour was upsetting things - the stupid woman. I was very angry that she was affecting my school, my staff and the children - and anxious because of what it was doing to others in the school - dividing us. I felt frustrated because it wasn't of my making. In a way, things have worsened because although she left the school three weeks ago, she's still spreading poison about the school - it's very annoying and very hurtful.

> (29B-F-FS)

Thus, perceptions of injustice stemming from moralistic ways of thinking can have powerful effects on emotional reactions to a problem both during and after the situation has been dealt with. Further, there is evidence that as Ostell (1988) recognizes, the dialogues and engendered emotions can initially be **consequences of** the problem situation but subsequently, become a **part of** the problem, interfering or detracting from problem solving behaviours (e.g., 'I was so angry I couldn't think clearly') and/or become a problem in their own right (e.g., 'I still feel angry').

Perfectionism/infallibility

According to Ellis (1962), absolutist beliefs about standards of behaviour are often underpinned by an individual's insistence on perfectionism or infallibility, whereby when events fall short of 'the standard', the individual finds it difficult to accept their own and/or other people's limitations. This can result in feelings of anger, anxiety, self-deprecatory ruminations or criticizing and blaming themselves and/or other people.

Demands for perfectionism or infallibility were readily apparent in the private dialogues of some headteachers when they were describing specific situations, and frequently they reinforced these attitudes by making general statements such as:

> I'm **never** satisfied with what I do. I criticize and blame myself all the time... I can't stop myself... it makes me feel angry in a way. I think it goes back to my childhood when I was always blamed for everything.

> (29B-F-FS)

> You do what you can and what is expected of you, but you never feel satisfied..... I don't **ever** think I'm doing enough.

> (80B-F-MS)

> Even when realistically there is nothing to blame myself for, I still do.... I **never** feel **totally** happy with things I've done.

> (56B-F-MS)

Other dialogues reflected what Burns (1980) describes as 'a perfectionist's sensitivity to disapproval' with absolutist demands that no matter what, everyone should like them:

I like to be popular with everyone, all of the time

(58A-M-FS)

I always want to keep everybody happy - it's a personality defect of mine....and knowing I haven't bugs me.

(26B-F-FS)

Along similar lines, other dialogues reflected an insistence that whatever the situation, they must be able to deal with it satisfactorily:

I find it hard to say to myself 'you can't win 'em all' and when things don't work out I get very depressed, moody and dejected.

(45B-M-MS)

The above examples reflect the all-or-nothing style of thinking which is commonly found in perfectionists (Burns, 1980; Ellis, 1962; Ostell, 1992). This dichotomous absolutist thinking style entails that actions, events, outcomes, etc., are evaluated as either all-black or all-white to the exclusion of any intermediary shades of grey. As a consequence, any 'imperfect' actions, events or outcomes generate critical ruminations about the self and/or others and/or the environment, each with the attendant emotions of anger, anxiety, guilt, depression and so on. In a less than perfect world, therefore, individuals who demand perfectionism or infallibility seem doomed to perpetual disappointments.

Inability or unwillingness to change

The fourth theme underlying absoluteness is described here as the inability or unwillingness to change, where change refers to beliefs and/or behaviours. Generally speaking, one could argue that unwillingness to change is not a sub-theme but rather, an overarching theme of absolutist thinking whereby the individual demands certain standards of belief and/or behaviour in an absolutistic, unchallengeable way (Ostell, 1992). Nonetheless, a more specific theme of unwillingness to change was detectable in some of the interview dialogues. For instance, consider the reactions of the following headteachers when there is a conflict of beliefs or opinion:

I felt so frustrated. I just could not get the parents to see that the discipline procedure was for the child's own good. I felt like gripping the parent warmly round the throat.

(57A-M-MS)

It made me so angry and frustrated. She just could not visualize the vision I had for the new unit. I'd fought and fought for this unit and I had a vision of how it could work. I'm very good at picturing final results and want it **regardless**. I'm arrogant, and once I've made a decision **I will not change my mind.**

(58B-M-FS)

In these examples, the insistent and unchallengeable, dogmatic nature of absoluteness mean that the headteachers are unwilling to identify with or understand a frame of reference other than their own. In the first example, the head finds it difficult to tolerate the parents who cannot see his point of view. Similarly, the head in the second example expresses his frustrations with a teacher who is unable to 'visualize' his plans for the teaching unit, yet admits to still wanting those plans 'regardless'. In both cases, the individual's inability or unwillingness to tolerate or try to understand another person's point of view or actions results in elevated levels of anger and frustration with negative implications for health.

In summary, the dialogues associated with absolutist thinking as defined in this study were found to generate strong, negative emotional reactions and often had adverse effects on coping behaviour. We have seen, for example, how the dialogues frequently gave rise to strong feelings of anger in particular, but also to anxiety, guilt and depressive reactions, be it anger at other people's behaviour, anxieties about the disapproval of others, guilt at letting other people down or depressive reactions at not being able to influence events. Moreover, the examples show how the dialogues and the emotions can actually detract from problem-solving behaviour, sometimes continuing to distress the individual long after the problem has been resolved, in effect, becoming a problem in their own right. Hence, both the quantitative and qualitative data analyses in this study show absolutist thinking to be a potentially dysfunctional mode of thinking which had negative consequences for both situational and personal outcomes for the headteachers

The qualitative data from this study are also of value, however, in identifying the kinds of dialogues which are indicative of non-absolutist thinking and which enabled some headteachers to avoid or ameliorate stress processes. A number of the non-absolutist dialogues reflect ideas commonly found in the counselling or cognitive therapy literature as examples of psychologically healthy ways of thinking. These dialogues are discussed below.

8.4 Non-absolutist thinking and health

Discussions in the section above have shown how absolutist individuals demand that they and/or others conform to particular beliefs and behaviours and how these beliefs are frequently underpinned by unrealistic expectations, unrealistic standards, low tolerance of their own or other people's shortcomings and a more general intolerance for the frustrations and discomforts of everyday living. By way of contrast, consider some of the dialogues of headteachers who were judged as 'non-absolutist'.

> I don't find it difficult to admit to myself or others that I'm not handling something well. I take a decision or act, and then live with whatever I've done - successful or not.

> (47B-M-MS)

> I know that sometimes I will make mistakes - some you win, some you lose - that's life.

> (40A-M-MS)

> Things don't always work out and I accept that as part of the job and development.

> (52B-F-MS)

> If you take the wrong road, recognize it, turn the car round and get on with redressing the balance.

> (36B-M-MS)

> I accept that I'm fallible. Just because you don't have success doesn't mean you've failed.

> (66A-M-MS)

There are no demands for perfectionism or infallibility in the above statements. Instead, the respondents acknowledge that to err is human; that people have strengths and weaknesses which vary over time and situations. Gone is the all-or-nothing, dichotomous thinking which was apparent in those respondents who demanded infallibility at all times. Also gone are the hostile reactions and self-defeating cognitions. This acceptance of human limitations and fallibility is reminiscent of Rational Emotive Therapy (Ellis, 1962) which helps clients dispute absolutist beliefs about behaviour or situations more generally. Here, individuals who are emotionally disturbed because of irrational, absolutist ways of thinking are encouraged to aspire to standards which are more attainable and acquire beliefs which are more realistic.

Realism was implicit in the dialogues of some non-absolutist headteachers who had been dealing with problem situations which, for various reasons, had unsuccessful outcomes:

> If you try and please everybody then it's a terrible job because it can't be done - and if you try, you're doing yourself a disservice, a great disservice.

> (69B-M-MS)

> Issues crop up all the time which don't always work first time. You can't envisage eradicating these sorts of problems, they are bound to happen with people.

> (28B-M-FS)

> You get to accept that things will take a long time and may never really be resolved. You get to accept the disappointing outcomes - that's the job.

> (68B-M-MS)

> You get used to dealing with situations and learn that you will lose some, and I accept that.

> (78B-F-MS)

Here the implicit themes are of not insisting on pleasing everyone all of the time and not expecting success in every task undertaken. As a result of this preferential, rather than demanding mode of thinking, the headteachers' emotional reactions to events and outcomes are altogether more benign (Ostell, 1992, 1995a). These dialogues reflect acceptance and tolerance of their own and other people's frailties and shortcomings, even though behaviours and outcomes may, at times, be disappointing.

Along this line, there was also evidence that non-absolutist individuals are prepared to be flexible in their thinking, are willing to change their views and are able to identify with another person's frame of reference. As one head remarked:

> I accept that it's difficult modifying people's views - it's like a balance or a knife-edge and it's very difficult. But what's important is that we all discuss and pool our ideas - a healthy exchange of each person's ideas and their input.

> (18A-M-FS)

Or, as another head put it:

> When you're dealing with people, or anything, you've got to be prepared
> to be flexible.

(75B-M-MS)

Finally, at a more general level, the dialogues of the non-absolutist individuals
indicated a particular orientation towards problem situations and having to deal with
them. Consider, for instance, the dialogues of the following headteachers:

> I expect that problems will occur and that they won't always turn out
> successfully.

(6B-F-FS)

> Problems are just a part of the job and I accept that - in fact, they're an
> integral part of life - that's the challenge.

(18A-M-FS)

In the dialogues quoted above it is evident that for these individuals, problems and
frustrations are an inevitable part of everyday living. They accept the fact that
sometimes problems will be very difficult to handle and will not always be resolved
satisfactorily. This orientation is of interest in the context of coping and health
because it has long been recognized that an individual's attitude in approaching a
problem situation can greatly influence behavioural and emotional responses and be
either facilitative or disruptive, depending on whether it moves the person toward or
away from an effective procedure and solution (D'Zurilla and Goldfried, 1971).
More specifically, D'Zurilla and Goldfried maintain that the type of orientation
which is likely to encourage independent problem-solving behaviour should include
the attitude to accept or verbally acknowledge that problem situations **will** occur
because they constitute a normal part of life and behave as though it is possible to
cope effectively with these problems. Evidence suggests that people who display
this general orientation are more likely to express confidence in their ability to
control aspects of their environment and tend to be better problem-solvers (Bloom
and Broder, 1950; Lefcourt, 1976; Rotter, 1966).

This general orientation to problems occurring is also referred to in Rational
Emotive Therapy. Ellis (1962) observed that many individuals tend to maintain
irrational expectations about the world around them. They expect, for example, that
problem situations 'should' or 'should not' occur when realistically it is unlikely (or
likely) that they will occur. As a consequence, anger, disappointment, frustration
and other emotional and behavioural disturbances occur whenever a problem

situation arises. Their reactions reflect the individual's failure to accept the fact that problematic situations are normal, inescapable parts of everyday living.

To summarize sections 8.3 and 8.4, the qualitative data have been used to explore and illustrate absoluteness as a potentially dysfunctional way of thinking and its more functional counterpart, non-absoluteness. The intention has been to illustrate the role of absolutist thinking in the aetiology of distressing emotional states and its potential for adversely influencing problem-solving behaviour, situational outcomes as well as the psychological well-being and physical health of the headteachers. Implications for training and recommendations for further research into absolutist thinking are discussed in the final chapters.

8.5 Attributional styles and headteacher health

Another major influence on the health of the headteachers was attributional styles. A person is said to have an attributional style when they consistently make particular kinds of judgements or attributions about situations. Attributional styles enable people both to make sense of circumstances and events by providing explanations for why and how they occur and to maintain a view of themselves which is consistent with their self-image or desired self-image (Taylor, 1983; Tennen and Herzberger, 1987). Thus, attributions are frequently subject to systematic **bias** in order for people to maintain for themselves or to portray to others a particular self-image.

As detailed in chapter 3, a major objective of this study was to identify the attributional styles of headteachers dealing with the two problem situations, one with a successful outcome and the other, an unsuccessful outcome. In line with theory, it was hypothesized that, irrespective of health, headteachers would make self-serving attributions for the successful outcome, thereby crediting the success to their efforts, skills, abilities and so on. Analysis of the interview scripts confirmed this hypothesis and revealed that all the heads used self-serving attributions to explain the situation with a successful outcome. Some did so quite unreservedly:

> I thought about it carefully and it worked well.

> (2A-F-FS)

> It sounds immodest, but I think I handled it as well as any teacher could and outsiders told me that too.

> (11A-F-FS)

> I am quite skilful at dealing with people and handled it to the best of my ability.

> (27A-M-FS)

167

I dealt with it really well.

(47A-M-MS)

Other headteachers' replies indicated that whilst the success was ultimately attributable to their personal skills and abilities, other people and/or factors such as external resources had played an influential role in the outcome.

> An awful lot of the resources I required were there - advice, information, emotional support and so on. It was a team effort - but I was co-ordinating it and I felt I handled it very well.

(3A-M-MS)

> My personal skills were extremely adequate and there were skilful people around me too.

(7A-M-FS)

> I had the advice, support and help I needed. My skills were in knowing which approach to take and where to put the right person at the right time.

(29A-F-FS)

Nevertheless, whether success was attributed exclusively to personal skills and abilities or whether other people or resources shared the credit, there was evident bias in the judgements of the headteachers in that **all** the respondents made self-serving attributions for the problem situation with a successful outcome. This is consistent with other research which has repeatedly shown that individuals tend to overemphasize the role of their own efforts, abilities or other dispositions in the successes with which they are associated (Arkin et al, 1976; Bradley, 1978; Greenberg et al, 1982). The self-serving attributional style stems from motives to maintain or enhance self-esteem and is called 'self-serving' because it reflects self-presentational concerns. By taking responsibility for praiseworthy acts, individuals can maximize both the esteem in which they are held by others and as a consequence, maximize their own self-esteem (Bradley, 1978).

A second hypothesis was that headteachers attributions for the unsuccessful outcome would differentiate between effective and non-effective copers as measured by the GHQ and SYMP scales. Specifically, it was predicted that heads who made self-serving attributions for the unsuccessful outcome would have better health than those making non-self-serving attributions. Again, in line with predictions, the data analyses revealed that a non-self-serving attributional style was strongly associated with both GHQ ($r = .67$) and SYMP ($r = .61$).and was a particularly powerful predictor of poor mental health in the hierarchical regression analyses. Analyses also showed that significantly more headteachers evidencing a non-self-serving style had visited their doctor in connection with stress-related symptoms. These findings are congruent with other studies reviewed in chapter 3 which demonstrated that non-self-serving attributional styles are related to lowered self-esteem (Ickes and Layden, 1978), depression (Peterson et al, 1981), and poor psychological well-being (Ostell and Divers, 1987).

Four attributional styles were identified in the explanations the headteachers gave for the situations with an unsuccessful outcome - two self-serving and two non-self-serving. All four are important for better understanding the potential impact of attributional styles on health and the qualitative data illustrate the differences between each one.

Self-serving attributional styles

External-exonerated

This self-serving style was evident when heads effectively exonerated themselves from blame and attributed the unsuccessful outcome to external, uncontrollable factors such as other people, inadequate external resources or a combination of attenuating factors. Consider what the following headteachers said about the failed outcome:

> I don't blame myself because I genuinely felt it was not my fault. The information from the office was clearly inadequate.

> (76B-M-MS)

> I feel I've set things up and they haven't taken advantage of it. It's difficult, because you can take a horse to water but you can't make it drink and there's little point in getting worked up about things over which I have very little control.

> (66B-M-MS)

The above quotations indicate that these headteachers feel they have done everything possible given the situational constraints, (i.e. lack of co-operation-operation, inadequate information) and have externalized, disowned or exonerated themselves from blame for the failed outcome. Such attributions allow the headteachers not to feel personally responsible or culpable for the negative outcome and as a result, negative emotional reactions are tempered or minimized.

The second self-serving style was apparent in the dialogues of headteachers who attributed the negative outcome to internal, transient and potentially controllable factors. Consider for instance, what these headteachers said about the unsuccessful outcomes:

> In a way the outcome is a bit disappointing because it emanated from a group decision. But these things happen in management and I'll just have to go back to the drawing board and try again.
>
> (28B-M-FS)

> In a sense it was my fault in the first place, but I learnt from my mistake and now, I will only pick a child up if I know him well first.
>
> (38B-M-MS)

> I did not question the teacher and I should have - but I've learned from the situation and it won't happen again like that.
>
> (50B-F-MS)

In these examples, the headteachers make attributions which blame the unsuccessful outcomes on potentially changeable factors such as amount of effort or behaviours at the time. These attributions are self-serving in the sense that they lead the headteacher to believe that as long as s/he exerts more effort or behaves differently in the future, s/he will be influential and have control over similar situations. As Baumgardner et al (1986) point out, a person who ascribes negative outcomes to internal and potentially controllable causes may persist longer and be more motivated in confronting further problems. Further, internal, controllable and variant attributions (i.e. effort) about outcomes can rarely be challenged or disputed, since the actual amount of effort expended can be manipulated or disguised by the individual to his or her advantage. But whether attributions are external-exonerated or internal-changeable, this self-serving pattern protects confidence in cases of failure and allows the headteacher maximum reinforcement in evaluative settings. In either case, the headteacher's self-serving attributions appeared to result in minimal or temperate negative emotional reactions. Markedly different themes were apparent in the dialogues of the headteachers who made non-self-serving attributions for the situation with an unsuccessful outcome.

Non-self-serving attributional styles

Internal-unchangeable

A non-self-serving attributional style was apparent in respondents who attributed the unsuccessful outcome to internal, unchangeable factors such as personality or character. In the following dialogues, it is evident that these headteachers feel responsible for the negative outcome and view the failure as a reflection of their personality and/or personal shortcomings.

> I should have been more forceful and directive but I kept putting it off. It niggles at my mind. I need to be more forceful. I worry about my skills. I'm not sure I'm management material.
>
> (71B-M-MS)

> I've tried everything to no avail and nothing has worked. I criticize and blame myself because I've never had discipline problems before. I ask myself 'Where have I gone wrong?' Nothing works, so my skills are inadequate - if I was handling it better I wouldn't be getting all this hassle.
>
> (13B-F-FS)

> I blame myself for making the appointment in the first place and I'm still questioning whether or not I supported her soon enough or even enough, I don't know. But it's happened and I'm responsible and I blame myself - I always do - even when the caretaker slips on the snow I blame myself.
>
> (56B-F-FS)

The above dialogues illustrate how attributions to internal, uncontrollable causes can lead to self-deprecatory ruminations about skills and abilities and low evaluations of self-worth more generally. These characterological-blame attributions are thus non-self-serving, maladaptive responses related to low esteem and perceptions of uncontrollability (Janoff-Bulman, 1979) which give rise to anxieties and concerns about performance and character.

External-implicated

During analysis and coding of the interview scripts, it became apparent that the three categories commonly used in research on attributional styles (namely, internal-changeable, internal-unchangeable and external-exonerated) were not adequate for the data in this study. Specifically, some respondents attributed the negative outcomes to external factors, but in so doing, did not exonerate themselves

171

from blame. Rather, they blamed the outcome on external, attenuating factors but still it seems, felt responsible for or implicated in the failed outcome. For instance, consider what the following headteachers said about the unsuccessful outcomes:

> I lack the managerial skills which are **fundamental** to a problem like this but there are no finances available for training. It's so annoying and frustrating - the Authority should be sorting this out, but it's left up to me. I should be teaching, not coping with this lot.

(1B-M-FS)

> The whole thing hinges on special needs, lack of resourcing and bad parenting, **not** management skills. It's so unsatisfactory - my emotions are exhausted and drained with this case. We'd like to have been able to give him 1:1 attention to modify his behaviour, but we can't - yet I'm responsible for him.

(11B-F-FS)

> I did everything I could as regards diplomacy and management skills but there are no finances - that's the problem. It makes me so angry.

(31B-M-FS)

> I'm not in control of this, it's determined by external resourcing. Decisions are made and I take the flack. I feel helpless and guilty that I haven't the power to sort it out. It's like punching blancmange. Yet I feel I **am** responsible.

(78B-F-MS)

The above quotations illustrate that attributions to external factors are not, as previous attribution studies have suggested, always self-serving attributions. For whilst each one of the headteachers quoted above attributes the unsuccessful problem outcome to a fundamental lack of external resources, the emotions expressed indicate that they still feel implicated in and responsible for the failed outcome. These emotions range from anger and frustration at the lack of finances, to self-criticism and guilt because the inadequate resources thwart their problem-solving efforts and goals to feelings of exhaustion, helplessness and powerlessness. In each case, the head feels responsible and very much implicated in the failure.

To summarize, it would seem that the attributions headteachers make regarding the outcomes of problem situations they have coped with can have important implications for their psychological well-being and physical health. The content of both self-serving and non-self-serving attributional styles have been described in relation to markedly different emotional responses and behaviours. This has revealed an inevitable overlap between attributional styles and absolutist thinking. For instance, we saw how absolutist beliefs about infallibility often led to self-criticism and blame when events challenged those beliefs. Similarly, we have seen how internal-characterological attributions comprise statements of self-blame and ruminations about self-worth. Likewise, attributions for failure being due to external constraints where the headteacher reacts with hostility and indignation (external-implicated) inevitably overlap with the concept of absoluteness where, for example, the headteacher is angered by circumstances because s/he insists that the required resources 'should be' available and it is 'unfair' if they are not available. Moreover, this conceptual overlap is reflected in the highly significant association found between absolutist thinking and attributional style ($r = .76$). Nonetheless, although there is a commonness in ideation, it is important to recognize that there are differences as demonstrated by the statistical analyses and quotations in the foregoing pages and that both cognitive variables contribute to our understanding of the aetiology of psychological stress reactions in appraisal and the impact on longer-term health outcomes.

8.6 Job demands and headteacher health

The final major influence on the health of the headteachers in this study was perceived job demands, as measured by the Affective Job Experience (AJE) scale. The AJE was designed specifically to explore:

- individual differences in appraisal of job demands

- the relationship between different appraisals and headteacher health.

Item analysis (see chapter 5) has already shown that individual headteachers appraise the same work demands in markedly different ways. It would be wrong to assume, therefore, that a work demand such as increased financial responsibilities is necessarily a source of pressure for every headteacher. For instance, one head, when referring to the Local Management of Schools (LMS) said:

> I'm not trained as an accountant, nor have I any interest in it. It's just a waste of my educational expertise. It makes me very cross because it prises me away from the real job of educating.

> (33B-F-FS)

Whereas another head, also referring to LMS said:

> I get a lot of job satisfaction from some of the recent management changes. For example, I find it very rewarding working with figures for LMS. I really enjoy that.

(49A-M-MS)

It might be expected then, that headteachers who appraise certain work demands differently will have different health. This was supported by the statistical analyses.

Analyses showed that perceived work demands (AJE) was strongly associated with negative emotionality ($r = .54$), with absolutist thinking ($r = .39$), with attributional style ($r = .49$) as well as with psychological health and physical symptoms. AJE's relationship with NEM, ABSOL and ATTRIB is understandable given their pervading nature and the way in which they inevitably influence perceptions of the environment generally, or work demands specifically. Yet, even when AJE was introduced into the regression equations after these major variables were entered, AJE accounted for between 8% and 10% unique variance in psychological health scores depending upon the model used. Rather than discuss occupational demands and the implications for headteacher health in general terms however, it is more instructive to focus discussion in the two main dimensions of the AJE derived from the factor analysis reported in chapter 5 - namely, AJE2 relating to 'Role changes' and AJE3 to 'Interpersonal duties'. When overall AJE scores were used as the sole predictors of GHQ and SYMP scores in regression analyses, AJE accounted for 42.3% and 21.2% respectively of the variance in the dependent measures. Using AJE2 and AJE3 as predictors of health scores in similar analyses, they accounted for 30% of the variance in GHQ scores (AJE2 = 16%; AJE3 = 14%) and 20% of the variance in SYMP scores (AJE2 = 7%; AJE3 = 13%;).

Role changes and headteacher health

The AJE2 factor was comprised of three items concerning the headteachers' changing role due to the Education Reform Act (ERA). These items related to:

- increased financial responsibilities

- planning ahead amidst the changes

- managing or adapting to organizational changes

It was readily apparent in the interviews that the changes in education are proving difficult and distressing for some headteachers. Indeed, as detailed in chapter 5, simple content analysis revealed that the educational changes were mentioned most frequently as a major difficulty in the role of headship. Following more detailed content analyses, these difficulties can be grouped under five sub-headings.

Lack of managerial training

One difficulty concerning the changes is that as trained educationalists, some headteachers are anxious about their abilities to meet the managerial requirements of the Education Reform Act. Sometimes this anxiety was expressed in terms of their lack of managerial training:

> It's worrying - since the changes I'm having to deal with all sorts of things I've never had any training for. I've never been on a management course in my life.

> (46A-M-MS)

> My role is changing fast from educationalist to business manager and that's difficult and quite threatening because I've only been trained to teach.

> (2A-F-FS)

Increased workload

Another difficulty is the increased workload, particularly in administrative duties which have arisen as a result of the changes. As one head put it:

> The major difficulty is the sheer diversity of what has to be done and the constant bombardment of documents and questionnaires relating to the changes which must be read and responded to within a very short space of time - time being the problem.

> (80A-F-MS)

This head expressed similar administrative anxieties coupled with ecological concerns:

> The main difficulty is the mountains of paper that have resulted from these changes. I can't help but have a serious concern for the world's woodland and the destruction of trees. The paper is unbelievable, there's just so much.

> (63A-M-MS)

Diminishing teaching duties

A further difficulty relating to the educational changes is expressed in terms of anxieties and often, sadness at the fast-diminishing opportunities for headteachers to teach and be involved with pupils and staff.

> It's a worry, because the changes are more and more taking me away from the role of educator. I'm now having to deal with management tasks which lead me away from the job for which I was appointed, and sadly of course, away from the children and staff.

(23A-F-FS)

Others expressed an entrenched reluctance to relinquish totally their teaching duties in order to attend to the newly-required managerial tasks.

> I find my rapidly changing role very frustrating. I like to be in amongst the staff and children. Often I just leave everything else and go into the classroom, which gives me problems, but I absolutely refuse to give up what I do best.

(60A-F-FS)

Bureaucratic frustrations

Closely allied to the anxieties and frustrations about the current changes in role are feelings of anger and indignation pertaining to the introduction of the changes per se. One head expressed his anger at the:

> ....insensitivity of those in bureaucratic positions, politicians and decision makers who have no insight into this job and therefore their ideologies are totally impractical and unworkable within a school. It makes me so mad.

(28A-M-FS)

Similarly, other heads talked about the changes having been imposed upon them with little thought having been given to how or even whether the changes will be practicable.

Rapidity of changes

Finally, a problem of central concern to some heads is the pace or speed of change. Worries and hostile reactions were expressed concerning the rapidity of the educational changes, which not only exacerbate administrative problems, but also entail that the heads are unable to assimilate new information. The following two heads illustrated this well when they said:

> There are far too many changes being introduced too quickly. I'm not against progress, but I am when it's too fast - teachers and headteachers just do not get time to read the paperwork that comes from various quarters - it's just impossible. It's too much, too fast, and no time to assimilate.

(61A-M-MS)

> You've no sooner begun to feel you've got a grasp of what has come in than the next week brings in a pile of new initiatives.

(59A-F-FS)

In summary, the enforced change of role from educator to manager, lack of managerial training, increased workload, diminishing opportunities to teach and the pace and timing of the changes are the main difficulties facing these headteachers as a result of the ERA and, as the above quotes illustrate, these difficulties frequently arouse strong, negative and distressing emotions.

If we consider these feelings of anger, anxiety, sadness and frustration and so on in terms of the occupational stress literature, it is hardly surprising that the AJE2 factor which represented 'Role changes' was a good predictor of psychological health. For instance, consider the headteachers' complaints about work overload. In the occupational stress literature, work overload has been given substantial empirical attention and is usually found to be associated with poor health (e.g. Cooper, Davidson and Robinson, 1982; French and Caplan, 1972; Margolis, Kroes and Quinn, 1974) as well as with behaviour malfunctions such as increased cigarette consumption (French and Caplan, 1972). Further, French and Caplan classified work overload as either quantitative (i.e. having too much to do) or qualitative (i.e. being beyond the individual's capabilities) and showed that either and/or both can produce differing symptoms of psychological and physical strain including job dissatisfaction, lowered self-esteem, threat, high cholesterol levels, increased heart rate. In the heads' complaints above about the amount of work and their lack of expertise, it is evident that **both** quantitative and qualitative work overload are being experienced by some headteachers.

The changes in education have also brought about role conflict and role ambiguity, again phenomena which are commonly reported as major sources of occupational stress. According to Cooper and Marshall (1976), role conflict exists when an individual in a particular work role is torn by conflicting job demands or doing things s/he really does not want to do or does not think are part of the job specification. Role ambiguity exists when there is lack of clarity about the work role, scope and responsibilities. Both were evident in the above quotations when

177

the headteachers bemoan their diminishing teaching role, complain that their job should entail different functions, express uncertainties about their job specifications and feel compelled to endure unwanted changes to their role. Given that quantitative/qualitative work overload, role ambiguity and role conflict appear to be some of the main consequences of the educational changes and that these concepts are frequently cited as major sources of poor psychological and health, it is understandable that the factor representing role changes was a significant predictor of headteacher well-being.

Interpersonal duties and headteacher health

The AJE3 factor was also a good predictor of GHQ and contained items relating to interpersonal duties a headteacher is involved with, such as supervising or managing the work of others, dealing with staff conflicts and making decisions that affect other people. Broadly speaking, the qualitative data indicated that the most distressing aspects of these duties were:

- the number of people the heads were responsible for, and

- the heads' relationship with other people, but particularly staff.

Responsibility for large numbers of people

On conducting the interviews, it was apparent that a great deal of the headteacher's role involved dealing with other people, in particular staff and children. This observation is congruent with Hall, Mackay and Morgan (1988) who, in their in-depth study of headteachers over an extended period of time, found that the majority of heads' activities were interpersonal and predominantly with individuals and groups within the school. As reported in chapter 5, most headteachers (85%) said they were responsible for the education, welfare, safety and general development of the children as well as for the professional development and personal welfare of the non-teaching and teaching staff (79%). In the smallest school this entailed responsibility for 80 children and 6 staff, whilst in the largest school, the head was responsible for 600 children and 39 staff. Thus any head, irrespective of school size, is responsible for a considerable number of people.

This is important because in the job stress literature, responsibilities for other people at work have been suggested as potential stressors, although relatively few studies have provided any substantive results (Glowinkowski and Cooper, 1987). An exception, however, is a study by Wardwell, Hyman and Bahnson (1964). They differentiated between 'responsibility for people' and 'responsibility for things' (e.g. building, equipment, etc.) and found that responsibility for people was significantly more likely to lead to coronary heart disease than responsibility for things. Similarly, research by French and Caplan (1970) found that responsibility for people was significantly related to serum cholesterol, diastolic blood pressure and heavy smoking; the more the individual had responsibility for things as opposed to people, the lower the risk of these heart disease factors.

The strain of having responsibilities for large numbers of people was reflected in some of the headteachers' replies to the question about the major difficulties in the job. One head, for example, simply stated:

> The major difficulty is the management of **so many** people.

> (22A-M-FS)

Another head said:

> It's difficult being responsible for absolutely everything - the teachers, the children, the non-teaching staff, the cleaners, etc., etc. They all make demands on my time. It's the sheer weight and bombardment of information and problems sometimes. It's a big strain.

> (34A-F-MS)

Here, the emphasis is very much on the number of people for whom the head is responsible, the time-consuming nature of these responsibilities and the difficulties in trying to cope with such diverse interactions. Similar psychological effects were described by another head who said the major difficulty in headship was:

> ....constantly having to shift between different tasks relating to many different groups of people. Constantly shifting from a child, to a parent, to a constable, to an adviser, to a child, to teaching, to counselling, etc., etc., etc., is exhausting and very draining.

> (77A-F-MS)

For another head it was the nature of certain interactions with other people which were distressing:

> The biggest difficulty is when I have to confront children, staff and/or parents. That's what I dread the most. I worry about it all the evening beforehand.

> (49A-M-MS)

Thus, having responsibilities for large numbers of colleagues and subordinates is, for some headteachers, a source of psychological strain.

Relationships with other people

Implicit in many of the above responsibilities for large numbers of people is the relationship headteachers have with these people. For instance, if a head feels responsible for the professional development and personal welfare of members of staff, this cannot be isolated from the relationship s/he has with the staff. In the general context of job stress and health, this is of interest because like responsibilities for other people, relationships with other people, e.g. superiors, colleagues and subordinates have also been suggested as potential sources of occupational stress (Cooper, 1986, 1988) although surprisingly, research in this area (i.e. relationships) is relatively scarce (Glowinkowski and Cooper, 1987). Yet for some heads, their relationship with the staff presents a major difficulty. This was reflected in terms such as:

> ...the main difficulty is dealing with staff who can be very set in their ways.

> (73A-M-MS)

> My biggest problem is trying to weld together disparate teachers when you have a philosophy which does not equate with those working with you. It can create a whole impetus of insecurity.

> (45A-M-MS)

So, the relationships with and responsibilities for large numbers of other people clearly is a source of distress for some headteachers, leading to anxieties, frustrations, increased workload, demands on time and often entailing a rapid switching of roles. It would seem then that little has changed in the character of a head's interpersonal role since Lyons' (1974) description of its 'fragmentary' quality. Indeed, an excellent example of the fragmentary nature of typical interpersonal duties was given to the authors, by a headmaster of his own initiative, and can be found in Appendix E.

Summarizing the findings relating to occupational demands it is clear that the headteachers appraise and react very differently to the many facets of headship with differing implications for their psychological health. Quantitative and qualitative work overload, role ambiguity and role conflict have been identified as some of the main consequences of the changes in education since 1988. Responsibilities for and relationships with large numbers of people have been identified as particularly difficult facets of the interpersonal duties a head has to perform. Since all of these concepts are frequently cited as major sources of poor psychological, it is hardly surprising that the two factors relating to these aspects of headship were significant predictors of GHQ scores.

8.7 Chapter summary

In this chapter, negative emotionality, absolutist thinking, attributional style and perceived job demands have been discussed as four major influences on the health of the headteachers in this study. The qualitative data have helped to illustrate the role of these variables in affecting the headteachers' appraisals of reactions to difficult work situations and ultimately, their psychological and physical health. It was argued that negative emotionality is strongly associated with headteacher health for a combination of three reasons: NEM acts as a dispositional factor whereby heads high in negativity tend to report more negative appraisals of and reactions to all kinds of situations than heads low on NEM; NEM possibly acts as a vulnerability factor such that heads high in NEM react with high levels of distress to stressful situations; some items in the NEM measure overlap conceptually with items in health measures typically used in stress studies, thus inflating the relationship between these variables. For these reasons it was suggested that future studies of stress and health using the NEM measure should acknowledge and try to isolate these confounding effects.

The cognitive variables absolutist thinking and attributional style were also identified as powerful influences of headteacher health, even after the effects of the dispositional variable negative emotionality had been partialled out from the analyses. The profile of absolutist headteachers which emerged in this chapter is of headteachers who interpret events or appraise situations in a rigid, black and white fashion. They become emotionally upset, usually angry, when people or circumstances do not conform to their inflexible 'standards' and frequently find it difficult to 'let go' of the negative reactions (e.g. ruminating angrily about an event which happened in the past). Not surprisingly, such heads were found to be experiencing poorer psychological and physical symptoms than the non-absolutist heads who evidenced a more pragmatic, flexible and less emotional approach to dealing with problem situations at work.

Along similar lines, those headteachers who made the two types of non-self-serving attributions for the situation which turned out unsuccessfully were found to have poor psychological health and physical symptoms. Heads who blamed the failed outcome on themselves (internal, characterological attributions) were shown to ruminate about self-worth and make self-deprecatory remarks. Likewise, headteachers who attributed the failure to external constraints but felt responsible for the failed outcome (external, implicated attributions) were shown to react with hostility and indignation towards those constraints. Again, as might be expected, heads making these non-self-serving attributions reported poor psychological and physical health.

Finally, role conflict and the diverse nature of interpersonal duties in headship were identified as significant influences of the psychological health of the headteachers. Work overload, lack of management training, diminishing opportunities to teach, bureaucratic frustrations and responsibilities for and relationships with large numbers of people were also identified as principle sources of difficulty for the headteachers.

9 Headteacher stress, coping and health: Summary findings and recommendations

The main objectives of this research were to:

- investigate how headteachers react to and attempt to cope with problem work situations;

- explore the factors which best predict successful and unsuccessful outcomes for these problem situations at work;

- assess the adaptational outcomes for headteachers in terms of their psychological well-being and physical symptoms.

Through a critical review of existing research, a rationale was developed for designing a methodology which, unlike most other studies, combined quantitative and qualitative data in order to fulfil the above objectives. In this chapter, the main findings from the study are summarized and recommendations made regarding how headteachers can be helped to cope better with the demands of their current rules.

9.1   Summary of main findings

The main findings from this study show that of all the changes which have taken place within the educational system over the past two decades, the introduction of the 1988 Education Reform Act has presented headteachers in particular with profound changes to the institutions they manage and the role they perform. They are now required to act as business managers responsible for the financial management of their schools and for attracting the numbers of students they need. These changes have often resulted in heads finding themselves unable to devote much, if any, time to teaching activities as their work load has increased, usually considerably. In the eyes of many headteachers these changes have been imposed by government but have not been adequately funded so that the necessary resources are unavailable for the physical maintenance of (some) schools and the efficient management of the educational process within schools. Many heads also feel that they are not being given adequate training in the management skills they need to meet the demands of their changed role.

Considering the impact of these changes it is perhaps surprising that the vast majority of headteachers in this Bradford sample perceived the range of demands with which they now have to deal, taken as a whole, as at least **moderately pleasant**. Less than 7% saw their job demands as being unpleasant. These findings are potentially misleading, however, as the psychological health of the Bradford headteachers, as a group, is poor relative to data available for other employed samples. Fifty per cent (50%) of the headteachers **exceed** the cut-off which defines normal, healthy functioning on the GHQ compared to less than 20% for other employed samples. Nearly 28% of the heads had mental health scores indicative of definite psychological distress; 13% of the sample had scores indicative of even poorer psychological health. These headteachers also reported relatively high levels of physical symptoms, particularly symptoms reflecting states of physical exhaustion and nervous sickness.

The apparent conflict between these findings for psychological health status and perception of job demands can be explained largely through more precise analysis of the heads' ratings for items in the AJE scale. Analysis revealed that **only certain kinds of job demands** assessed by the AJE were associated with poor health status for the sample, namely, those identified by the role changes and interpersonal duties factors. For example, items from the AJE concerning coping with role changes, (e.g., increased financial responsibilities) and the process of change itself (e.g., planning ahead amidst change, adapting to organizational changes) were more predictive of the psychological and physical health status of headteachers than any other items in the scale. Negative ratings for these changes were associated with poorer mental and physical health. Similarly, ratings of unpleasantness for items comprising the interpersonal duties factor (e.g., dealing with staff-related issues, supervising the work of others) were also associated with poorer health scores. The breakdown of the kinds of problems the heads described during their interviews indicated that many were ones dealing with change or interpersonal problems. Although the statistical analyses cannot prove that these job demands and problems were important factors leading to the headteachers' health problems, many of the heads with poor psychological and physical health volunteered this view themselves.

It is important to recognize, however, that although these demands and problems deriving from them almost certainly proved difficult for **all** heads at times, not all heads became psychologically distressed as a result. Some heads seemed to be challenged, even excited by them instead. Nevertheless, the analyses identified four variables (negative emotionality, absolutist thinking, attributional style and the perceived adequacy of external resources) one or more of which played an important role in the process of some headteachers becoming psychologically and physically distressed as they attempted to cope with problem situations at work.

Negative emotionality (NEM)

The regression analyses indicated that NEM contributed to distress generation and maintenance in headteachers in two ways. First, heads who score high on NEM have a general predisposition to see the world in negative terms. They see problems more readily in situations and feel more anxious and less optimistic about how events will turn out, regardless of whether they can identify genuine problems or not. They tend to have more concerns about their physical health and report higher levels of unpleasant physical symptoms without suffering higher levels of diagnosed illnesses (Costa and McCrae, 1985; Watson and Clark, 1984). Consequently they have a less sanguine, more distressed view of life in general than heads low on NEM.

Second, the hierarchical regression analyses indicated a marginally significant NEM and Job Demands (AJE) interaction suggesting that heads high on NEM, when faced with demanding problems, reacted more negatively than did heads low on NEM when faced with similar problems (see chapter 8, section 8.2).

NEM is a trait believed to have a strong genetic component to it and life experiences for people high on NEM often reinforce their inbuilt tendencies. This does not mean, however, that those who score highly on the NEM scale are consigned to a life of problems, pessimism and pain. It is possible to learn positive and constructive ways of viewing and reacting to situations which combat both inbuilt reactions and learned experience. The means of acquiring more constructive reactions are discussed later in this chapter.

Absolutist thinking

A major contribution of this study is the identification and empirical measurement of the characteristic mode of thinking labelled absolutist thinking (Ostell, 1992). Identified for the first time in any study of stress and coping, an absolutist way of thinking proved to be a powerful predictor of poorer psychological health and physical symptoms in the headteachers. There was also evidence that absolutist thinking was associated with less success at problem solving. Sixty two per cent (62%) of heads were classified as absolutist and seventy five per cent (75%) of these heads had GHQ scores which exceeded the cut-off score for healthy functioning whereas this was true for only nine per cent (9%) of the remaining heads (38%) who were classified as non-absolutist. Absolutist heads also had the highest (worst) physical symptoms scores.

The research design enabled the qualitative data to provide some insights as to why this mode of thinking can be dysfunctional in terms of negative emotional arousal and ultimately, health and situational outcomes. The data showed how absolutist headteachers have a categorical and demanding style of thinking which often results in them experiencing anger and other strong emotions when their demands are not met, that is, when things happen which contravene what the absolutist head believes ought or ought not to have happened. Their ability and willingness to cope effectively with job demands and derivative problems then tends to be reduced as they engage in morally evaluative and judgemental reactions about the 'offending' behaviour of either themselves or others and this interferes with the problem solving process. Absolutist heads do not necessarily fail to solve their problems but tend to manage them less efficiently than non-absolutist heads and (often) at considerable emotional cost to themselves.

Attributional style

Four attributional styles were identified in headteachers' attributions about the causes of their problems and the reasons for problems having successful or unsuccessful outcomes. Two of the attributional styles were described as evidencing a **self-serving** bias because they essentially provided explanations for events and outcomes which protected the headteacher from criticisms and offered the headteacher credit for successes, even when credit was not necessarily or, only partly due. This style is seen as a biased way of viewing events which protects and promotes an individual's self-esteem. The remaining two attributional styles were labelled **non-self-serving** because the attributions made by headteachers with this style either blamed or implicated the heads in unsatisfactory problem outcomes even, at times, when an 'objective' analysis of the facts suggested that this was inappropriate.

Heads using non-self-serving attributional styles had poor psychological health and a higher level of symptoms indicative of physical ill-health. Significantly more had also visited their doctor around the time of the study than was true for heads with self-serving attributional styles. The variables absolutist thinking and attributional style are strongly correlated ($r = 0.76$) indicating that absolutist thinkers tend to have non-self-serving attributional styles. There is a commonness in ideation between these variables but it is, as yet, unclear whether they are distinct variables or different ways of measuring a basic underlying construct.

External resource adequacy

The fact that the health of so many headteachers in this sample (50%) seemed to have been affected adversely through their attempts to cope with their job demands and problems indicates that they were not simply a small group of 'typical missorts' but people, whatever their vulnerabilities, confronted by a genuinely difficult role. One factor emerged from this study which almost certainly exacerbates the problems of coping with the demands of the headteacher role. Headteachers repeatedly mentioned the importance of having adequate external resources in the form of information, advice and emotional support for successful problem solving. In line with this, the quantitative analyses showed that (perceived) adequate external resources were a predictor of successful situational outcomes. The qualitative data showed how resource adequacy can influence appraisals and determine coping options and thereby further amplified the crucial role of external resources in the relationship between stress reactions, coping, health and outcomes.

It should be remembered that we are talking about **perceived** external resource adequacy not actual adequacy, as there was no way of obtaining direct measures of adequacy. Yet there is no reason for assuming that the reported perceptions were not reasonably accurate. First, external resource adequacy did not interact with any of the other major variables in the regression analyses indicating that these perceptions were not simply a reflection of the biased beliefs of particular groups of headteachers. Second, it could be argued that it is hardly self-serving for heads to admit that a major reason which accounted for their success in problem solving was the availability of appropriate external resources.

9.2 Recommendations

On the basis of the main findings from this research, recommendations for three initiatives merit serious consideration. These recommendations concern provision of certain external resources, support systems and training for headteachers.

External resource provision

The findings in this study show that it is crucial that headteachers have available the necessary information, advice and emotional support, particularly for coping with many of the complex, protracted interpersonal issues arising from certain staff-related problems, 'problem children', conflicts between parents, the school and Social Services, and so on. The educational system currently provides expert information, advice and support for heads through such people as educational advisers or inspectors and educational psychologists. Heads commented positively on the help provided by these sources but also indicated that, at times, the help offered was not sufficient for their needs.

One recommendation therefore is that a thorough examination is made of the adequacy of the external resources available to headteachers for performing their roles and that improvements are made when necessary and feasible. Clearly, in the current economic and political climate it will be difficult to improve significantly upon the availability of certain resources, particularly financial ones. It is recommended, however, that the adequacy of the expert information, advice, etc., available to heads for certain problems (e.g., financial, legal, pupil behaviour, etc.,) is examined and improvements made if any significant limitations are identified. Headteachers' views and experiences could be canvassed through discussions and questionnaires where the emphasis is constructive and upon identifying potential improvements rather than simply amassing criticisms.

Support systems

The results of this study highlight the need for providing emotional and behavioural support systems for headteachers. Whilst it is acknowledged that only a few UK organizations are able and/or prepared to provide comprehensive health promotion programmes with gymnasiums, saunas, running tracks, dietary advice and so on (Cooper et al., 1988a), at the very least efforts should be made to provide headteachers with practical support for dealing with their problems, particularly when they develop a strong, negative emotional component. This might involve the provision of regional professional counselling services for headteachers, but issues of access to the service and confidentiality would have to be carefully thought through (Ostell, 1986). Whilst such services are likely to be welcomed by a good proportion of headteachers, newly-appointed heads may find this particularly useful.

Provision of training

Management training

The enforced change of role from trained educationalists to managers makes it hard to believe that any deputy headteacher, however competent and wide the experience in that post, could be ready for elevation to headship without prior formal training and management development. Thus, it can be argued that the best long-term policy would be to give management training provision for deputies.

With regard to headteachers already in post however, the data in this study indicate that management training for headteachers needs to be tailored to specific needs. For example, the headteachers described themselves as having highly varying strengths and weaknesses when dealing with members of staff, handling financial budgets, decision making and so on. Hence, any training and management development policy needs to be tailored to meet this variety of individual need: bespoke headteacher training is required rather than large scale courses which all heads are expected to undertake.

Although it might only be possible to provide limited training opportunities in the immediate future, a detailed assessment of headteacher and deputies' perceptions of their current training needs should be conducted. The findings will then help shape both the current and future training agenda for headteachers and deputies and ensure that training modules are developed in the areas where needs are greatest. Certain modules would almost certainly need to be mandatory, at least for new appointees, others could be offered on a cafeteria basis according to need, interest and specialism.

Stress-management training

More specific recommendations for helping headteachers arise exclusively from the findings in this research relating to absolutist thinking and attributional styles.

Absolutist thinking. In chapter 8, the dialogues associated with absolutist and non-absolutist thinking were described and contrasted. On the one hand, the thoughts of absolutist headteachers frequently reflected irrational expectations, unrealistic standards and low tolerance of their own and/or other people's shortcomings. In contrast, non-absolutist heads evidenced more realistic expectations and standards, a tolerant attitude towards themselves, others or the environment and in general, responded to situations in a preferential rather than a demanding manner.

The differences between absolutist and non-absolutist thinking identified here have significant implications for training needs. Arguably, training related to the nature and emotional consequences of absoluteness would be of value to any group of individuals, but particularly to highly absolutist subjects. Given the lack of theoretical and empirical attention to absoluteness, the 'person in the street' is not likely to be aware of the potentially dysfunctional consequences of this mode of thinking. Hence any level of training relating to absoluteness would constitute an increment in knowledge and self-awareness.

Further, training would not necessarily entail complex cognitive-behavioural interventions over protracted periods of time. At the simplest level, one awareness-raising session would be of value in helping headteachers understand the components of absoluteness and its implications for emotional well-being and health. Indeed, both researchers and practitioners emphasize the importance of awareness or self-knowledge in coping with stress. The psychotherapist Meichenbaum (1977) claims that awareness is the main characteristic of his therapeutic interventions. Ostell (1992) describes how it is possible to alert clients to the adverse effects of absoluteness and bring about improvements with only a few therapeutic intervention sessions. In line with this, Ladouceur and Mercier (1984) reviewed extensive literature on behaviour therapy and highlighted the important role played by awareness in learning and in behaviour modification. Their main conclusion was that awareness can increase self-monitoring of a habit and serve as a cue for interacting with the external environment in a more adaptive, less stress-evoking manner, thereby permitting the individual to modify his or her own behaviour. So whether it results in the acquisition of new behaviours or in the extinction of maladaptive habits, general awareness-raising training as to the nature of absoluteness and its potential consequences would most likely be of value to headteachers.

Training programmes could be designed along the lines of Rational Emotive Therapy (RET) whereby the therapist aims to induce subjects to become less demanding or dictatorial and more tolerant. RET for instance teaches subjects how to recognize their 'shoulds', 'oughts', 'musts', etc., and how to separate rational (non-absolutistic) from irrational (absolutistic) beliefs and how to accept reality, even when it is pretty grim. In essence then, training programmes could be designed to encourage the headteachers to minimize their demanding, dogmatic, absolutistic core philosophy and to adopt a more preferential and benign mode of thinking and reacting. Moreover, the training sessions would not involve a one-to-one Socratic-type dialogue between a headteacher and a trainer but could be conducted along the lines of group therapy, where group members are taught the underlying characteristics of absoluteness and then encouraged to discuss, explain and reason through with ineffectually thinking members. Extending this idea further, Cooper et al., point out that groups composed of a cross-section of employees, e.g., headteachers, deputies, teachers and auxiliary staff) may prove particularly valuable in helping to 'dispel the prejudice that is still inherent in attitudes towards stress problems' (1988a, p.184). More recently, role-playing scenarios have been advocated as a means of teaching people to better manage both their own emotional reactions and those of others (Ostell 1995a).

Attributional styles. The findings relating to attributional styles and health also have implications for stress management training for headteachers. As this study has shown, headteachers who make non-self-serving attributions in situations which turn out unsuccessfully had significantly poorer psychological health and physical symptoms than heads making self-serving attributions. Thus, training related to attributional processes could be targeted at:

1. alerting headteachers to the four main styles of attribution and the differences between each;

2. understanding why and how the self-serving and non-self-serving styles can have functional/dysfunctional implications for health outcomes;

3. cognitive-behavioural change, whereby the heads learn to protect self-esteem, enhance coping confidence and encourage relatively benign emotional reactions by making self-serving attributions for the inevitable failure situations which occur in everyday living.

A simple training programme such as the one outlined above could have significant implications for headteachers in terms of health and general well-being. It is feasible that even a brief training session would help headteachers with a tendency for non-self-serving attributions to both recognize the potentially dysfunctional nature of their attributional style and to make cognitive-behavioural efforts to change in the future.

To summarize: recommendations have been made for helping headteachers cope with difficult situations at work and for improving their psychological and physical health. These suggestions relate to an assessment and provision of certain external resources, providing a counselling support system for headteachers, offering training modules tailored to the current needs of deputies and heads and specific stress management training. The recommendations are not meant to be exhaustive; they do not consider government policy on implementing changes in schools, job descriptions and other grievances which are important in the context of headship and health. Rather, these suggestions arise directly from the data and findings in this study.

10   Future directions

Innovative methodologies normally open up new possibilities for research and the focus of this chapter is to consider a number of these possibilities. Indeed, since this research was completed (Oakland, 1991) a number of researchers have already adopted or advocated similar approaches to that used in the study (Bunce and West, 1994; O'Driscoll and Cooper, 1994). First, however, several limitations in the current study, which arise in part from the methodology adopted, will be examined as these make possible a realistic appraisal of the findings reviewed in chapters 7 to 9 and provide direction for future research. These limitations relate to causal directionality, the use of self-report data, the headteacher sample and the measurement of certain variables.

10.1   Limitations of the study

Causal directionality

Foremost regarding limitations in this study is the issue of causality and the direction of influence. From the findings, it is tempting to infer that certain styles of appraising and responding to problem situations influence both situational outcomes and health. Indeed, such inferences have been encouraged by assuming that outcome A, outcome B and the mental health (GHQ) and physical symptoms (SYMP) of the headteachers are dependent criteria. However, the cross-sectional, retrospective design of this study does not determine causal direction. Although appraisal may affect well-being independent of prior mental health status, it is equally likely that people in poorer mental health appraise situations in less effective ways than those in better mental health. A number of studies have shown, for example, that depressives exhibit different coping patterns than non-depressives (e.g. Billings and Moos, 1984) but it is not clear whether ineffective coping efforts cause, or are a result of, depression.

Most likely, a mutually reinforcing causal cycle exists between poor mental health and maladaptive appraisals in coping. This issue could only have been addressed with a prospective research design which was not a feasible option for this study for a number of reasons. Firstly, longitudinal designs can pose methodological and statistical problems if the time lag between samplings is too short (Dwyer, 1983) and funding for this study was only for three years. Secondly, because of factors such as retirements, promotions and staff-turnover, work environments are rarely constant places. This raises potential difficulties of repeated sampling with the same respondents (Frese 1984). Above all, longitudinal research into stress and coping behaviour is particularly prone to 'reactivity' whereby respondents are influenced and react to initial interventions by the researcher which in turn can influence subsequent reports about behaviours as well as actual behaviours. This point, of course, is not an argument against the use of longitudinal studies, it simply indicates that all research designs have their limitations.

Self-report data

Another limitation concerns the method of self-report used in this study to assess personality, health and to learn what subjects did, thought and felt in the context of a particular event. Whilst most researchers would admit that self-report measures are potentially problematic, in the stress and coping field they are still considered necessary (Folkman and Lazarus, 1985) since many coping strategies are cognitive and respondents must be asked to report their thoughts, feelings and actions. The problem is not that self-report is inherently more fallible than other methods of inquiry, but rather that it ultimately requires verification by other methods such as the observation of direct behaviours, physiological assessments and objective sources of data such as the observations of colleagues and peers for assessing the convergence of the headteachers' perceptions of personal abilities, environmental demands and constraints. Had some of these alternative approaches been feasible, they may have improved this research. It is, however, well-documented that these methods are also potentially problematic (see, for instance, Fried's (1988) critique of physiological measures).

Both the conceptualization of variables and the dependence on self-report procedures in this study have led to inevitable blurred distinctions among the appraisal variables. It was shown, for example, how subjects high on negative emotionality are more likely to report a lack of confidence in a situation and that absolutist individuals are more likely to make non-self-serving attributions about situational outcomes. This problem exists in all research of this kind (Folkman and Lazarus, 1985) with the result that the concepts are often difficult to disentangle for discussion, not because of sloppy definitions, but because they are inevitably fused. Constructs such as absolutist thinking, attributional style and confidence judgements simply represent operational aspects of the information-processing/decision-making system which mediates a person's exchange with the outside world (Ostell, 1991).

Again, this is not to imply that self-report methods are not needed in future stress research or that they are necessarily more prone to bias than other methods. Indeed there are limited alternatives to self-report methods. Bailey and Bhagat (1987), for example, advocate the use of non-reactive measures such as a 'worn carpet that leads to the employee lounge' (1987, p.222) or data on absenteeism as possible indicators of job dissatisfaction. Yet such measures are based on highly debatable inferences that absenteeism and worn carpets are related to job satisfaction. Therefore, although the inherent problems of self-report data are acknowledged, in the absence of feasible alternatives, it was considered more useful in this research to employ a combination of self-report methods, (i.e. questionnaire and interview) and to take steps in the design of these measures for minimizing the social desirability response bias whilst maximizing data reliability and validity (see chapter 4 for details). Moreover, efforts were made to minimize subjective researcher bias in the qualitative data analyses by precisely referencing all the quotations to demonstrate that data from a wide sample of the respondents was used (Wolcott, 1990). In sum, this is not to deny the value of multi-method approaches (e.g. self-report + observations from colleagues + physiological assessments) but simply to say that in this study, it was only possible to employ a combination of self-report methods in order to best achieve the major research objectives.

Headteacher sample

Other limitations are related to the sample. Since there is always risk of bias in a small-scale survey, the sample size of eighty respondents may be viewed as a potentially limiting factor in this study, particularly with respect to the quantitative data analyses. However, choices about the number of participants had to be tempered with considerations for the collection and analyses of the qualitative data, both of which are well-documented as time-consuming and labour-intensive activities (Green, 1995; Miles and Huberman, 1994). Consequently, eighty respondents were considered to be an optimal number taking account of practical and methodological considerations.

It might be argued that the findings may have been distorted by the localized nature of the sample group and that some of the conclusions (for example, about resourcing) may be relevant only to the Bradford Local Education Authority. One suspects, however, that this is not the case. There is no reason to suppose that the eighty headteachers who participated in this study differ greatly from other headteachers employed in statutory education services in other parts of the UK. Moreover, media coverage about the national problem of under-resourcing in schools is prolific. Ultimately though, only further studies of other groups of headteachers will establish whether in/adequate external resources influence appraisals, coping and situational outcomes.

The choice of headteachers as a sample constrained the nature of the problem situations described. Inevitably, the situations were oriented to occupational problems in headship and the analyses therefore could only encompass responses about appraisal, resources, coping behaviour and so on used in this context. These responses may, therefore, be somewhat limited in terms of generalizability to other samples. Further, the type of situation the headteachers reported was not specified beforehand by the researcher. Thus, differences in situations (to the extent they existed) may have added an extraneous source of variance to the headteachers' responses. Nonetheless, by not pre-specifying the problem situations this did guard against flaccid data and permit rich, descriptions of appraisals and coping in an educational context.

Variable measurement

Methodological issues arise because of the way in which certain variables in the study were measured. The NEM, PEM and GHQ measures used were well-established scales with known psychometric characteristics. The AJE and SYMP scales constructed specifically for this study also proved to be acceptably reliable, multi-item scales. However, not all the variables could be assessed with multiple items. Absoluteness and attributional style, for instance, had to be assessed and analyzed for the most part as dichotomous variables comprising somewhat gross categories of absoluteness/non-absoluteness and self-serving attributional style/non-self-serving attributional style respectively.

With attributional style, it was possible to categorize respondents (with a high degree of reliability) into four modes of attribution. These were of value heuristically and were then collapsed into self-serving and non-self-serving categories for subsequent analyses. With regard to absoluteness, however, only dichotomous categories could be agreed upon with an acceptable level of reliability. This was somewhat disappointing since the original intention had been to categorize respondents on a four-point scale ranging from highly absolutist to not at all absolutist. When this was attempted the resulting Kappa value of .30 was considered to be unacceptably low.

With hindsight, the unacceptable coefficient of reliability is understandable for one or a combination of the following reasons. First, inter-rater reliability was calculated using the particularly stringent statistic Kappa which inevitably yields lower reliability coefficients than the more commonly-reported method of calculating simple percentage agreement (Cicchetti and Sparrow, 1981).

Second, the disappointing level of agreement for coding absoluteness on a four-point scale may be a function of the complexity of the data and the inherent difficulties of defining mutually exclusive categories for the concepts which theoretically underpin absolutist thinking. As pointed out in chapter 3, as yet there is a paucity of data concerning this potentially dysfunctional mode of thinking and the major aim of this study was to explore rather than predefine the underlying concepts. Moreover, the concepts are inherently related further exacerbating mutually exclusive definitions of categories.

Arguably though, the most salient reason for the disappointing Kappa result may concern an issue raised by Ostell (1992) namely, that one criterion for identifying absoluteness is the manner in which the person conveys him or herself. More specifically, Ostell contends that highly absolutist individuals frequently advertise themselves in the ways they speak and act by speaking loudly and/or emphatically and using words or phrases such as should/not, must/not, ought/not and so on. This is an important issue here because whilst initial coding judgements were based on both **what** respondents said and **how** they said it, the independent judge could only make judgements based on **what** was said. In other words, information about the subject's manner of responding was available only to the researcher who conducted and transcribed the interviews. Because of time considerations, it was impractical for the independent judge to listen to all the interview tapes. It is likely therefore that this unavoidable disparity of available information to the researcher and the independent judge contributed to the disappointing level of agreement.

Research into Type A or 'coronary-prone' behaviour adds further credence to this point. For instance, the Rosenman structured interview (SI) (Rosenman, 1978), a primary technique for assessing Type A behaviour, can be reliably scored according to the subject's style of responding (e.g. loud/explosive, potential-for-hostility) as well as according to the contents of the interviewees' replies. In retrospect then, although it was not practically feasible for content and stylistic information to be available to both coders, it would have been ideal and would have probably resulted in acceptable levels of agreement for coding absoluteness on a four-point scale.

A final issue concerns the measurement of the variable relating to situational outcome. Regression analysis encourages the use of variables whose amounts can be measured with numeric precision, that is, interval variables such as NEM or GHQ. In addition, non-interval variables (such as absoluteness) may also be incorporated into a regression framework, since dichotomous variables enter the equation as 'dummy variables' (or an interval variable with just two values) and do not cause the regression estimates to lose any of their desirable properties (Lewis-Beck, 1980). However, the outcome variable was coded 1=Resolved, 2=Improved, 3=Unchanged, 4=Worsened and was thus an ordinal variable, which strictly speaking, is not an ideal candidate for regression. Nevertheless, some researchers argue that ordinal variables can be used in regression analyses. In brief, advocates argue that conclusions are usually equivalent to those generated by interval-level statistics and that multiple regression analysis is so powerful, compared to ordinal-level techniques, that the risk of error is acceptable (Lewis-Beck, 1980).

10.2 Suggestions for further work

A number of suggestions for further work emanate from the results of this study and concern negative emotionality, absolutist thinking, attributional styles, assessing coping and external resource adequacy and methodology.

Negative emotionality

With regard to negative emotionality (NEM) the results showed that congruent with other studies, NEM not only influences the individual's appraisal of work demands but also their psychological and somatic health reporting. The qualitative data were used to explore whether NEM influenced appraisal and reported health as a dispositional or a vulnerability/reactivity factor whilst further discussion highlighted the possibility of conceptual overlap and confounding between NEM and typical job stress and health measures. It was argued that NEM's influence may well be an interaction of all three factors, i.e. disposition/reactivity/conceptual overlap.

If NEM had been the only appraisal variable measured in this study, it would be tempting to conclude, along with other authors (e.g. Brief et al., 1988; Parkes, 1990; Payne et al., 1988) that future studies employing self-report methods must employ a measure of negative affectivity and partial out its effects before testing hypotheses about environmental conditions and psychological states. However, the findings relating to absolutist thinking and attributional style indicate that NEM is not the only, nor even the best appraisal variable worthy of future attention.

Absolutist thinking

A major contribution of this study is the identification and empirical measurement of absolutist thinking. Identified for the first time in a study of stress and coping, an absolutist way of thinking has been shown to generate strong, negative emotions and to be a powerful predictor of psychological health, physical symptoms and a less powerful but nonetheless (marginally) significant predictor of situational outcomes. Clearly these findings have implications for empirical developments in the stress field and indicate that a measure of absolutist thinking would be valuable.

Developing and construct validating a measure of absoluteness, however, would not necessarily be a straightforward procedure. The paucity of data relating to absoluteness suggests, as Ostell (1992) points out, that the role of this mode of thinking in generating emotional distress is either not well understood and/or has not been given not given priority. Thus, initial research efforts will have to focus on modelling more precisely the role of absolutist thinking in emotional disorders.

Next, just as theorists have distinguished between state and trait self-awareness (Wicklund, 1979) or anxiety (Spielberger et al., 1970) this distinction would need to

197

be addressed in developing a measure of absoluteness (Ostell, 1992). Briefly, a distinction would have to be made between individuals who respond in an absolutist manner to wide and varying issues (trait-absoluteness) as opposed to those individuals who respond in a preferential manner to most issues until a particular event or state of affairs causes them to respond in an absolutist way (state-absoluteness).

Finally, it may well be that the most effective way of measuring absolutist thinking would entail developing indicators which assess both **what** an individual says and **how** it is said. For whilst theory indicates that the content of absolutist dialogues frequently relates to criticism and blame, and is interjected with words such as 'must', 'should', 'ought', (Ellis, 1962; Ostell, 1992), theory also indicates that absolutist people often express their thoughts loudly and/or emphatically. Thus, along the lines of the Rosenman structured interview for assessing Type A behaviour (Rosenman, 1978) an interview will have to be developed which assesses absolutist thinking and which classifies the respondent in terms of both speech **content** and the subject's **manner** of responding.

Attributional styles

Congruent with previous studies, a non-self-serving attributional style was found to be a strong predictor of poor psychological and physical health. Extending previous research, this study assessed attributional styles in the context of everyday coping with work problems, revealed an important addition to the usually-reported self-serving 'external' category and permitted qualitative description of the differences between the four attributional styles identified.

These findings are not only of value in contributing to existing knowledge of attributional processes, but they also have implications for developing a new measure of attributional styles. For although a number of attributional style measures already exist (e.g. Seligman et al., 1979), the data in this study indicate that for completeness, measures should tap into:

• two self-serving styles (external-exonerated and internal-changeable)

• two non-self-serving styles (external-implicated and internal-unchangeable)

Existing measures do not assess the external-implicated category.

Developing a new measure of attributional styles would be valuable for three reasons. First, such a measure would not only be a good predictor of health and physical symptoms but would have some advantage (over measures such as NEM) in that questions about attributional processes would not overlap so obviously with items measuring health. Questions about attributional style would not require information relating to loss of sleep, feelings of tension or the tendency to worry - all of which are found in measures of negative emotionality and overlap conceptually with items in health measures such as the GHQ. Instead, items in an attributional style measure would be focused on factors such as external constraints in situations, personal skills, behaviours or effort and the extent to which individuals feel 'responsible' or culpable for situations with unsuccessful outcomes. It might be argued, of course, that whilst such factors may not conceptually overlap with typical health items they would, nevertheless, be problematic in that they would be subject to social desirability bias. In other words, individuals would simply 'blame' failed outcomes on, say, external factors thus presenting themselves in the best possible light. However, the results of this study have illustrated that if questions about failed outcomes are asked unobtrusively in an interview setting, then individuals do report other than 'socially desirable' attributions.

The second reason for developing a new measure of attributional styles is that it could be of practical value in identifying potential vulnerabilities in the attributional styles of individuals and therefore, in determining stress management training needs as discussed in chapter 9.

Thirdly, and perhaps most appealingly, the value of a measure of attributional style is that it taps into fundamental and characteristic ways in which individuals interpret and respond to situations and would not therefore be restricted to further studies of headteachers, but could be used with virtually any group of individuals in any context involving coping with problem situations.

Assessing coping behaviours and external resources

Together, the qualitative data on coping and the quantitative findings relating to external resources in this study highlight a number of important issues for future coping research (Oakland and Ostell, 1995). The qualitative data illustrate the tremendous diversity and complexity of coping behaviour and the dynamic nature of a process in which coping actions are often used reiteratively or on a trial-and error basis according to a complex and ever-changing interaction of personal and situational factors. In some cases, actions are immediately effective, in others, strategies are initially effective but then cease to be so. Sometimes, wide varieties of strategies employed over long periods of time prove totally ineffectual leaving the problem unchanged or worsened. At no time is coping a static, unitary event.
So can this extremely complex, changing process, often involving multiple permutations of situational and personal variables, be represented adequately by the quantitative coping measures which are so widely used in research? It seems not, for three main reasons relating to coping efficacy, external resource adequacy and the dynamic nature of the coping process.

Coping efficacy

Firstly, current methods of assessing coping are preoccupied with the type of strategy and/or how often it is used and how these factors relate to personal and situational outcomes. Yet qualitative data indicates that a more important factor regarding outcomes is the **efficacy** of the chosen strategies. It is coping efficacy which can have profound effects on psychological stress reactions, subsequent coping behaviors and ultimately, on personal and situational outcomes. In the future, therefore, research efforts need to concentrate on refining quantitative measures of coping to integrate ways of assessing coping effectiveness. Initially, this might entail modifying inventories which contain predefined categories of coping to include quantitative scales for reporting action effectiveness, as well as open-ended questions to collect qualitative data about why a particular strategy was chosen, why the strategy was effective or otherwise and what effects this had on psychological reactions and on the situation. Only then will we be in a better position, as Dewe (1992) says, to understand and explain why individuals use different strategies, why they feel the strategies are appropriate, the factors which affect coping efficacy and ultimately, to better understand the links between coping and various situational and adaptational outcomes.

External resource adequacy

The second reason why quantitative methods of assessing coping need refining is that they include items which are targeted only at whether and /or how often external resources such as advice, finances, information, emotional support and so on were sought. Yet the qualitative coping data in this study clearly indicate that **external resource adequacy** is a more important determinant of situational outcomes and psychological stress. It is vital , therefore, that future quantitative measures of coping are modified to include items which are targeted not only at whether advice, information, finances etc., were sought, but also, to what extent they were perceived as adequate.

  Here, one idea may be to modify the approach which was used by Roy and Steptoe (1994) in their study of daily stressors and social support availability amongst male firefighters. They used the Social Support Questionnaire (SSQ) (Sarason, Levine, Basham and Sarason, 1983) which includes items such as 'Whom can you count on to console you when you are very upset?' and respondents are required to give a list of support providers. Additionally, the SSQ provides a rating of satisfaction with the available support on a six-point scale ranging from very dissatisfied to very satisfied. This approach could be adapted to give quantitative data about:

- the **availability** of external resources such as money, advice, emotional support, practical assistance etc.

- the respondent's satisfaction with the **adequacy** of a particular resource.

Even though the above modifications would improve our current understanding of the role of external resources in the coping process, researchers face yet further challenges. For instance, one main area of difficulty concerns the perceptual process. Both the literature review and the headteachers' quotations in this book make it clear that an individual's perceptions of resource adequacy are important in shaping coping behaviours. Yet, in any problem situation, the individual's perceptions of the situation will be affected by a myriad of variables including personality, what is at stake for them in the situation (e.g. loss of job, loss of self-esteem), the extent of other problems they are having to deal with, the role of other people in the problem, the timeliness of otherwise of resource provision and so on. Thus, it may be useful in the future to consider ways of distinguishing between subjective perceptions of resource adequacy and their objective existence. Here, the first task in any study will be to determine those external resources which can be measured in a reasonably objective way (e.g. money, provision of equipment, tools, documented information etc.) and when feasible, to collect objective data. The advantage if this approach would be that if the subjective and objective data were congruent, then this would validate the individual's perceptions of resource adequacy (Patton, 1987). If the subjective and objective data were found to be incongruent, then the individual's perceptions would be questionable but could, perhaps, be illuminated by additional data relating to factors such as personality, low self-esteem, attributional style or negative emotionality. Either way, collecting objective data concerning external resource adequacy would give further insights into the coping process.

However, a compounding problem facing researchers is that objective data cannot be reasonably collected for all external resources. For example, it would be both difficult and of dubious value to collect objective data about the adequacy of resources such as emotional support or advice. Nonetheless, as this study has demonstrated, in an interview setting it is possible to follow the questions on resource availability and adequacy with open-ended questions asking why emotional support was 'Not at all adequate' or why they were only 'Moderately satisfied' with the advice they were given in a particular situation. These data at least provide some measure of consistency and internally validate or invalidate the responses to earlier questions (Patton, 1987). In sum, the modifications outlined above would help to redress the apparent imbalance between theory and practice and allow the importance of external resources to be stressed theoretically and their adequacy to be studied empirically (Newton, 1989; Oakland, 1991; Oakland and Ostell, 1995; Patterson et al., 1990).

Coping is a dynamic process

Effective coping can be achieved at times through a simple act or sequence of actions such as paying a bill, applying brakes while driving and steering to avoid an obstacle, or perhaps by a person changing their goals. But coping is often much more complicated and becomes a **dynamic** process of self-regulation and of the management of interpersonal events and environmental contingencies (both of which can change through time according to the actions and reactions of those involved) so that an acceptable outcome can be achieved as far as the coper is concerned. A manager handling a conflict between staff, a headteacher dealing with the parents of a disruptive child and the consequences of the child's behaviour within a school, a married couple attempting to establish better ways of avoiding quarrels and a wife caring for a husband dying of cancer while also managing her children and home, all illustrate the dynamic complexities of the coping process.

The inevitable question concerns how best to capture the changing nature of this process (Oakland and Ostell, 1995). Folkman and Lazarus (1985) took repeated measures of students' thoughts, feelings and actions using questionnaires in a longitudinal study of coping with college examinations. This event had three natural stages to it: the revision period, time prior to the examination and after the examination; the coping examples described above are much more unstructured, lacking any guaranteed sequence and in fact, often involve repetitive cycles of 'failure to cope effectively' (e.g. couples failing to avoid arguments).

The challenge here is to identify the complexities and crudeness or subtleties of the coping process while limiting the reactive effects of repeated measurement upon the coper's thoughts and actions. This cannot be achieved simply through the repeated administration of questionnaires but by the sensitive use of structured interviews. The latter might include the use of questionnaires, but will rely more upon the systematic and sensitive probing of the subjects involved to understand what they did, why, how they felt and so on. Even the reactive effects of prior measurement can be identified to some extent through this process by questioning subjects about whether previous interviews have changed their coping behaviour, in what ways and to what extent. Such information does not invalidate studies but provides vital detail about how the people involved actually coped.

In the social, behavioural sciences there is no way of avoiding totally the reactive effects of prior measurements upon future behavior. Thus, the key is to find ways of using any reactive effects to advantage so that they illuminate further the process being studied. The objective, ultimately, is not to identify every nuance in a person's coping behaviour but to identify the key factors and processes which mediated that person's reactions both at the moment in time and through time. The methodology used in the current study, when applied to longitudinal studies and adapted as suggested above, seems to provide the best approach currently available for achieving this goal.

10.3 Concluding remarks

The research reported in this book was concerned with the ways in which headteachers react to and attempt to cope with situations which they perceive to be stressful, the factors which influenced the situational outcomes and the implications for health. The rationale for the research design was derived from a critical review of existing stress and coping studies and represents an initial attempt to explore, describe and better understand the stress, coping and health relationship. Whilst the methodology chosen here is not without limitations, this is not to deny the value of the study. The major strengths of the study are threefold: theoretical, practical and methodological.

Foremost, the study has identified, described and assessed for the first time in stress research the impact of cognitive appraisal, external resource adequacy and headteacher work demands in the stress/health process. In particular, the identification of absolutist thinking and attributional style is of immediate and heuristic value in understanding the aetiology of stress reactions and ultimately health outcomes. Moreover, because of their strong relationship with psychological well-being, physical health and, in the case of absolutist thinking, situational outcomes, absolutist thinking and attributional style warrant further research efforts to develop measures which can be included in future studies of stress and health. Above all the current study indicates that future research must focus attention on such variables and partial out their effects before concluding that situational factors are the cause of maladaptive personal outcomes. It is also essential that future coping studies target questions on the adequacy of external resources rather than their availability (Oakland and Ostell, 1995) since the data here have provided insights into the impact of in/adequate resources on both situational and personal outcomes for the headteachers.

Together, the theoretical contributions arising from this study reinforce its practical strengths. A major strength of this work lies in the practical implications the results have for stress management training. The findings suggest that the ways in which a headteacher appraises, reacts to and handles his or her reactions to a problem situation can have significant effects on situational and health outcomes. In turn, this means that training headteachers to appraise situations and handle their emotional reactions more effectively would be of great value. As pointed out in chapter 9, such training would not necessarily have to be complicated, or protracted, or conducted on a one-to-one basis. Nor would training be only relevant and of value to headteachers. Indeed, both the theoretical and practical implications of this work have relevance beyond the sample of headteachers and are arguably, generalizable to virtually any group of individuals coping with everyday problem situations in any context.

The methodology chosen here confirms the benefits that can be derived when qualitative data and quantitative data are combined to investigate the stress process. The semi-structured interview schedule not only proved to be an effective data gathering instrument but also, when used in conjunction with the questionnaire, the information it yielded was a powerful predictor of psychological well-being and physical symptoms. Therefore, one contribution of this work concerns the development of a data-gathering, quasi-diagnostic interview schedule which, with only minor modifications to the introductory sections, could be readily adapted and used with other groups. Further, using the schedule with other groups need not be restricted to enquiry about occupational problems. Indeed, the wording and ordering of the questions in the schedule are such that they could apply to virtually any problematic situation, involving any individual in any context.

The methodology chosen here has also highlighted the potential limitations of studies which use only a questionnaire approach. Having access to both qualitative and quantitative data it was possible to highlight the limitations of studies which adhere rigidly to quantification and the much-used practice of simply relating either, events themselves to stress reactions or coping strategies to stress reactions, thereby leaving out a crucial intermediary step - cognitive appraisal. This point has particular salience for many occupational stress studies where the much-used practice when measuring work stressors has been to simply ask individuals to comment on the degree to which certain situations are perceived to be present. Such practice should now be reviewed if we are to avoid what Payne, Jick and Burke (1982) describe as the 'over-simplification assumption', that is, the belief that by reporting the presence of a demanding situation necessarily results in those situations being experienced in an unpleasant way.

The qualitative data have provided an insight into the stress and coping process to show that problems are dynamic and multidimensional in nature. We saw, for example, how some of the quantitative items in the interview schedule had to be treated as missing data because respondents found it impossible to give a 'static' answer about confidence, when their confidence throughout an encounter had fluctuated as events changed or unfolded. The qualitative data illustrated how problem situations frequently involve other people who not only influence appraisal but who also are often involved in the actual coping process. Individuals often joined forces with a headteacher in coping with a problem situation indicating that coping is sometimes a collaborative process. This is never addressed in purely quantitative assessments of coping.

The qualitative data also revealed the reiterative, trial-and-error nature of coping, with complex interactions of personal and situational variants determining coping effectiveness. Such observations surely call into question the utility of studies which use only single, retrospective assessments of coping, assessing the type of and/or frequency with which strategies are used but do not (indeed, cannot) address some of the more dynamic elements of the stress process which have been identified in this study. Researchers now must face the challenge of developing better measures of coping which tap into these elements (Oakland and Ostell, 1995).

The quantitative/qualitative data provide important insights into appraisal processes. The data make it clear that events themselves are not a necessary precursor to stress reactions but that the individual meaning of events (i.e. the private dialogues relating to the perceived costs of the situation) are a powerful predictor of affect, and ultimately, health. The results indicate that the meaning individuals attribute to events intervenes between the stressor and individual affective outcomes making individual evaluations a more powerful predictor of stress reactions than the actual events themselves. This is congruent, of course, with the transactional definition of stress on which this research is based. The results therefore lend empirical support for the vital role of cognitive appraisal in the arousal of stress reactions.

More generally, the methodology used in this study raises important issues concerning traditional stress measurement practices which clearly need modification in future stress research. Until now, most research efforts have been primarily concerned with investigating the stressor-stress interaction and have focused attention predominantly on elements of the interaction rather than the interaction itself. The methodologies developed to support such research have largely remained unchallenged, even though researchers have, for at least a decade, been emphasizing the transactional nature of stress and the need for understanding the role of appraisal in the stress process. The current study represents an initial effort at doing just this, using an alternative methodology which addresses contemporary theoretical issues and translates these into practical steps for collecting quantitative and qualitative data about stress processes within individuals. The qualitative/quantitative design of this study challenges therefore the more typically-used nomothetic approaches which mask important subtleties in the stress process.

For centuries different philosophers have expounded views which illustrate the basic principle upon which this research study was based, namely, that cognitive appraisal is central to an understanding of the generation and maintenance of stress processes. Epicetus, the Stoic philosopher, wrote in the Enchiridion during the first century A.D. that 'People are disturbed not by things but by the view which they take of them'. This research study has explored empirically and provided significant insights into the role of appraisal in stress processes.

The challenges for future research are two-fold. First, to develop better models of the key aspects of cognition which lead to the arousal and subsequent maintenance of stress processes. This will require researchers to look beyond current paradigms and explore new methods of measurement and alternative methods of data collection. Second, 'No man is an island', although some attempt to live as such! Occupational stress researchers also need to contribute to the even more demanding challenge of going beyond the individual and his or her transactions with a problematic and changing work environment to identify more healthy ways for **individuals to work together** in organizational contexts. This will involve an examination of work practices, work design and modes of motivating and managing individuals with differing goals and values and to promote more effective ways of working that are less injurious to psychological and physical health.

Semi-structured interview schedule

Date:.................................
Name of respondent: ...... (omitted for confidentiality)
Sex:.................................. (omitted for confidentiality)
Name of school:.............. (omitted for confidentiality)
Address of school:.......... (omitted for confidentiality)
Type of school: .... (omitted for confidentiality)
LEA district: .... Bradford

- Introductions

- Funded by the Economic and Science Research Council to look at the different ways in which people behave, think and feel when they are dealing with difficult tasks and responsibilities at work.

- Headteachers are a special group because they deal with a wide variety of tasks and responsibilities, many of which are undergoing rapid change.

- The study is not an evaluation of how effective headteachers are in dealing with their work demands but rather, aims to gain a better understanding of the different ways in which headteachers feel, think and react when dealing with work-related tasks and responsibilities.

- We are prepared to offer a feedback session, perhaps in the form of a 1-day course, tailored to the interests of heads who have taken part.

- All information will be held in the strictest confidence and no names of schools or individuals will appear anywhere in the results.

Background details:

Number of pupils on roll ....
Number of staff ....
Number of deputies ....
Secretarial staff ....

How long have you been headteacher of this school? ....

Are you employed on a full time or part time contract? ....

Is it a permanent or temporary contract? ....

How many years have you been teaching? ....

For how many of those years have you been a headteacher? ....

How many years were you in the role of deputy? ....

Which of the following qualifications do you hold?   GCE '0' levels
   GCE 'A' levels
   First degree
   Higher/Diploma/Certificates

Have you had any work experience other than teaching? ....

Outside work do you have any hobbies or interests? ....

Does this lead to any formal involvement in clubs etc.? ....

To complete the background information I need one or two personal details, please.

a) How old are you? ....

b) Are you married? ....

c) Does your partner work? ....

d) Do you have any children? ....

A.   **To help me gain some insight into your job, I'd like you to begin by briefly summarizing the responsibilities you have as headteacher.**

I am responsible to the children in School re. attainment levels and targets and responsible to members of staff insofar as facilitating their effectiveness really. And also, over recent years, responsible for their well-being because over and above their responsibilities they have personal problems which crop up, interactive problems with other members of staff because of their extra responsibilities and the Education Reform Act. So quite a lot of my time is spent with staff. And I am responsible for non-teaching staff as well, that includes caretaking, cleaning and auxiliary staff and responsibilities to the community because you know, we are a very active part of this community. So I have a responsibility to parents and obviously to the governing body now and the LEA - Quite a lot of time has to be spent on forging very positive links with the governing body because we are going to be working very ..... extremely closely with them in the future ... very much so.

B.   What would you say are the most rewarding or satisfying aspects of your job?

If I isolate the role of teaching, because in your role as headteacher these days teaching becomes much more limited... but I have got to mention that because that gives lots of rewards; seeing children getting benefits over the course of a year. Within the whole school, I enjoy looking at developments and seeing them come to fruition is great... it's very time consuming though - nothing in education is speedy, everything is slow. But one of the biggest kicks is the children without a doubt - their smiles and enthusiasm and working with staff who are friends as well as colleagues.

C.   What, if any, would you say are the special difficulties or problems your job gives rise to?

At the moment, the amount of paperwork that's coming in basically. In his wisdom, the Secretary of State has decreed a lot of things which in the long-term will benefit schools - but it is coming too fast and too much together. What with LMS, National Curriculum and governing body responsibilities and so on, you tend to be running round too quick and my fear is that I only do a partial job on it.... you cannot do justice to the reforms that are coming through ... and the legislation changes so much. I mean the goalposts with National Curriculum have moved quite dramatically. So as a general rule I try to build in flexibility on the path so that I might be going down one path and then quickly I have to change route ... it's difficult to hit the balance because yes, you have got to be realistic in your expectations, but at the end of the day you have got to have achieved something - you cannot be so flexible that you bend and end up where you started off! So I try to develop within the staff, people who are able to accept delegation ... it's difficult and very, very time consuming.

SECTION A

What I am interested in now are the different ways in which people react to various events or difficult situations at work. In particular, what I would like you to do is think back and recall an event or difficult situation which you have had to deal with recently at work, say in the past few weeks or so. Try to think of an event or situation, not a trivial matter, but something which posed you with genuine difficulties.... perhaps other people were involved ... maybe not ... but a situation that in the end, you felt had a successful outcome.

1. **Take your time to think ... then would you briefly describe any recent work-related incident or difficult situation which you have had to deal with and which you feel turned out successfully?**

I have had to deal with a very difficult situation concerning a long-term staff absence. I have a teacher who has only worked eight days since last September and has not been in school since. What happened is that the nature of the illness was such that the teacher was not fit to work but was keen to get back to work. So after short-term sick notes and long-term sick notes it was clear to me that in no way would the teacher be fit to return to work and that it had to be resolved in a way that would be satisfying to the teacher, to the Local Authority, to the management of the school, but above all else - to the pupils who were in the teacher's charge. So it involved ' balancing' - thats a key word in headship - and that is what I have tried to do ... its been so difficult but in fact it's finished today ... that is why it is on my mind.

2. **Who else was involved?**

Apart from myself, the teacher and the LEA and staff.

3. **Was the situation unexpected or expected?**

It was expected because I knew the teacher's background and I predicted that something like this would happen at some point. The trick was getting a satisfactory, balanced conclusion without anybody limping - without the teacher feeling deeply wounded and without unpleasantness and anxieties in the staff room and without the children's education unscathed, above all.

Looking at this rating scale, where 1 = very expected and 6 = very unexpected, where would you rate the event?

Show scale card: Expectedness = 2

4. **Have you had to deal with something like this before?**

Oh yes. I have dealt with it lots of times before so I am extremely familiar with this sort of issue.

On the scale, how familiar/unfamiliar would you say the situation was?

Show scale card: Familiar = 1

5. **Thinking back to what happened, do you remember it as a predominantly pleasant or unpleasant experience?**

Very unpleasant because we are talking about somebody's job ... their income ... and having to be word perfect in your presentation because you have to be mindful that anything you say will be recorded and reported and could be brought to Court - but above all its very, very hard to confront people with failure professionally - you get tremendous guilt having to tell them.

On the scale, how would you rate the pleasantness/unpleasantness of the events/situation

Show scale card: Unpleasant = 5

6. **And thinking back to the time this situation arose, do you remember it as a time when you had any other difficult situations or problems that you were dealing with - either at work, or socially or at home?**

Right up at the top end of the scale because everybody's teaching including me - I am teaching 50% of the time to cover **plus** all the other day to day problems to cope with - so you are at a major disadvantage when you are in the classroom most of the day with everything else going on.

So if I asked you to rate on the scale the extent to which there were other problems or difficulties going on in your life at the time, how would you rate the extent of other problems?

Show scale card: Other Problems = 7

7. **And generally speaking, how much control would you say you felt you had over being able to sort the problem out to your satisfaction?**

It changed - at first I was in almost total control of it because all the decisions were down to me - but then when the LEA were involved I felt I wasn't in control of it at all - I was least happy at that point and an additional complexity was that the LEA were undergoing lots of changes and that made it worse because there was no continuity of personnel. Then, the ball was back in my court as they say.

On the scale, where would you rate the amount of control you felt you had over the situation/events?

Show scale card: Control = 6→1→6

8. How confident did you feel that you would be able to deal with the situation?

Very confident - when the decisions were mine to make because I have dealt with this sort of situation so many times before. That might not be a typical response from some other headteachers. One of the things I hope your study will show is that heads will give different, complex answers which reflect the complexity of the job - that is what makes it difficult.

How would you rate your confidence on the scale?

Show scale card: Confidence = 6

Thank you, those details help me to get a clearer picture of the problem and were useful for putting the problem in context for me. What I am interested in now is what you did, what you thought and how you felt when this was happening.

9. First of all, can you elaborate on just what it was about this situation that made it seem problematic or difficult for you?

The first thing of primary importance was that the teacher was absent for such a long time and the children's education was suffering. Linked to this was the extra workload which of course, fell on me and the other members of staff. Also, it was difficult to really know when or indeed, if, the teacher would be coming back to school at all, so planning was difficult and another thing is that it is very time consuming dealing with something like this. What was frustrating as well was that the staff at the LEA were changing all the time - there was no continuity - so each time I had to relate the tale to someone new and then again to someone new a couple of weeks later and so on.

As people attempt to handle difficult situations, they often experience different emotions - these may change as the situation develops or as events unfold. What I would like you to do now is think back and try to recall how you felt when this was happening.

10. How did you feel when the situation first arose?

I felt guilty - guilty about what was happening to staff, colleagues who were having to carry the extra workload and about the standard of education that we were not giving the pupils - we **should** have been offering them much more, but were unable to - that is very frustrating.

Show emotion prompt card: EMOTIONS = Angry, Frustrated, Guilty, Anxious

I felt angry at the change of personnel in the LEA and because of some of the double-talk that was going on - where people say one thing and mean another. I got really cross when people would not confront the reality of the situation. If you like, I am at the sharp end and reality is outside my door. Those in the LEA are removed from that reality and have a different perspective.

From those emotions you say you experienced, which two would you say were predominant ones

Anger and guilt

When people feel say, angry or guilty they often have private conversations with themselves, saying such things as .... or ....

11. When you felt angry can you recall the sorts of things that were going through your mind at the time?

Quite frankly, you are in a ridiculous position because you have the reality of turmoil in the school, over-worked staff and so on and yet on some of the issues your hands are tied - it is ludicrous. That is what makes me cross.

You mentioned that you also felt guilty. What sort of things were you thinking to make you feel guilty?

Well, the staff are working at full pelt anyway and all I do is add to their workload and because that is the only option open to me I wondered and worried at lot about whether they think I am the sort of head who dismisses staff for illness.

Not only do people engage in these private conversations, but also they sometimes actually do something in response to their feelings.

12. Thinking back, what if anything, did you do when you felt angry and guilty?

I tend to go ... not so much at school but more at home ... I tend to go very quiet, I put on 'a face' at school and stay fairly 'level' .... obviously I do not go home and kick the cat or my wife, but I do go very quiet at home and brood a lot ... you know, I am moody and a bit snappy - then I feel guilty about that! But you have got to hide your aggressive feelings haven't you?

When faced with difficult situations like the one you have described, people decide on what they are going to do in very different ways and react or behave very differently. Frequently, these plans or actions change as the situation changes and events unfold.

13. What did you do initially to deal with the situation?

At first I just monitored the teacher's absence - then monitored it with a view to determining how long it might go on - then I set target dates for the teacher's return ... I set and failed on four dates. So I devised a system for phasing the teacher back into school gradually and the LEA supported and financed this. But the goals had to change when the teacher failed to return again. The trick was identifying the point at which to try and re-introduce the teacher so that you were deemed to be fair by all concerned, including my own staff because I was not scheming to get rid of someone who was genuinely sick. Anyway, the teacher failed to return on any of the dates and today has resigned.

14. And before you actually did this, can you remember considering any alternative possible courses of action or other ways of dealing with the situation?

I could have done nothing and just let it ride or, I could have had a classic row with the teacher and let them know the position I was in.

Why did you decide to reject the first alternative?

I rejected this because of concern for the pupils, because an absence like this has to be covered for their sakes.

And why didn't you pursue the second idea?

Because it would not have been professional dealing with it by getting angry.

15. You have already described what you actually did in response to the situation ... if I show you this list of possible responses to difficult or problematic situations, can you recognize any other responses which you had?

Show coping response prompt card:

1.   I made more than one plan of action but the teacher did not return to school, that was the problem.

2. I did not vent my emotions - I bottled them up.

3. I did criticize myself to some degree because my colleagues were taking the brunt of the workload.

4. I talked with my partner about it which helped a lot.

5. The adviser gave me good advice which I acted on.

16. And when you were handling the situation ... were you still feeling angry and guilty, for instance, as you were when the situation first arose?

I suppose so, yes, because the lack of continuity at the LEA was so frustrating. But I now also feel sad - sad for the teacher involved because they had such potential as a teacher and now, that potential will never be developed.

What I am interested in now is what happened and how or if things changed.

17. In relation to the problem, what happened as a result of what you did?

Although I set target dates to phase the teacher back into school, the teacher is still not well enough to return and has recognized that now and resigned this morning.

So, would you describe the situation as:

Show outcome card: OUTCOME = Resolved

in that the school as an institution can appoint someone else.

(Use questions 18-22 as appropriate, depending on whether outcome is resolved, improved, unchanged or worsened)

18. How did you feel at the time about the way things had worked out?

Relief in one sense, but the sad thing is that the teacher did not come back to school in the first place.

(IF IMPROVED, WORSENED, UNCHANGED)

19. What did you decide to do next?

20. Why? What were you hoping that would achieve?

21. Did things eventually get sorted out?

22. How do you feel now that the situation has ended?   Relieved, but sad

In difficult situations such as the one you have described, having access to certain resources such as financial resources, support or help from friends and colleagues, or having certain personal skills and so on can greatly influence the outcome of a situation like this.

23. Thinking back to what happened, which of the following resources would you say were available to you in the situation you have described?

Show resources card:

ADVICE ☑
EMOTIONAL SUPPORT ☑
PERSONAL SKILLS ☑
FINANCIAL ☑
MORE INFORMATION ☒
PRACTICAL ASSISTANCE ☑

24. Which of those resources (if any) were not available to you but if they had been available, might have facilitated things or led to a satisfactory solution sooner?

The LEA only offered teaching 'assistance' which fell far short of the practical assistance I would have liked - the help just was not forthcoming.

Why? How would that have helped?

It would have distributed the teaching load.

25. How adequate were the actual resources that were available to you and can you explain why?

Show 7-point scale card:

ADVICE = 6
SUPPORT = 7
SKILLS = 6
FINANCIAL = 5
INFORMATION = N/A
ASSISTANCE = 1

Advice from the adviser was good and I acted on it. Support from my partner and colleagues was excellent. Modesty apart - I feel I handled it well. The finances were there to support phasing her back but what I really needed was practical assistance at the time - that just was not available.

26. Reflecting on events as you have described them, how well would you say you handled the situation?

I am quite pleased with how things have worked out.

And on the scale, how well would you say you handled events?

Show scale card: HANDLED = 6

Why?

I think I did everything I could given the situation.

SECTION B

Thank you for your patience and co-operation so far ... the interview is progressing well ... your answers have been very thoughtful and some interesting issues are emerging.

27. What I would like you to do now is somewhat similar to what you have already done. This time I would like you to recall a recent event or difficult situation which you have had to deal with at work ... but a situation which you feel had an unsuccessful outcome. As before, the situation may have involved other people or may not, but this time would you recall a recent, difficult situation which you feel turned out unsuccessfully.

I can think of something recently that involves a child who has come to this school almost as a last resort. He had 'failed' behaviour-wise everywhere else. As a child he had been severely sexually molested - he is 12 now. We have a reputation for accepting 'last resorters' because our parameters for 'acceptable behaviour' are much wider than anyone else's. And there is an underlying general philosophy amongst the staff that certain kids **will** do *x* or **will** do *y* anyway.

He came to us from another school - having 'failed' there. He was living in a children's home having been taken away from his natural parents. Things were not too bad to start with but we had to invent strategies in school to help him because he has a deep mistrust of adults - not surprisingly because he has been through terrible experiences. But by and large the staff were prepared to put up with his tantrums and inappropriate behaviour - we work very hard at learning to tolerate. Then, after last weeks holiday he came back to school having mixed with a lot of older boys in the home and was a lot wilder than before. At this point the staff were beginning to feel that the camel's back had been broken and we had bent as far as we could bend. But I was still determined to keep him in school. Then, the other lunchtime, he assaulted another child very savagely. And so, for the first time ever in my years here, I suspended a child ... and that has caused me a tremendous amount of grief.

Can I stop you there a moment to clarify one or two details about the situation you have just described,

28. Who else was involved?

Child, staff, Social Services, police, advisers.

29. Was the situation unexpected or expected?

Somewhat expected given the history of the boy.

Looking at this rating scale, where 1= very expected and 6= very unexpected, where would you rate the event?

Show scale card: EXPECTEDNESS = 3

30. Have you had to deal with something like this before?

Sadly, yes - not quite as extreme as this case but I do deal with similar incidents quite frequently.

On the scale, how familiar/unfamiliar would you say the situation was?

Show scale card: FAMILIAR = 2

31. Thinking back to what happened, do you remember it as a predominantly pleasant or unpleasant experience?

Extremely, extremely unpleasant. It has upset me personally a great deal.

On the scale, how would you rate the pleasantness/unpleasantness of the events/situation?

Show scale card: UNPLEASANT = 6

32. And thinking back to the time this situation arose, do you remember it as a time when you had any other difficult situations or problems that you were dealing with - either at work, or socially or at home?

There are always many problems going on in school - you are never in one channel for long - although this has been uppermost in my mind for a few weeks even though it gets crowded out now and again by everything else.

So if I asked you to rate on the scale the extent to which there were other problems or difficulties going on in your life at the time, how would you rate the extent of other problems?

Show 7-Point scale card: OTHER PROBLEMS = 5

33. And generally speaking, how much control would you say you felt you had over what was happening?

That is a very good question. It was very limited ... very, very limited - and I felt that when I wanted to hold the line and make decisions (even if they went against the staff) that it wasn't a holdable line. My hands were tied. So many agencies were involved and the buck kept being passed between the LEA and the Social Services and there is conflict between those two anyway.

On the scale, where would you rate the amount of control you felt you had over the situation?

Show scale card: CONTROL = 2

34. How confident did you feel that you would be able to deal with the situation?

I wasn't confident at all - I felt as if I was left in the middle holding the can - receiving messages from one source, passing it on to another source and never a straight tale from any of them. The only time I had authority in the whole saga was in suspending him - and even then he has been re-instated now - so it's not really 'authority'.

How would you rate your confidence on the scale?

Show scale card: CONFIDENCE =2

Thank you, those details help me to get a clearer picture of the problem and was useful for putting the problem in context for me. What I am interested in now is what you did, what you thought and how you felt when this was happening.

35. First of all, can you elaborate on just what it was about this situation that made it seem problematic or difficult for you?

Foremost, its not being able to really get 'hold' of the situation and help him. I am not a trained psychologist so I cannot get to the bottom of what his feelings are, nor can I understand the thinking behind special educational needs or the Social Services. Nobody seemed to have a clear vision of how to deal with it and the bottom line feeling coming through from other people involved is that **we have not done enough**! Now I cannot take that - I find that very, very hurtful and so did my senior staff - we had bent as far as possible. I found the representative from the Social Services - their whole demeanour and attitude were offensive - they were clearly saying we had not done enough. The scheme they suggested for modifying the boy's behaviour was totally inappropriate - we tried it for a week - it was hopeless.

36. How did you feel when the situation first arose?

I vacillated from feeling very, very angry about the way the boy was being treated to feeling angry about the way I was being treated, and the school. I felt hurt that the school's name was being undermined and there was a constant pressure on me to do something that wasn't deliverable.

Can you remember experiencing any other emotions at the time?

Show emotions prompt card: EMOTIONS = Angry
                                                                       Dejected
                                                                       Anxious
                                                                       Hurt

Very, very dejected. I felt everything we had worked for six years was being pulled out from under us. I still feel very down and desperately hope that we do not get a similar child until the memories have died down. Also angry because I jealously guard the reputation we have carefully built up here - I simply **cannot** and **will not** accept that we did not 'do enough'.

From those emotions you say you experienced, which two would you say were the predominant ones?

Angry and anxious

37. When you felt angry can you recall the sorts of things that were going through your mind at the time?

I was angry because I felt impotent and it should not be that a child like that is allowed to 'slip down the slope' and follow his father's footsteps to prison. In my experience it is nearly always inevitable that they do follow their fathers - so I felt angry **for** him.

What sort of things were you thinking when you felt anxious?

Well, after suspending him I had to take him round to the children's home and deposit him there and their reaction was 'We do not know how you have put up with him for as long as you have'. Now he is wandering the streets and will eventually become prison fodder.

38. Thinking back, what, if anything, did you do when you felt angry and anxious?

I have had a lot of very bad nights where I have had kind of 'pressure' type dreams - I have been waking up sweating and shaking. But I also eat too much - I eat quite ridiculously and put on weight like you would not believe. - I **force** sugar into my body by whatever means - comfort eating has always been a severe problem with me.

39. What did you do initially to deal with the situation?

At first I did a lot of talking to the staff to encourage them in what we were trying to do for the boy, but when his behaviour deteriorated further I then had to counsel the bruised staff to restore their confidence in me and the school. A scheme we tried only worked for a week: the advice I got from Social Services was to introduce a scheme of behaviour modification for the boy whereby he would get different coloured counters for certain behaviours and then exchange the counters for a Mars Bar or something. Fine - the idea is fine - but it is **not** appropriate for this boy - his basic problem is a deep-seated mistrust of adults.

40. And before you actually did this, can you remember considering any alternative possible courses of action or any other ways of dealing with the situation?

I could have had him taken away to a residential home at the beginning.

And why did you decide to reject the first alternative?

I was determined to keep trying for the boy's sake even though the staff did not like it at all in the latter weeks.

41. You have already described what you actually did in response to the situation ... if I show you the list of possible responses to difficult or problematic situations, can you recognize any other responses which you had?

Show coping response prompt card:

There are some things on this list which I would love to have done but I simply could not:

1. I could not make a plan of action because I did not have the authority to make one.
2. There were times when I **had to** accept the situation but I did not like that one bit - I hated every minute of it.
3. There was some self-criticism - I still wonder whether there were better ways of dealing with it.
4. I could not consider the problem carefully because the goalposts kept shifting.
5. I am a Christian - I find my faith helps.

42. And how did you feel while this was going on ...... were you still feeling angry and anxious, for instance, as you were when the situation first arose?

To me the whole thing is horribly unsatisfactory and it is still very painful for me and I still feel it should not have happened as it did. I took the brunt of it.

43. In relation to the problem, what happened as a result of what you did?

Arguably, the situation's worsened hasn't it? He is wandering the streets now and somehow I feel responsible. In school though, the situation's improved because the staff and the other children are happier now - they are no longer threatened by the boy. But his full time care assistant had to be laid off when he left - that is not a pleasant task.

So, would you describe the situation as:

Show outcome card: OUTCOME = Worsened

(Use questions 44-47 as appropriate, depending on whether outcome is resolved, improved, unchanged or worsened.)

44. How did you feel at the time about the way things had worked out?

I still feel bad about things but having said that, I still do not know what else I could have done - yet I feel so responsible for the fact that he's out there in the streets - it's dreadful.

45. What did you decide to do next?

46. Why? What were you hoping that would achieve?

47. Did things eventually get sorted out?

48. How do you feel now that the situation has ended?

49. Thinking back to what happened, which of the following resources would you say were available to you in the situation you have described?

Show resources card: ADVICE ☑
EMOTIONAL SUPPORT ☑
PERSONAL SKILLS ☑
FINANCIAL ☑
MORE INFORMATION ☒
PRACTICAL ASSISTANCE ☑

50. Which of those resources (if any) were not available to you but if they had been available, might have facilitated things or led to a satisfactory solution sooner?

Help in the form of a full-time teacher for him might have helped - I really don't know though.

Why? How would that have helped?

It would have relieved the staff who were already overworked.

51. How adequate were the actual resources that were available to you and can you explain why?

Show 7-point scale card:

ADVICE = 2
SUPPORT = 6
SKILLS = 3
FINANCIAL = 4
INFORMATION = N/A
ASSISTANCE = 1

Advice was not too useful from colleagues because they didn't know how to handle it either. The staff supported me for the main part. My skills were under the microscope in this one - maybe they were not adequate. I felt I was perhaps lacking the power to make decisions. I just did not have the power even if I'd had the moral fibre. The finances were partially there for a non-teaching assistant but a full-time teacher's help would have probably been more use.

52. Reflecting on events as you have described them, how well would you say you handled the situation?

I felt my skills were severely tested with this one and I am certainly not happy with how things have turned out. My deputy and I took the brunt of it and we were both very, very upset by it.

And finally, on the scale, how well would you say you handled events?

Show scale card:

HANDLED = 3

POST INTERVIEW NOTES

A Profile of Health, Behaviour

and

Personal Characteristics

Private and confidential

Section A

Personal characteristics

The first section focuses on individual differences in people's attitudes and personal characteristics.

Listed below is a series of statements a person might use to describe his or her attitudes or personal characteristics. If a statement is **true** or largely true, as applied to you, circle the 'T' in the space next to that item. If a statement is **false**, circle the 'F' in the space next to that item.

Please answer **every** statement.

1.	I often find myself worrying about something	T	F
2.	My feelings are hurt rather easily	T	F
3.	It is easy for me to be enthusiastic about things I'm doing	T	F
4.	Often I get irritated at little annoyances	T	F
5.	I often feel happy and satisfied for no particular reason	T	F
6.	I suffer from nervousness	T	F
7.	I live a very interesting life	T	F
8.	Every day I do some things that I enjoy	T	F
9.	My mood often goes up and down	T	F
10.	I sometimes feel miserable for no good reason	T	F
11.	Occasionally I experience strong emotions, anxiety, anger, etc., without really knowing what causes them	T	F
12.	I usually find ways to liven up my days	T	F
13.	I am easily startled by things that happen unexpectedly	T	F
14.	I sometimes get myself into a state of tension and turmoil as I think of the day's events	T	F
15.	Most days I have feelings of real fun or joy	T	F
16.	I often feel sort of lucky for no special reason	T	F
17.	Every day interesting and exciting things happen to me	T	F
18.	Minor setbacks sometimes irritate me too much	T	F
19.	In my spare time I usually find something interesting to do	T	F
20.	I often lose sleep over my worries	T	F
21.	For me life is a great adventure	T	F
22.	There are days when I'm on edge all of the time	T	F
23.	I am too sensitive for my own good	T	F
24.	I sometimes change from happy to sad, or vice versa, without good reason	T	F
25.	I always seem to have something pleasant to look forward to	T	F

226

Section B

How you experience your job

This section is concerned with how people in the same occupational role, experience that role in different ways.

In any occupation there are features of a job which may be experienced as either:

Pleasant - leading to feelings of satisfaction, enjoyment, pride, feeling challenged, etc.

or

Unpleasant - leading to anxiety, anger, tension, frustration, and so on.

Listed below are 17 features of a Headteacher's job. Against **each** item please circle the number which most accurately describes how you generally experience that particular feature of your job.

Extremely unpleasant	**6**
Very unpleasant	**5**
Somewhat unpleasant	**4**
Somewhat pleasant	**3**
Very pleasant	**2**
Extremely pleasant	**1**

1.	Managing or supervising the work of other people	6	5	4	3	2	1
2.	Dealing with the demands of various people to whom you are responsible (Governors, LEA, etc.)	6	5	4	3	2	1
3.	Dealing with staff related issues, e.g., motivation	6	5	4	3	2	1
4.	Having a wide variety of tasks in your job	6	5	4	3	2	1
5.	Handling some aspects of your job for which you feel you have inappropriate training	6	5	4	3	2	1
6.	Making decisions that affect others	6	5	4	3	2	1
7.	Not being able to influence some decisions and actions that affect you	6	5	4	3	2	1
8.	Choosing your own method of working	6	5	4	3	2	1
9.	Exercising independent thought and action in your job	6	5	4	3	2	1
10.	Keeping up with new ideas, technology, etc.	6	5	4	3	2	1
11.	Having authority to influence school management methods and procedures	6	5	4	3	2	1
12.	Having authority to delegate some responsibilities	6	5	4	3	2	1
13.	Being responsible for setting goals for the school	6	5	4	3	2	1
14.	Trying to equate perceived objectives of the school with external demands and constraints	6	5	4	3	2	1
15.	Preparing for increased financial responsibilities	6	5	4	3	2	1
16.	Managing or adapting to organizational change	6	5	4	3	2	1
17.	Planning ahead amidst organizational and curricular changes	6	5	4	3	2	1

Section C

Health

The final section is concerned with: i) your general health, and ii) any physical complaints you may have experienced over the past few weeks.

i)   General health

From the 12 questions listed below, please **UNDERLINE** the answer which you think most accurately applies to you. It is important to answer as accurately and honestly as you can.

Have you recently:

been unable to concentrate on whatever you are doing?	More so than usual	Same as usual	Less so than usual	Much less than usual
lost much sleep over worry?	Not at all	No more than usual	Rather more	Much more than usual
felt that you are playing a useful part in things?	More so than usual	Same as usual	Less useful than usual	Much less useful
felt capable of making decisions about things	More so than usual	Same as usual	Less so than usual	Much less capable
felt constantly under strain?	Not at all	No more than usual	Rather more than usual	Much more than usual
felt you couldn't overcome your difficulties?	Not at all	No more than usual	Rather more than usual	Much more than usual
been able to enjoy your normal day to day activities?	More so than usual	Same as usual	Less so than usual	Much less able
been able to face up to your problems?	More so than usual	Same as usual	Less so than usual	Much less than usual
been feeling unhappy or depressed?	Not at all	No more than usual	Rather more than usual	Much more than usual
been losing confidence in yourself?	Not at all	No more than usual	Rather more than usual	Much more than usual
been thinking of yourself as a worthless person?	Not at all	No more than usual	Rather more than usual	Much more than usual
been feeling reasonably happy all things considered?	More so than usual	Same as usual	Less so than usual	Much less than usual

ii)   **Physical complaints**

Examine the list below and indicate the frequency of occurrence of these complaints, as applied to you, over the past few weeks.
  Please answer by circling the appropriate number on the scale shown.

Very frequently	**6**
Frequently	**5**
Sometimes	**4**
Infrequently	**3**
Very infrequently	**2**
Never	**1**

Headaches or pains in the head	6	5	4	3	2	1
Acid stomach, nausea or indigestion	6	5	4	3	2	1
Nervousness or shakiness inside (e.g., 'butterflies')	6	5	4	3	2	1
Breathing difficulties or shortness of breath	6	5	4	3	2	1
Irregular heart beat, palpitations, etc.	6	5	4	3	2	1
Faintness or dizziness	6	5	4	3	2	1
Lack of energy, apathy or constant tiredness	6	5	4	3	2	1
Feelings of heaviness or weakness in your arms and legs	6	5	4	3	2	1
Soreness or trembling of muscles, twitches or tics, etc.	6	5	4	3	2	1
Minor skin irritations - rashes, itching	6	5	4	3	2	1
Soreness or discomfort in the eyes	6	5	4	3	2	1
Tendency to hot or cold spells	6	5	4	3	2	1
Numbness or tingling in parts of your body	6	5	4	3	2	1
Chest pains	6	5	4	3	2	1
Pains in lower back	6	5	4	3	2	1
Difficulty getting to sleep or staying asleep	6	5	4	3	2	1
Feeling unrested following a night's sleep	6	5	4	3	2	1

Have you visited your doctor recently in relation to any of the above complaints? (Please answer Yes or No)   ....

Thank you for your patience and co-operation with this study.

Data Reduction Proforma

Interview No: **Name:**   **Sex:**   **School:**

Main responsibilities:

To children re. attainment and staff well-being
For non-teaching staff
To community, parents and governing body
Lot time forging links with governing body

Job satisfaction/rewards:

Teaching - lots rewards seeing benefits to children
Enjoy but time-consuming school developments
Biggest kicks from smiles/enthusiasm of children

Main difficulties:

Amount of paperwork - too much too fast (since educational changes)
Fear only doing partial job
Try to build in flexibility to cope - difficult and time consuming re. staff
development

Section A

Problem description

Long-term staff absence - set target dates and plans to phase teacher back into
school - all failed because teacher not well enough to return. Head seeks solution
that suits teacher, LEA and education of children but worries about other staff.

Who else involved?

Head, absent teacher LEA, staff

Un/expected	2	Expected because of teachers background but worried about other staff as well as teacher
Un/familiar	1	Familiar, extremely - dealt with lots times before.
Un/pleasant	5	Very unpleasant - someone's job, income, needs very careful handling - guilt telling teacher.
Other problems	7	Very much so - everyone is teaching including myself plus all day-to-day problems.
Control	6→1→6	Changed - at first almost total - all decisions down to me - then LEA involved - then decision mine in the end
Confidence	6	Very confident - dealt with this before many times - hope study shows complexity

Why problematic?

1. Children's education suffering because of teacher's absence.
2. Extra workload for me and staff.
3. Planning difficult because uncertain when/if coming back.
4. LEA personnel changing all time - no continuity.

Emotional reactions(s):

Guilty - because staff carrying extra workload
Angry - at change of LEA personnel and because of double-talk - really cross
    when others won't confront reality - hands are tied.
Anxious - worried re. staff thinking I dismiss for illness.

Handling emotions:

Go very quiet - put on a face - brood - moody at home then guilty - got to hide aggressive feelings.

Coping responses and intentions:

Monitored absence
Set target dates for teacher's return - to no avail
Devised a phase-in system - also failed

Made number of plans - to no avail
Didn't vent emotions - bottled them up
Criticized staff because colleagues had increased workload
Talked with partner- helpful
Asked adviser for advice - helped

Alternative strategies and why rejected:

Could have just let it ride but children's education suffering.
Could have had row with teacher but not professional.

Situation outcome:

Resolved - teacher has resigned and now school can appoint someone else.

Residual emotions or events:

Still frustrated and sad now for teacher because potential will never be developed -
but relief in another sense.

Resources required and adequacy:

Advice	6	Good advice from adviser
Emotional support	7	Support from partner excellent
Personal skills	6	Modesty apart, I handled it well
Financial	5	Finances were there to support phasing scheme but really needed practical assistance
More information	N/A	
Assistance/help	1	Help was not forthcoming
How well handled	6	Think I did everything I could given situation

SECTION B

Problem description

Child with abuse background accepted in school - school has reputation for
tolerating 'last resorters' - strategies to build confidence of boy with adults -
assaulted another child - staff fed up - behaviour scheme didn't work - boy
suspended - head devastated re. child and others comments.

232

Who else involved?

Child, staff, Social Services, police, advisers

Un/Expected	3	Somewhat expected because of boy's history
Unfamiliar	2	Very familiar because similar incidents
Un/Pleasant	6	Extremely unpleasant: upset me personally a great deal
Other Problems	5	Always many problems in school
Control	2	Very, very limited - hands tied re. decision - many agencies involved
Confidence	2	Wasn't at all confident - I was in middle passing messages - even suspension re-instated

Why problematic?

1. I am not a trained psychologist therefore difficult to understand boy or
2. Social Services' thinking.
3. Others saying school hadn't done enough - very hurtful
4. Behaviour modification scheme inappropriate - hopeless

Emotional reactions(s):

Very, very angry at way boy treated and way school being treated - hurt re. school's name and reputation undermined - and because boy 'slipping down prison slope'.
Very, very dejected - because everything worked for for 6 years being threatened.
Anxious - because boy now wandering streets and prison fodder.

Handling emotions:

Pressure dreams - wake up sweating, shaking, overeating sugary food - always been a problem re. comfort eating.

Coping responses and intentions:

Talked with staff to encourage
'Counselled' staff when plans didn't materialize
Plan to modify behaviour only worked for a week
Couldn't make plans because lacked authority
Had to accept situation at times - hated every minute of it

233

Some self criticism - are there better ways of dealing with him?
Christian faith helps

Alternative strategies and why rejected:

Could have taken boy in first place to residential home but determined to keep trying for boy's sake.

Situation outcome:

Worsened - because boy now wandering streets although staff and children happier.

Residual emotions or events:

Horribly unsatisfactory - very painful - still feel bad about things and responsible for boy - dreadful.

Resources required and adequacy:

Advice	2	Not too useful because they didn't know what to do either
Emotional support	6	Staff supported me
Personal skills	3	Skills under microscope - severely tested in this one - perhaps I lack the power to make decisions
Financial	4	Finances partially there for NTA but full-time teacher would have been better
More information	N/A	
Assistance/help	1	The practical assistance was totally inappropriate from Social Services
How well handled	3	

Coding self-serving attributional biases: training script

Attribution theory is concerned with the reasons people give for successful and unsuccessful situational outcomes. Research has indicated that success is usually considered to be due to one's own personal characteristics, whilst failure is seen as caused by situational factors. These attributions are described as internal and external attributions respectively and can be understood as attempts to explain one's own behaviour, either to others as a self-presentational tactic or to oneself if its meaning is not immediately clear.

Attribution research has indicated that individuals take credit for success, and blame external factors for failure for two reasons. On the one hand, attributions offered to oneself about behaviour can serve an egocentric function by protecting, maintaining or enhancing self-esteem. On the other hand, attributions can convey impressions to others that are as favourable as possible. But in either case, attributions can be biased by the idiosyncratic perspective of the individual offering them, resulting in self-serving explanations for behaviour. It is this self-serving attributional bias which is of particular interest in this study.

In recent years there has been increasing interest in the attributional concomitants of various individual difference variables. This work has demonstrated that certain attributional styles are related to psychological well-being. More specifically, causal attributions have been examined in relation to self-esteem, unemployment and personal problem-solving. For example, differences have been found between depressed and non-depressed subjects primarily in causal attributions for failing performances; depressed subjects viewed their failing performances as due more to their own personal responsibility than did non-depressed subjects.

Similarly, whilst self-appraised effective problem-solvers did not differ from their counterparts in their ability attributions for successful performances, they did for failing attempts. Following failure, self-appraised effective problem-solvers attributed their failing performances less to ability and more to external factors or lack of effort.

To elaborate, ability is a property of the person, and although environmental factors may augment or deplete ability, it essentially describes the person and not the environment. Thus, because ability is an internal, stable and relatively uncontrollable factor, individuals who make attributions to poor ability believe that there is little they can do to control the situation and succeed. In contrast, attributions to external factors allow the individual to disown the failure and not feel personally responsible. Effort attributions lead the individual to believe that as long as s/he tries harder, s/he will be able to exert control over the situational outcome. Effort offers a unique opportunity for self-serving attributions; as an internal, variable and potentially controllable factor, the amount of effort expended ranges from none to as much as possible and is entirely at the individual's discretion. Further it is possible to disguise the actual amount of effort given by appropriately managed impressions, e.g., making a great show of exerting effort (or not). Furthermore, it is possible to make claims about effort without much fear that they will be contradicted by other performance-relevant information since there are few independent checks on a subject's claims about effort that cannot be manipulated to his or her advantage. But whether attributions are made to external, uncontrollable or internal, controllable factors, one implication of this self-serving pattern of attribution is that it allows the individual maximum reinforcement in evaluative settings: in cases of success, confidence is bolstered; in cases of failure, confidence is protected.

Other studies have also provided evidence of a self-protective attributional bias but distinguished between two different types of self-blame:

(i) behavioural self-blame representing an adaptive, control oriented response, and

(ii) characterological self-blame, a maladaptive, self-deprecating response generally related to harsh self-criticism and low evaluation of one's worth.

In the current study the distinction between these two types of self-blame is important and warrants further discussion. The nature of the focus of the blame is the primary distinction between these two attributions. On the one hand, behavioural self-blame focuses on behaviour - an internal, variable, controllable source and is associated with a belief in future avoidability of other negative outcomes in similar situations. Characterological self-blame on the other hand is esteem-related and involves attributions to an internal, stable and non-controllable source, i.e., character or disposition, and is associated with a belief in personal deservingness for past and present negative outcomes. Utilizing this distinction, one study showed that depressed college students engaged in more characterological self-blame than non-depressed students. Using the same internal behavioural/characterological distinction, another study found that unemployed managers making characterological attributions for negative events had poor mental health and those managers making behavioural attributions had better mental health.

The causal attribution theory outlined above has been used as a framework for developing a coding scheme for respondents' attributional tendencies. The interview scripts are to be coded or assigned to one of the three categories detailed below:

Category A. When attributions are external, stable, uncontrollable and refer to situational factors, material resources, other people fate, luck, God and so on.

Category B. Scripts are assigned to this category when attributions are internal-behavioural and refer to some transient and potentially controllable action or behaviours by the subject.

Category C. When internal-characterological attributions are made referring to stable, uncontrollable factors such as personality, character, personal skills or abilities.

Scripts coded either A or B evidence presence of the self-serving attributional bias. Scripts coded C are evidence of the non-self-serving attributional bias.

'One day in the life of a headteacher'

A brief outline of 1 day in the life of a headteacher. Please note that the intention of this document is merely to give an indication of the number of 'hats' to be worn during the day, indicating the number of interruptions, and the range of minor issues constantly demanding attention.

In order to provide individual anonymity the following codes have been used to identify people and/or activity concerned:

H	=	Head
C	=	Child in school
T	=	Teacher on staff
N	=	Nursery nurse on staff
A	=	Non-teaching assistant
S	=	Secretary
L	=	Lunchtime supervisor
P	=	Parent
O	=	Officer (nominally anybody working for LEA)
I	=	Unexpected telephone interruption
X	=	Other

Time	Code	Issue
08.25	T + T	Visit to Middle School with leavers group
08.30	T + T	Discussion re Advisers impending visit
08.50	T	More Discussion re Advisers visit
08.55	H	Completed items for internal mail
09.00	S	Query re tomorrow's dinners
09.10		Whole school Assembly
09.50	A	Query re exchange of 'A's' working hours
09.55	I	Colleague head querying transfer of Nursery child
10.05	H	Finalized arrangements for staff meeting
10.15	I	Local Middle School rang about transfers
10.18	H	Tried to ring 'O' - engaged
10.20	O	'O' arrived to introduce new colleague
10.25	T	Report of damage to outdoor pipes followed by 'phone call to Buildings Section - engaged
10.25	H	Continued from 10.05
10.40	I	'L' rang to say would be arriving late
10.45	H	Rang colleague 'H' to arrange visits - engaged

Time	Code	Issue
10.50	S	Discussed implications for impending industrial action
10.54	I	'X' rang to confirm personal arrangements
10.55	H	Completed arrangements for staff meeting
11.02	T	Head from nearby Middle School came to confirm our new designation of class names
11.05	H	Began writing rough draft for this! (Impending Adviser has not arrived)
11.10	S	Presented with minutes of previous staff meeting
11.15	H	Coffee - actually managed to drink it!!
11.10	H	Rang Buildings Section re damaged pipes - engaged so rang colleague Head (re 10.48) - also engaged
11.23	H	Contacted Buildings Section at last
11.28	T + C	Recognition of good work
11.30	H	Rang Schools Psychological Service - left message
11.35	H	Began letters to invite candidates for interview for teaching posts
11.36	S	Informed of fumes problem with photocopier so rang 'O' for information - engaged
11.40	H	Continued letters (re 11.35)
11.45	H	Rang 'O' re photocopier - success!
11.50	H	Began letters asking for references (re 11.35)
12.00	H	Draft letters completed
12.02	S	Brought internal mail - queried stamps for application letters, etc.
12.04	T	Deputy came in for a quick break and we discussed how to use school camera
12.15	I	'Impending Adviser' rang to apologize for not arriving - re-arranged for 11.00 am tomorrow
12.19	H	Went for lunch
12.32	T + T	Short meeting re next Senior Management Team meeting
12.37	H	Began sorting Middle School transfers
12.50	P	Came in to ask about forthcoming Local Festival
12.53	P	Came in to query transfer of child between schools (re 09.55)
12.58	T	Deputy came to add item to agenda for staff meeting
13.00	A	Query about waste-paper collection
13.04	I	Colleague Head rang me about visits (re 10.48)
13.08	T	Liaison meeting about admission of Nursery children to Reception for September
13.12	H	Went to Hall for singing, released 4 teachers for non-contact time. I was 2 minutes late!

Time	Code	Issue	
13.52	H	Returned to office to begin sorting internal mail. Made a list of what had arrived. Key as follows:	

I = Information for me
T = To be passed on to other members of staff
A = Action required by me
B = Sorry but 'binned'

		1. Leaflets re industrial action	I + T
		2. Outline of curriculum development funding bids procedure	I + A
		3. Transfer of records for new child from other school	I + T
		4. Outline of new procedures for allocation of furniture budget	I + A
		5. Details of appointment for new temporary Support Assistant	I + A
		6. N.A.H.T. update	I
		7. 'Headfirst' newsletter	I
		8. 30 page document relating to S.E.N. provision	I
		9. Document related to Physical Education	I
		10. Document re fans	I + A
		12. Circular from Leprosy Mission	B
		13. Circular re outdoor sports	B
		14. Request from LEA for updated documents	I
14.00	S	Query about letters drafted this a.m.	
14.05	H	Finished sorting (but not acting on!) internal mail	
14.08	I	Parent rang about a place in school for her child	
14.12	H	Tried to contact 2 'O' re transfer of child from other school (re 09.55). 1st one engaged, 2nd one away ill - could it be stress?	
14.14	S	Update on school booklet Query on milk letters Further clarification re industrial action	
14.21	H	Repeated attempts to contact 'O' by 'phone (re 14.12) left message to contact me	
14.21	H	Managed a cup of coffee	
14.26	S	Brought letters in for signature	
14.28	T	Requested early release to visit another school	
14.30	H	Into staffroom to enquire about late records for a new child	
	T	Request for funding	
14.33	I	'O' phoned me back to clarify 09.55 situation	
14.36	H	Saw Secretary re requests for funding	
14.40	H	Rang 'O' re photocopier fumes and query on furniture for new classroom	

Time	Code	Issue
14.44	H	Gone singing! Into the hall with another 4 classes - more non-contact time for staff
15.16	H	Back to the office, met by 'P' requesting permission to pick child up early tomorrow for dentists appointment
15.19	I	'O' rang to query free meals list - asked her to call Secretary tomorrow
15.22	T	Final query on agenda for staff meeting
15.28	I	Colleague Head rang about Thursday's meeting
		Staff meeting began
16.50		Staff meeting ended
16.50	T	Clarification on decision made during meeting
16.56	T + T	Follow-up discussion on another item from agenda
17.05	X	Caretaker queried arrangements of chairs for meeting on Wednesday a.m.
17.11	T	Arranged lift home for 17.20
17.13	I	Personal call
17.17	T	Feed-back on this morning's visit to Middle School
17.22		Escaped home to prepare for the evening
19.30		Interviewed about 'Stress in headship'!

Bibliography

Achen, C.H. (1982), *Interpreting and Using Regression*, Sage Publications, London.

Ader, R. (1971), 'Experimentally Induced Gastric Lesions', in *Advances in Psychosomatic Medicine,* Vol. 6, Karger, Basel.

Aldwin, C.M. (1985), 'Cultural Influences on the Stress Process', paper presented at the International Symposium on the Management of Stress: Biological, Psychological and Clinical Implications, Ensenada, Mexico.

Aldwin, C.M., Folkman, S., Schaefer, C., Coyne, J.C., and Lazarus, R.S. (1980), 'Ways of Coping: A Process Measure', paper presented at the 88th Annual Meeting of the American Psychological Association, Montreal, Quebec, Canada.

Aldwin, C.M., and Revenson, T.A. (1987), 'Does coping help? A re-examination of the relation between coping and mental health', *Journal of Personality and Social Psychology*, Vol. 53, No. 2, pp. 337-48.

Allpert, R., and Haber, R.N. (1960), 'Anxiety in academic achievement situations', *Journal of Abnormal and Social Psychology*, Vol. 61, pp. 207-15.

Anderson, C.A., Horowitz, L.M., and French, R. (1993), 'Attributional style of lonely and depressed people', *Journal of Personality and Social Psychology*, Vol. 45, pp. 127-36.

Antonovsky, A. (1979), *Health, Stress and Coping*, Jossey-Bass, San Francisco.

Argyris, C., and Schon, D. (1974), *Theory in Practice*, Josey-Bass, San Francisco.

Arkin, R.M., Gleason, J.M., and Johnston, S. (1976), 'Effect of perceived choice, expected outcome and observed outcome of an action of the causal attributions of actors', *Journal of Experimental Social Psychology*, Vol. 12, pp. 151-58.

Arnold, M.B. (1960), *Emotion and Personality*, Columbia University Press, New York.

Averill, J.R. (1982), *Anger and Aggression: An essay of emotion*, Springer-Verlag, New York.

242

Bailey, J.M., and Bhagat, R.S. (1987), 'Meaning and Measurement of Stressors in the Work Environment: An Evaluation', in Kasl, S.V., and Cooper, C.L. (eds.), *Stress and Health: Issues in Research Methodology*, Wiley, Chichester.

Bakeman, R., and Gottman, J.M. (1987), 'Applying Observational Methods: A Systematic View', in Osofsky, J.D. (ed.), *Handbook of Infant Development*, (2nd ed.), John Wiley & Sons, Chichester.

Bandura, A. (1977), 'Self-efficacy: Toward a unifying theory of behavioural change', *Psychological Review*, Vol. 84, No. 2, pp. 191-215.

Banks, M.H. (1983), 'Validation of the General Health Questionnaire in a young community sample', *Psychological Medicine*, Vol. 13, pp. 349-53.

Banks, M.H., Clegg, C.W., Jackson, P.R., Kemp, N.J., Stafford, E.M., and Wall, T.D. (1980), 'The use of the GHQ as an indicator of mental health in occupational studies', *Journal of Occupational Psychology*, Vol. 53, pp.187-94.

Baumgardner, A.H., Heppner, P.P., and Arkin, R.M. (1986), 'Role of causal attribution in personal problem solving', *Journal of Personality and Social Psychology*, Vol. 50, No. 3, pp. 636-43.

Beck, A.T., Rush, A.J., Shaw, B.F., and Emery, G. (1979), *Cognitive Therapy of Depression*, Guilford, New York.

Bem, D. (1972), 'Self-perception Theory', in Berkowitz, L. (ed.), *Advances in Experimental Social Psychology*, Vol. 6, Academy Press, New York.

Billings, A.G., and Moos, R.H. (1981), 'The role of coping responses and social resources in attenuating the stress of life events', *Journal of Behavioral Medicine*, Vol. 4, No. 2, pp. 139-57.

Billings, A.G., and Moos, R.H. (1984), 'Coping, stress and social resources among adults with unipolar depression', *Journal of Personality and Social Psychology*, Vol. 46, No. 4, pp. 877-91.

Bloom, B.S., and Broder, L.J. (1950), *Problem Solving Processes of College Students*, University of Chicago Press, Chicago.

Bowlby, J. (1970), 'Attachment', *Attachment and Loss*, Vol. 1, Hogarth Press, London.

Boyle, G.J., Borg, M.G., Falzon, J.M., and Baglioni, A.J., Jr (1995), 'A structural model of the dimensions of teacher stress', *British Journal of Educational Psychology*, Vol. 65, pp. 49-67.

Bradley, G. (1978), 'Self-serving biases in the attribution process: A re-examination of the fact or fiction question', *Journal of Personality and Social Psychology*, Vol. 36, pp. 56-71.

Braham, B.J. (1994), *Managing Stress*, Irwin Professional Publishing, New York.

Brief, A.P., and Atieh, J.M. (1987), 'Studying job stress: Are we making mountains out of molehills?', *Journal of Occupational Behaviour*, Vol. 8, pp. 115-26.

Brief, A.P., Burke, M.J., George, J.M., Robinson, B.S., and Webster, J. (1988), 'Should negative affectivity remain an unmeasured variable in the study of job stress?', *Journal of Applied Psychology*, Vol. 73, No. 2, pp. 193-98.

Bunce, D., and West, M. (1994), 'Changing work environments: Innovative coping responses to occupational stress', *Work and Stress*, Vol. 8, No. 4, pp. 319-331.

Burgess, R. (1983), *Experiencing Comprehensive Education: A Study of Bishop McGregor School*, Methuen, London.

Burke, M.J., Brief, A.P., and George, J.M. (1993), 'The role of negative affectivity in understanding relations between self-reports of stressors and strains: a comment on the applied psychology literature', *Journal of Applied Psychology*, No. 78, pp. 402-412.

Burke, R.J., and Belcourt, M.L. (1974), 'Managerial role stress and coping responses', *Journal of Business Administration*, Vol. 5, No. 2, pp. 55-68.

Burke, R.J., and Greenglass, E., 'A longitudinal study of psychological burnout in teachers', *Human Relations*, Vol. 48, No. 2, Feb., 1995, pp. 187-202.

Burns, D.D. (1980), 'The perfectionists' script for self-defeat', *Psychology Today*, Nov., pp. 34-52.

Buunk, B.P., and Peeters, M.C.W. (1994), 'Stress at work, social support and companionship: Towards an event - contingent recording approach', *Work and Stress*, Vol. 8, No. 2, pp. 177-190.

Byrne, D. (1961), 'The repression-sensitization scale: Rationale, reliability and validity', *Journal of Personality*, Vol. 29, pp. 334-49.

Calden, G., Dupertuis, C.W., Hokanson, J.E., and Lewis, W.C. (1960), 'Psychosomatic factors in the rate of recovery from tuberculosis', *Psychosomatic Medicine*, Vol. 22, pp. 345-55.

Cannon, W.B. (1936), *Bodily Changes in Pain, Hunger, Fear and Rage*, (2nd ed.), Appleton-Century, New York.

Carmines, E.G., and Zeller, R.S. (1982), *Reliability and Validity Assessment*, Sage Publications, London.

Carver, C.S., Scheier, M.F., and Weintraub, J.K. (1989), 'Assessing coping strategies: A theoretically based approach', *Journal of Personality and Social Psychology*, Vol. 56, No. 2, pp. 267-83.

Cicchetti, D.V., and Sparrow, S.S. (1981), 'Developing criteria for establishing interrater reliability of specific items: Applications to assessment of adaptive behavior', *American Journal of Mental Deficiency*, Vol. 86, pp. 127-137.

Coehlo, G.V., Hamburg, D.A., and Adams, J.E. (eds.) (1974), *Coping and Adaptation*, Basic Books, New York.

Cohen, F., and Lazarus, R.S. (1973), 'Active coping processes, coping dispositions and recovery from surgery', *Psychosomatic Medicine*, Vol. 35, No. 5, pp. 375-389.

Cohen, F., and Lazarus, R.S. (1979), 'Coping with the Stresses of Illness', in Stone, G.C., Cohen, F., and Adler, N.E. (eds.), *Health Psychology*, Jossey-Bass, San Francisco.

Cohen, J. (1960), 'A coefficient of agreement for nominal scales', *Educational and Psychological Measurement*, Vol. 20, pp. 37-46.

Cohen, J. and Cohen, P. (1983), *Applied Multiple Regression/Correlation Analysis for the Behavioral Sciences*, Erlbaum, Hillsdale, New Jersey.

Cohen, L., and Holliday, M. (1982), *Statistics for Social Scientists*, Harper and Row, London.

Cohen, S., and Edwards, J.R. (1988), 'Personality Characteristics as Moderators of the Relationship between Stress and Disorder', in Neufeld, W.J. (ed.), *Advances in the Investigation of Psychological Stress*, John Wiley and Sons, New York.

Collins, D.L., Baum, A., and Singer, J.E. (1983), 'Coping with chronic stress at Three Mile Island: Psychological and biochemical evidence', *Health Psychology*, Vol. 2, pp. 149-66.

Cooper, C.L. (1986), 'Job distress: Recent research and the emerging role of the clinical occupational psychologist', *Bulletin of The British Psychological Society*, Vol. 39, pp. 325-31.

Cooper, C.L. (1988), 'Stress in the workplace: Recent research evidence', in Pettigrew, A.M. (ed.), *Competitiveness and the Management Process*, Blackwell, Oxford.

Cooper, C.L., (1995), 'Life at the chalkface - identifying and measuring teacher stress', *British Journal of Educational Psychology*, Vol. 65, No. 1, March 1995.

Cooper, C.L., Cooper, R.D., and Eaker, L.H. (1988a), *Living With Stress*, Penguin Books Ltd, Middlesex.

Cooper, C.L., Davidson, M.J., and Robinson, P. (1982), 'Stress in the police service', *Journal of Occupational Medicine*, Vol. 24, pp. 30-36.

Cooper, C.L., and Kelly, M. (1993), 'Occupational stress in headteachers: A national UK study', *British Journal of Educational Psychology*, Vol. 63, pp. 130-143.

Cooper, C.L., and Marshall, J. (1976), 'Occupational sources of stress: A review of the literature relating to coronary heart disease and mental ill-health', *Journal of Occupational Psychology*, Vol. 49, pp. 11-28.

Cooper, C.L., and Marshall, J. (1978), *Understanding Executive Stress*, Macmillan Press, London.

Cooper, C.L., Watts, J., Baglioni, A.J. (Jnr), and Kelly, M. (1988b), 'Occupational stress amongst general practice dentists', *Journal of Occupational Psychology*, Vol. 61, pp. 163-74.

Costa, P.T. (Jnr), and McCrae, R.R. (1985), 'Hypochondriasis, neuroticism and ageing: When are somatic complaints unfounded?', *American Psychologist*, Vol. 40, pp. 19-28.

Cox, T. (1977), 'The Nature and Management of Stress in Schools', Education Department, Clwyd County Council, Mold.

Cox, T. (1978), *Stress*, Macmillan, London.

Cox, T. (1987), 'Stress, coping and problem solving', *Work and Stress*, Vol. 1, No. 1, pp. 5-14.

Cox, T., Boot, N., and Cox, S. (1989), 'Stress in Schools: A Problem-solving Approach', in Cole, M., and Walker, S. (eds.), *Teaching and Stress*, Open University Press, Milton Keynes.

Cox, T., and Ferguson, E. (1994), 'Measurement of the subjective work environment', *Work and Stress*, Vol. 8, No. 2, pp. 98-109.

Cronbach, L.J. (1984), *Essentials of Psychological* Testing (4th ed.), Harper and Row, New York.

Cummings, T.G., and Cooper, C.L. (1979), 'A cybernetic framework for studying occupational stress, *Human Relations*, Vol. 32, pp. 395-418.

Cvetanovski, J., and Jex, S.M. (1994), 'Locus of control of unemployed people and its relationship to psychological and physical well-being', *Work and Stress*, Vol. 8, No. 1, pp. 60-67.

D'Zurilla, T.J., and Goldfried, M.R. (1971), 'Problem solving and behavior modification', *Journal of Abnormal Psychology*, Vol. 78, No. 1, pp. 107-26.

Depue, R.A., and Monroe, S.M. (1986), 'Conceptualization and measurement of human disorder in life stress research: The problem of chronic disturbance', *Psychological Bulletin*, Vol. 99, pp. 36-51.

Derogatis, L.R., Lipman, R.S., and Covi, L. (1973), 'SCL-90: An outpatient psychiatric rating scale', *Psychopharmacology Bulletin*, Vol. 9, pp. 13-27.

Dewe, P.J. (1985), 'Coping with work stress: An investigation of teachers' action', *Research in Education*, 33, pp. 27-40.

Dewe, P.J. (1986), 'An investigation into the causes and consequences of teacher stress', *New Zealand Journal of Educational Studies*, Vol. 21, pp. 145-157.

Dewe, P.J. (1989), 'Examining the nature of work stress: Individual evaluation of stressful experiences and coping', *Human Relations*, Vol. 42, No. 11, pp. 993-1013.

Dewe, P.J. (1991), 'Primary appraisal, secondary appraisal and coping: Their role in stressful work encounters', *Journal of Occupational Psychology*, Vol. 64, pp. 331-351.

Dewe, P.J. (1992), 'Applying the concept of appraisal to work stressors: Some exploratory analysis', *Human Relations*, Vol. 45, pp. 143-164.

Dewe, P., Cox, T., and Ferguson, E. (1993), 'Individual strategies for coping with stress at work: A review', *Work and Stress*, Vol. 7, No. 1, pp. 5-15.

Dijkstra, W., and Vander Zouwen, J. (1982), *Response behaviour in the Survey - Interview*, Academic Press, London.

Dobson, C.B. (1982), *Stress: The Hidden Adversary*, MTP Press Limited, Lancaster.

Dunham, J. (1984), *Stress in Teaching*, Croom Helm, London.

Dwyer, J.E. (1983), *Statistical Models for the Social and Behavioral Sciences*, Oxford University Press, New York.

Earley, P., and Baker, L. (1989), 'The recruitment and retention of headteachers: The LEA survey', National Foundation for Educational Research in England and Wales.

Easterbrook, J.A. (1959), 'The effect of emotion on cue utilization and the organization of behavior', *Psychological Review*, Vol. 66, pp. 183-201.

Edwards, J.R. (1988), 'The Determinants and Consequences of Coping with Stress', in Cooper, C.L., and Payne, R. (eds.), *Causes, Coping and Consequences of Stress at Work*, John Wiley and Sons, Chichester.

Edwards, J.R., Baglioni, A.J., and Cooper, C.L. (1990), 'Stress, Type-A, coping and psychological and physical symptoms: A multi-sample test of alternative models', *Human Relations*, Vol. 43, No. 10, pp. 919-56.

Edwards, T., Fitz, J., and Whitty, G. (1989), *The State and Private Education: An Evaluation of the Assisted Places Scheme,* Falmer Press, London.

Elliott, G.C. (1989), 'Self-serving attributions in the face of reality: The effect of task outcome and potential causes on self-other attributions', *Human Relations*, Vol. 42, No. 11, pp. 1015-32.

Ellis, A. (1962), *Reason and Emotion in Psychotherapy*, Lyle Stuart and Citadel Press, New York.

Ellis, A., and Harper, R.A. (1975), *A New Guide to Rational Living*, Prentice-Hall, Englewood Cliffs, New Jersey.

Endler, N.S., and Parker, J.D.A. (1990), 'Multidimensional assessment of coping: A critical evaluation', *Journal of Personality and Social Psychology*, Vol. 58, pp. 844-854.

Eysenck, H.J., and Eysenck, S.B.G. (1964), *Manual of the Eysenck Personality Inventory*, University of London Press, London.

Eysenck, H.J., and Eysenck, S.B.G. (1975), *Manual of the Eysenck Personality Questionnaire*, Hodder and Stoughton, London.

Felton, B.J., and Revenson, T.A. (1984), 'Coping with chronic illness: A study of illness controllability and the influence of coping strategies on psychological adjustment', *Journal of Consulting and Clinical Psychology*, Vol. 53, pp. 343-53.

Firth, J. (1985), 'Personal meanings of occupational stress: Cases from the clinic', *Journal of Occupational Psychology*, Vol. 58, pp. 139-48.

Firth-Cozens, J. (1992), 'Why me?: A case study of the process of perceived occupational stress', *Human Relations*, Vol. 45, No. 2, pp. 131-141.

Fleiss, J.L. (1981), *Statistical Methods for Rates and Proportions*, Wiley, New York.

Fleming, R., Baum, A., and Singer, J.E. (1984), 'Toward an integrative approach to the study of stress', *Journal of Personality and Social Psychology*, Vol. 46, No. 4, pp. 939-49.

Fletcher, B.C. (1989), 'The Epidemiology of Occupational Stress', in Cooper, C.L., and Payne, R. (eds.), *Causes, Coping and Consequences of Stress at Work*, John Wiley and Sons, Chichester.

Folkman, S. (1984), 'Personal control and stress and coping processes: A theoretical analysis', *Journal of Personality and Social Psychology*, Vol. 46, pp. 839-52.

Folkman, S., and Lazarus, R.S. (1980), 'An analysis of coping in a middle-aged community sample', *Journal of Health and Social Behaviour*, Vol. 21 (Sept), pp. 219-39.

Folkman, S., and Lazarus, R.S. (1985), 'If it changes it must be a process: A study of emotion and coping during three stages of a college examination', *Journal of Personality and Social Psychology*, Vol. 48, No. 1, pp. 150-70.

Folkman, S., and Lazarus, R.S. (1986), 'Stress processes and depressive symptomology', *Journal of Abnormal Psychology*, Vol. 95, pp. 107-13.

Folkman, S., and Lazarus, R.S. (1988), 'Coping as a mediator of emotion', *Journal of Personality and Social Psychology*, Vol. 54, No. 3, pp. 466-75.

Folkman, S., Lazarus, R.S., Dunkel-Schetter, C., Delongis, A., and Gruen, R.J. (1986b), 'Dynamics of a stressful encounter: Cognitive appraisal, coping and encounter outcomes', *Journal of Personality and Social Psychology*, Vol. 50, No. 5, pp. 992-1003.

Folkman, S., Lazarus, R.S., Gruen, R.J., and DeLongis, A. (1986a), 'Appraisal, coping, health status and psychological symptoms', *Journal of Personality and Social Psychology*, Vol. 50, No. 3, pp. 571-79.

Folkman, S., Schaefer, C., and Lazarus, R.S. (1979), 'Cognitive Processes as Mediators of Stress and Coping', in Hamilton, V. and Warburton, D.M. (eds.), *Human Stress and Cognition: An Information Processing Approach*, John Wiley and Sons, Chichester.

Fontana, D., and Abouserie, R. (1993), 'Stress levels, gender and personality factors in teachers', *British Journal of Educational Psychology*, Vol. 63, pp. 261-270.

Frank, R.G., Umlauf, R.L., Wonderlich, S.A., Askanazi, G.S., Buckelew, S.P., and Elliott, T.R. (1987), 'Differences in coping styles among persons with spinal cord injury: A cluster-analytic approach', *Journal of Consulting and Clinical Psychology*, Vol. 55, No. 5, pp. 727-31.

French, J.R.P., and Caplan, R.D. (1970), 'Psychosocial factors in coronary heart disease', *Industrial Medicine*, 39 (9), pp. 383-97.

French, J.R.P., and Caplan, R.D. (1972), 'Organizational Stress and Individual Strain', in Marrow, A.J. (ed.), *The Failure of Success*, Amacon, New York.

Frese, M. (1984), 'Job Transitions, Occupational Socialization and Strain', in Allen, V. and Vliert, E.V.D. (eds.), *Role Transitions*, Plenum Press, New York.

Frey, J.H. (1983), *Survey Research by Telephone*, Sage Publications, London.

Fried, Y. (1988), 'The Future of Physiological Assessments in Work Situations', in Cooper, C.L., and Payne, R. (eds.), *Causes, Coping and Consequences of Stress at Work*, John Wiley and Sons, Chichester.

Friedman, M., and Rosenman, R.H. (1959), 'Association of specific overt behavior pattern with blood cardiovascular findings', *Journal of the American Medical Association*, Vol. 169, pp. 1286-96.

Glass, D.C., Reim, B., and Singer, J.E. (1971), 'Behavioral sequences of adaptation to controllable and uncontrollable noise', *Journal of Experimental Social Psychology*, Vol. 7, pp. 244-57.

Glowinkowski, S.P., and Cooper, C.L. (1987), 'Managers and Professionals in Business/industrial settings: The Research Evidence', in Ivancevich, J.M. and Ganster, D.C. (eds.), *Job Stress: From Theory to Suggestion*, Haworth Press, London.

Goffman, E. (1959), *The Presentation of Self in Everyday Life*, Anchor, New York.

Goldberg, D. (1978), *Manual of the General Health Questionnaire*, National Foundation for Educational Research, Windsor, England.

Goldberg, D., and Williams, P. (1988), *A User's Guide to the General Health Questionnaire*, NFER-Nelson, Windsor, England.

Goldstein, D.S. (1979), 'Instrumental cardiovascular conditioning: A review', *Pavlovian Journal of Biological Science*, Vol. 14, pp. 108-27

Gooding, R.Z., and Kinicki A.J. (1995), 'Interpreting event causes: The complementary role of categorization and attribution processes', *Journal of Management Studies*, Vol. 32, No. 1, January 1995, pp. 1-22,

Green, A. (1995), 'Verbal protocol analysis', *The Psychologist*, Vol. 8, No. 3, pp. 126-129.

Greenberg, J., Pyszczynski, T., and Solomon, S. (1982), 'The self-serving attributional bias: Beyond self-presentation', *Journal of Experimental Social Psychology*, Vol. 18, pp. 56-67.

Guilford, J.P., and Fruchter, B. (1978), *Fundamental Statistics in Psychology and Education* (6th ed.), McGraw-Hill, Singapore.

Gummesson, E. (1991), *Qualitative Methods in Management Research*, Sage Publications, London.

Haan, N. (1977), *Coping and Defending*, Academic Press, New York.

Hall, V., Mackay, H., and Morgan, C. (1988), 'Headteachers at Work: Practice and Policy', in Glatter, R., Preedy, M., Riches, C. and Masterton, M. (eds.), *Understanding School Management*, Open University Press, Milton Keynes.

Halstead, M. (1994), 'Accountability and Values', in Scott, D. (Ed.), *Accountability and Control in Educational Settings*, Cassell, London.

Hamburg, D.A., and Adams, J.E. (1967), 'A perspective on coping: Seeking and utilizing information in major transitions', *Archives of General Psychiatry*, Vol. 17, pp. 277-284.

Hamilton, E., and Cairns, H. (eds.) (1961), *The Collected Dialogues of Plato*, Princeton University Press, Princeton, New Jersey.

Hamilton, V. (1975), 'Socialization, Anxiety and Information Processing: A Capacity Model of Anxiety-induced Performance Deficits', in Sarason, I.G. and Spielberger, C.D. (eds.), *Stress and Anxiety*, Vol. 2, Wiley, Washington D.C.

Hanke, J.E. and Reitsch, A.G. (1940), *Business Forecasting*, Allyn and Bacon, London.

Hawkins, L., White, M., and Morris, L. (1983), 'Smoking, stress and nurses', *Nursing Mirror*, 13 October 1983.

Heider, F. (1958), *The Psychology of Interpersonal Relations*, Wiley, New York.

Henwood, K., and Nicolson, P. (1995), 'Qualitative research', *The Psychologist*, Vol. 8, No. 3, March 1995.

Henwood, K., and Pidgeon, N. (1995), 'Grounded theory and psychological research', *The Psychologist*, Vol. 8, No. 3, March 1995.

Hepworth, S.J. (1980), 'Moderating factors of the psychological impact of unemployment', *Journal of Occupational Psychology*, Vol. 53, pp. 139-45.

Hollon, S.D., Kendall, P.C., and Lumry, A. (1986), 'Specificity of depressotypic cognitions in clinical depression', *Journal of Abnormal Psychology*, Vol. 95, pp. 52-59.

Holroyd, K.A., and Lazarus, R.S. (1982), 'Stress, Coping and Somatic Adaptation', in Goldberger, L. and Breznitz, S. (eds.), *Handbook of Stress*, Free Press, New York.

Holsti, O.R. (1969), *Content Analysis for the Social Sciences and Humanities*, Addison-Wesley Publishing Company Inc, California.

Horney, K. (1950), *Neurosis and Human Growth*, Norton, New York.

Horowitz, M. (1976), *Stress Response Syndromes,* Aronson, New York.

Horowitz, M. (1979), 'Psychological response to serious life events', in Hamilton, V. and Warburton, D.M. (eds.), *Human Stress and Cognition: An Information Processing Approach*, Wiley, Chichester.

Houston, B.K. (1977), 'Dispositional Anxiety and the Effectiveness of Cognitive Strategies in Stressful Laboratory and Classroom Situations', in Spielberger, C.D. and Sarason, I.G. (eds.), *Stress and Anxiety* (Vol. 4), Wiley, New York.

Huberman, A.M., and Miles, M.B. (1983), 'Drawing valid meaning from qualitative data: Some techniques of data reduction and display', *Quality and Quantity*, Vol. 17, pp. 281-339.

Hughes, M. (1975), 'The innovating school head: Autocratic initiator or catalyst of cooperation', *Educational Administration*, Vol. 4, No. 1, pp. 43-54.

Ickes, W., and Layden, M.A. (1978), 'Attributional Styles', in Harvey, J., Ickes, W., and Kidd, R. (eds.), *New Directions in Attribution Research*, (Vol. 2), Erlbaum, Hillsdale, New Jersey.

Jackson, S.E., and Schuler, R.S. (1985), 'A meta-analysis and conceptual critique of research on role ambiguity and role conflict in work settings', *Organizational Behaviour and Human Decision Processes*, Vol. 36, pp. 16-78.

Janis, I.L. (1959), 'Decisional conflicts: A theoretical analysis', *Journal of Conflict Resolution*, Vol. 3, pp. 6-27.

Janis, I.L., and Mann, L. (1977), *Decision Making*, Free Press, New York.

Janman, K., Jones, J.C., Payne, R.L., and Rick, J.T. (1988), 'Clustering individuals as a way of dealing with multiple predictors in occupational stress research', *Behavioural Medicine*, Vol. 14, pp. 17-79.

Janoff-Bulman, R. (1979), 'Characterological versus behavioural self-blame: Inquiries into depression and rape', *Journal of Personality and Social Psychology*, Vol. 37, No. 10, pp. 1798-809.

Kahn, R.L. (1957), *The Dynamics of Interviewing*, Wiley, Chapman and Hall.

Kahn, R.L., Wolfe, R.P., Quinn, R.P., Snoeck, J.D., and Rosenthal, R.A. (1964), *Organizational Stress: Studies in Role Conflict and Ambiguity*, Wiley, New York.

Karasek, R.A. (1979), 'Job demands, job decision latitude and mental strain: Implications for job redesign', *Administrative Science Quarterly*, Vol. 24, pp. 285-308.

Kasl, S. (1983), 'Pursuing the Link between Stressful Life Experiences and Disease: A Time for Reappraisal', in Cooper, C.L. (ed.), *Stress Research: Issues for the Eighties*, Wiley, New York.

Keenan, A., and Newton, T.J. (1984), 'Frustration in organizations: Relationships to role stress, climate and psychological strain', *Journal of Occupational Psychology*, Vol. 57, pp. 57-65.

Keenan, A., and Newton, T.J. (1985), 'Stressful events, stressors and psychological strains in young professional engineers', *Journal of Occupational Behaviour*, Vol. 6, pp. 151-56.

Kelly, M.J. (1988), 'The Manchester survey of occupational stress among headteachers and principals in the United Kingdom', Manchester Polytechnic.

Kendall, P.C., Williams, L., Pechacek, T.F., Graham, L.E., Shesslak, C., and Herzoff, N. (1979), 'Cognitive-behavioral and patient education interventions in cardiac catheterization procedures: The Palo Alto medical psychology project', *Journal of Consulting and Clinical Psychology*, Vol. 47, pp. 49-58.

Kepner, C.H., and Tregoe, B.B. (1965), *The Rational Manager*, McGraw-Hill, New York.

Kim, J., and Mueller, C.W. (1982), *Factor Analysis*, Sage Publications, England.

Kinnunen, E., and Leskinen, E. (1989), 'Teacher stress during a school year: Covariance and mean structure analyses', *Journal of Occupational Psychology*, Vol. 62, pp. 111-22.

Kobasa, S.C. (1979), 'Stressful life events, personality and health: An inquiry into hardiness', *Journal of Personality and Social Psychology*, Vol. 37, No. 1, 1-11.

Kobasa, S.C., Maddi, S.R., and Courington, S. (1981), 'Personality and constitution as mediators in the stress-illness relationship', *Journal of Health and Social Behaviour*, Vol. 22 (Dec), pp. 368-78.

Krause, N., and Stryker, S. (1984), 'Stress and well-being: The buffering role of locus of control beliefs', *Social Science and Medicine*, Vol. 18, No. 9, pp. 783-90.

Kubler-Ross, E. (1969), *On Death and Dying*, Macmillan, New York.

Kuiper, N.A. (1979), 'Depression and causal attributions for success and failure', *Journal of Personality and Social Psychology*, Vol. 36, pp. 236-46.

Kyriacou, C. (1987), 'Teacher stress and burnout: An international review', *Educational Research*, Vol. 29, No. 2, pp. 146-52.

Kyriacou, C., and Pratt, J. (1985), 'Teacher stress and psychoneurotic symptoms', *British Journal of Educational Psychology*, Vol. 55, pp. 61-4.

Ladouceur, R., and Mercier, P. (1984), 'Awareness: An understudied cognitive factor in behavior therapy', *Psychological Reports*, Vol. 54, pp. 159-78.

Langner, T.S. (1962), 'A twenty-two item screening score of psychiatric symptoms indicating impairment', *Journal of Health and Human Behaviour*, Vol. 3, pp. 269-76.

Latack, J.C., and Havlovic, S.J. (1992), 'Coping with job stress: A conceptual evaluation framework for coping measures', *Journal of Occupational Behavior*, Vol. 13, pp. 479-508.

Lazarus, R.S. (1966), *Psychological Stress and the Coping Process*, McGraw-Hill, New York.

Lazarus, R.S., Cohen, J.B., Folkman, S., Kanner, A., and Schaeffer, C. (1980), 'Psychological Stress and Adaptation: Some Unresolved Issues', in Selye, H. (ed.), *Selye's Guide to Stress Research*, Van Nostrand Reinhold, New York.

Lazarus, R.S., and Folkman, S. (1984), *Stress, Appraisal and Coping*, Springer, New York.

Lazarus, R.S., and Launier, R. (1978), 'Stress-related Transactions between Person and Environment', in Pervin, L.A. and Lewis, M. (eds.), *Perspectives in Interactional Psychology*, Plenum, New York.

Leach, C. (1979), *Introduction to Statistics*, John Wiley & Sons, Chichester.

Lefcourt, H.M. (1976), *Locus of Control: Current Trends in Theory and Research*, Halstead, New York.

Lefcourt, H.M. (1985), 'Intimacy, Social Support and Locus of Control as Moderators of Stress', in Sarason, I.G., and Sarason, B.R. (eds.), *Social Support: Theory, Research and Applications*, Martinus Nijhoff, Dordrecht.

Levi, L. (1994), 'Work, worker and wellbeing: An overview', *Work and Stress*, Vol. 8, No. 2, pp.79-83.

Lewis, A. (1970), 'The ambiguous word 'anxiety'', *International Journal of Psychiatry*, Vol. 9, pp. 62-79.

Lewis-Beck, M.S. (1980), *Applied Regression*, Sage Publications, London.

Litt, M.D. (1988), 'Self-efficacy and perceived control: Cognitive mediators of pain tolerance', *Journal of Personality and Social Psychology*, Vol. 54, No. 1, pp. 149-60.

Loftus, E.F., and Loftus, G.R. (1980), 'On the permanence of stored information in the human brain', *American Psychologist*, Vol. 35, pp. 409-20.

Lyons, G. (1974), 'The administrative tasks of head and senior teachers in large secondary schools', working paper, University of Bristol.

McCracken, G. (1988), *The Long Interview*, Sage Publications, London.

McCrae, R.R. (1984), 'Situational determinants of coping responses: Loss, threat and challenge', *Journal of Personality and Social Psychology*, Vol. 46, No. 4, pp. 919-28.

McKenna, R.J. (1972), 'Some effects of anxiety level and food cues on the eating behaviour of obese and normal subjects', *Journal of Personality and Social Psychology*, Vol. 22, pp. 311-19.

Maclure, S. (1988), *Education Reformed*, Hodder and Stoughton, Kent.

Marascuilo, L.A., and Sweeney, M. (1977), *Non-parametric and Distribution-free Methods for the Social Sciences*, Brookes/Cole, Monterey, California.

Margolis, B.L., Kroes, W.H., and Quinn, R.P. (1974), 'Job stress: An unlisted occupational hazard', *Journal of Occupational Medicine*, Vol. 16, pp. 654-61.

Markus, H. (1977), 'Self-schemata and processing information about the self', *Journal of Personality and Social Psychology*, Vol. 42, pp. 38-50.

Mason, J. (1974), 'Specificity in the Organization of Neuroendocrine Response Profiles', in Seeman, P. and Brown, G. (eds.), *Frontiers in Neurology and Neuroscience Research: First International Symposium of the Neuroscience Institute*, University of Toronto Press, Toronto.

Mason, J., Maher, J., Hartley, L., Mougey, E., Perlow, M., and Jones, L. (1976), 'Selectivity in Corticosteroid and Catecholamine Responses to Various Natural Stimuli', in Serban, G. (ed.), *Psychopathology of Human Adaptation*, Plenum, New York.

Mechanic, D. (1962), *Students Under Stress*, Free Press of Glencoe, New York.

Meichenbaum, D. (1977), *Cognitive-Behavior Modification: An Integrative Approach*, Plenum Press, New York.

Meichenbaum, D. (1985), *Stress Inoculation Training*, Pergamon, Oxford.

Melhuish, A. (1978), *Executive Health*, Business Books, London.

Menninger, K., Mayman, M., and Pruyser, P. (1963), *The Vital Balance*, Viking Press, New York.

Miles, M.B. (1979), 'Qualitative data as an attractive nuisance: The problem of analysis', *Administrative Science Quarterly*, Vol. 24, pp. 590-601.

Miles, M.B., and Huberman, A.M. (1994), *Qualitative Data Analysis: An expanded sourcebook* (2nd ed.), Sage Publications, London.

Millar, R., Crute, V., and Hargie, O. (1992), *Professional Interviewing*, Routledge, London.

Miller, S.M., and Grant, R. (1979), 'The Blunting Hypothesis: A View of Predictability and Human Stress', in Sjoden, P.O., Bates, S., and Dockens, W.S. (eds.), *Trends in Behavior Therapy*, Academic Press, New York.

Mills, R.T., and Krantz, D.S. (1979), 'Information, choice and reactions to stress: A field experiment in a blood bank with laboratory analogue', *Journal of Personality and Social Psychology*, Vol. 37, pp. 608-20.

Moos, R.H. (1974), 'Psychological Techniques in the Assessment of Adaptive Behavior', in Coelho, G.V., Hamburg, D.A. and Adams, J.E. (eds), *Coping and Adaptation*, Basic Books, New York.

Moos, R.H., and Billings, A.G. (1982), 'Conceptualizing and Measuring Coping Resources and Processes', in *Handbook of Stress: Theoretical and Clinical Aspects*, Free Press, New York.

Moriarty, B., Douglas, G., Punch, K., and Hattie, J. (1995), 'The importance of self-efficacy as a mediating variable between learning environments and achievement', *British Journal of Educational Psychology*, Vol. 65, No. 1, March 1995, pp. 73-84.

Morris, V.C. (1981), *The Urban Principal*, NIE Report, University of Illinois, Chicago.

Morrissey, E., Becker, J., and Rubert, M.P. (1990), 'Coping resources and depression in the caregiving spouses of Alzheimer patients', *British Journal of Medical Psychology*, Vol. 63, pp. 161-71.

Nelson, D.W., and Cohen, L.H. (1983), 'Locus of control and control perceptions and the relationship between life stress and psychological disorder', *American Journal of Community Psychology*, Vol. 11, pp. 705-22.

Newton, T.J. (1989), 'Occupational stress and coping with stress: A critique', *Human Relations,* Vol. 42, pp. 441-461.

Nisbett, R.E., and Wilson, T.D. (1977), 'Telling more than we can know: Verbal reports on mental processes', *Psychological Review*, Vol. 84, pp. 231-59.

Norusis, M.J. (1983), *SPSS Introductory Statistics Guide,* SPSS Inc. Chicago, Illinois.

Novaco, R.W. (1976), 'The function and regulation of the arousal of anger', *American Journal of Psychiatry*, Vol. 133, pp. 1124-28.

Novaco, R.W. (1979), The Cognitive Regulation of Anger and Stress, in Kendall, P.C. and Hollon, S.D. (eds.), *Cognitive-Behavioral Interventions: Theory, Research and Procedures*, Academic Press, New York.

O'Driscoll, M.P., and Cooper, C.L. (1994), 'Coping with work-related stress: A critique of existing measures and proposal for an alternative methodology', *Journal of Occupational and Organizational Psychology*, Vol. 67, pp. 343-354..

Oakland, S. (1991), *Headteacher Stress, Coping and Health: A Study of Headteachers*, unpublished doctoral thesis, University of Bradford.

Oakland, S., and Ostell, A. (1995), 'Measuring coping: A review and critique', *Human Relations*, Vol. 48 (in press).

Osberg, T.M. (1989), 'Self-respect reconsidered: A further look at its advantages as an assessment technique', *Journal of Counselling and Development*, 68, Sept/Oct.

Ostell, A. (1974), *The Role of Belief Systems and Negative Information in the Resolution of Conflicting Information*, unpublished doctoral dissertation, University of Sussex.

Ostell, A., (1986), 'Where stress screening falls short', *Personnel Management*, September, pp. 34-37.

Ostell, A. (1988), 'The development of a diagnostic framework of problem solving and stress', *Counselling Psychology Quarterly*, Vol. 1, Nos. 2 and 3, pp. 189-209.

Ostell, A. (1991), 'Coping, problem solving and stress: A framework for intervention strategies', *British Journal of Medical Psychology*, Vol. 64, pp. 11-24.

Ostell, A. (1992), 'Absolutist thinking and emotional problems', *Counselling Psychology Quarterly*, No. 5, pp. 161-176.

Ostell, A. (1995a), 'Managing dysfunctional emotions in organizations', (in press).

Ostell, A. (1995b), 'Managing Stress at Work', in Molander. C. (ed.), *Human Resources at Work,* Chartwell-Bratt, Sweden.

Ostell, A., and Divers, P. (1987), 'Attribution style, unemployment and mental health', *Journal of Occupational Psychology*, 60, pp. 333-37.

Parkes, K.R. (1990), 'Coping, negative affectivity and the work environment: Additive and interactive predictors of mental health', *Journal of Applied Psychology*, Vol. 75, No. 4, pp. 399-409.

Parkes, K.R. (1994), 'Personality and coping as moderators of work stress processes: Models, methods and measures', *Work and Stress*, Vol. 8, No. 2, pp. 110-129.

Patterson, T.L., Smith, L.W., Grant, I., Clopton, P., Josepho, S., and Yager, J. (1990), 'Internal vs external determinants of coping responses to stressful life-events in the elderly', *British Journal of Medical Psychology*, Vol. 63, pp. 149-60.

Patton, M.Q. (1987), *How to Use Qualitative Methods in Evaluation*, Sage Publications, London.

Payne, R. (1988), 'A longitudinal study of the psychological well-being of unemployed men and the mediating effect of neuroticism', *Human Relations*, 41 (2), pp. 119-38.

Payne, R.A., Jick, T.D. and Burke, R.J. (1982), 'Whither stress research?: An agenda for the 1980s', *Journal of Occupational Behaviour*, Vol. 3, pp. 131-45.

Payne, R.L,. and Fletcher, B.C. (1983), 'Job demands, supports and constraints as predictors of psychological strain among school teachers', *Journal of Vocational Behaviour*, Vol. 22, pp. 136-147.

Payne, R.L. and Hartley, J. (1987), 'A test of a model for explaining the affective experience of unemployed men', *Journal of Occupational Psychology*, Vol. 60, pp. 31-47.

Payne, R.L., Jabri, M.M., and Pearson, A.W. (1988), 'On the importance of knowing the affective meaning of job demands', *Journal of Organizational Behaviour*, Vol. 9, pp. 149-158.

Pearlin, L.I., and Schooler, C. (1978), 'The structure of coping', *Journal of Health and Social Behaviour*, Vol. 19 (Mar), pp. 2-21.

Peterson, C., Schwartz, S.M., and Seligman, M.E.P. (1981), 'Self-blame and depressive symptoms', *Journal of Personality and Social Psychology*, Vol.41 No. 2, pp. 253-259.

Piaget, J. (1952), *The Origins of Intelligence in Children*, International Universities Press, New York.

Pithers, R.T., and Fogarty, G.J. (1995), 'Occupational stress among vocational teachers', *British Journal of Educational Psychology*, Vol. 65, No. 1, March 1995.

Proctor, J.L., and Alexander, D.A. (1992), 'Stress among primary teachers: Individuals in organisations', *Stress Medicine*, Vol. 8, pp. 233-236.

Pullis, M. (1992), 'An analysis of the occupational stress of teachers of the behaviourally disordered: Sources, effects and strategies for coping', *Behavioral Disorders*, Vol. 17, pp. 191-201

Quick, J.C., and Quick, J.D. (1984), *Organizational Stress and Preventive Management*, McGraw-Hill, New York.

Randell, G.A. (1979), 'Interviewing in research', unpublished paper, Human Resources Research Group, University of Bradford.

Regan, D.T., and Fazio, R.H. (1977), 'On the consistency between attitudes and behavior: A look at the method of attitude formation', *Journal of Experimental Social Psychology*, Vol. 13, pp. 28-45.

Richardson, S.A., Dohrenwend, B.S., and Klein, D. (1965), *Interviewing*, Basic Books Inc, New York.

Rizzo, J.R., House, R.J., and Lirtzman, S.I. (1970), 'Role conflict and ambiguity in complex organizations', *Administrative Science Quarterly*, Vol. 15, pp. 150-163.

Rogenstine, C.N., van-Kemmen, D.P., Fox, B.H., Docherty, J., Rosenblatt, J.E., Boyd, S.C., and Bunney, W.E. (1979), 'Psychological factors in the prognosis of malignant melanoma: A prospective study', *Psychosomatic Medicine*, Vol. 41, pp. 147-64.

Rosenberg, M. (1979), *Conceiving the Self*, Basic Books, New York.

Rosenman, R.H. (1978), 'The Interview Method of Assessment of the Coronary-prone Behavior Pattern', in Dembroski, T.M., Weiss, S.M., Shields, J.L., Haynes, S.G. and Feinleib (eds.), *Coronary-prone Behavior*, Springer-Verlag, New York.

Rotter, J.B. (1966), 'Generalized expectancies for internal versus external control of reinforcement', *Psychological Monographs: General and Applied*, Vol. 80, No. 1, (Whole no. 609).

Roy, M.P., and Steptoe, A. (1994), 'Daily stressors and social support availability as predictors of depressed mood in male firefighters', *Work and Stress*, Vol. 8, No. 3, pp. 210-219.

Ryle, G. (1949), *The Concept of Mind*, Harper and Row, New York.

Sarason, I.G. (1972), 'Experimental approaches to test anxiety: Attention and the use of information', in Spielberger, C.D. (ed.), *Anxiety - Current Trends in Theory and Research*, Vol. 2, Academic Press, New York.

Sarason, I.G., Johnson, J.H., and Siegel, J.M. (1978) *Journal of Consulting and Clinical Psychology*, Vol. 46, No. 5, pp. 932-946.

Sarason, I.G., Levine, H.M., Basham, R.B., and Sarason, B.R. (1983), 'Assessing social support: The Social Support Questionnaire', *Journal of Personality and Social Psychology*, Vol. 44, No. 1, pp. 127-39.

Schank, R.C., and Abelson, R.P.. (1977), *Scripts, Plans, Goals and Understanding*, Erlbaum, Hillsdale, New Jersey.

Schmied, L.A., and Lawler, K.A. (1986), 'Hardiness, Type A behavior and the stress-illness relation in working women', *Journal of Personality and Social Psychology*, Vol. 51, pp. 1218-1223.

Schuler, R.S. (1982), 'An integrative transactional process model of stress in organizations', *Journal of Occupational Behaviour*, Vol. 3, pp. 5-19.

Schutz, W.C. (1958), 'On categorizing qualitative data in content analysis', *Public Opinion Quarterly*, Vol. 22, pp. 503-15.

Schwartz, R.M. (1986), 'On the asymmetry between positive and negative coping thoughts', *Cognitive Therapy and Research*, Vol. 10, No. 6, pp. 591-605.

Schwartz, R.M., and Gottman, J.M. (1976), 'Towards a risk analysis of assertive behaviour', *Journal of Consulting and Clinical Psychology*, Vol. 44, No. 6, pp. 910-20.

Schwartz, J.E., and Stone, A.A. (1994), 'Coping with daily work problems: Contributions of problem content, appraisals and person factors', *Work and Stress*, Vol. 7, No. 1, pp. 47-62.

Scott, D. (1994), 'Introduction' in Scott, D. (ed.), *Accountability and Control in Educational Settings*, Cassell, London.

Seligman, M.E.P. (1975), *Helplessness*, Freeman, San Francisco.

Seligman, M.E.P., Abramson, L.Y., Semmel, A., and von Baeyer, C. (1979), 'Depressive attributional style', *Journal of Abnormal Psychology*, Vol. 38, pp. 242-47.

Selye, H. (1936), 'A syndrome produced by diverse nocuous agents', *Nature,* Vol. 138, p. 32.

Selye, H. (1956), *The Stress of Life*, McGraw-Hill, New York.

Selye, H. (1976), *The Stress of Life* (2nd ed.), McGraw-Hill, New York.

Sheffield, D., Dobbie, D., and Carroll, D. (1994), 'Stress, social support, and psychological and physical wellbeing in secondary school teachers', *Work and Stress*, Vol. 8, No. 3, pp. 235-243.

Shontz, F.C. (1975), *The Psychological Aspects of Physical Illness and Disability*, Macmillan, New York.

Sihera, E. (1989), *Heads Under Pressure*, Impact Connections, Berkshire.

Silver, R.L., and Wortman, C.B. (1980), 'Coping with Undesirable Life Events', in Garber, J., and Seligman, M.E.P. (eds.), *Human Helplessness: Theory and Applications*, Academic Press, New York.

Sloan, S., and Cooper, C.L. (1986), *Pilots Under Stress*, Routledge and Kegan Paul, London.

Solomon, G.E., and Amkraut, A.A. (1981), 'Psychoneuroendocrinological effects of the immune response', *Annual Review Microbiology*, 35, pp. 155-84.

Solomon, Z., Mikulincer, M., and Habershaim, N. (1990), 'Life-events, coping strategies, social resources and somatic complaints among combat stress reaction casualties', *British Journal of Medical Psychology*, Vol. 63, pp. 137-48.

Spector, P.E. (1975), 'Relationship of organizational frustration with behavioural reactions of employees', *Journal of Applied Psychology*, Vol. 60, pp. 635-37.

Speisman, J., Lazarus, R.S., Mordkoff, A. and Davison, L. (1964), 'Experimental reduction of stress based on ego defense theory', *Journal of Abnormal and Social Psychology*, Vol. 68, pp. 367-380.

Spielberger, C.D., Gorsuch, R.L. and Lushene, R.E. (1970), *Manual for the State - Trait Anxiety Inventory*, Consulting Psychologists Press, Palo Alto, California.

Stein, M., Keller, S. and Schleifer, S. (1976), 'The hypothalamus and the immune response', in Weiner, H., Hofer, M. and Stunkard, A. (eds.), *Brain, Behavior and Bodily Disease*, Raven. New York.

Stensrud, R., and Stensrud, K. (1983), 'Coping skills training: A systematic approach to stress management counselling', *The Personnel and Guidance Journal*, Vol. 62, No. 4, pp. 214-18.

Steptoe, A. (1991), 'Psychological Coping, Individual Differences and Physiological Stress Responses', in Cooper, C.L., and Payne, R. (Eds.), *Personality and Stress: Individual Differences in the Stress Process*, Wiley, Chichester.

Stone, A.A., and Neale, J.M. (1984), 'New measure of daily coping: Development and preliminary results', *Journal of Personality and Social Psychology*, Vol. 46 No. 4, pp. 892-906.

Stone, A.A., Reed, B.R., and Neale, J.M. (1987), 'Changes in daily event frequency precede episodes of physical symptoms', *Journal of Human Stress*, Vol. 13, pp. 70-74.

Storms, P.L., and Spector, P.E. (1987), 'Relationships of organizational frustration with reported behavioural reactions: The moderating effect of locus of control', *Journal of Occupational Psychology*, Vol. 60, No. 3, pp. 227-35.

Stratton, P., Heard, D., Hanks, H.G.I., Munton, A.G., Nrewin, C.R., and Davidson, C. (1986),, 'Coding causal beliefs in natural discourse', *British Journal of Social Psychology*, Vol. 25, pp. 299-313.

Sudman, S., and Bradburn, N.H. (1982), *Asking Questions*, Jossey-Bass, London.

Suls, J. and Fletcher, B. (1985), 'The relative efficacy of avoidant and non-avoidant coping strategies: A meta-analysis', *Health Psychology*, Vol. 4, No. 3, pp. 249-288.

Suls, J., and Sanders, G.S. (1988), 'Type A behavior as a general risk factor for physical disorder', *Journal of Behavioral Medicine*, Vol. 11, pp. 201-226.

Szpiler, F.A., and Epstein, S. (1976), 'Availability of an avoidance response as related to autonomic arousal', *Journal of Abnormal Psychology*, Vol. 85, pp. 73-82.

Taylor, D.S., and Wright, P.L. (1988), *Developing Interpersonal Skills*, Prentice-Hall International (UK) Ltd, Hertfordshire.

Taylor, J.A. (1953), 'A personality scale of manifest anxiety', *Journal of Abnormal and Social Psychology*, Vol. 48, pp. 285-290.

Taylor, S.E. (1983), 'Adjustment to threatening events: A theory of cognitive adaptation', *American Psychologist,* (Nov), pp. 1161-173.

Tellegen, A. (1982), *Brief Manual of the Differential Personality Questionnaire*, University of Minnesota Press, Minneapolis.

Tennen, H., and Herzberger, S. (1987), 'Depression, self-esteem and the absence of self-protective attributional biases', *Journal of Personality and Social Psychology*, Vol. 52, pp. 72-80.

Thompson, S.C. (1981), 'Will it hurt less if I can control it? A complex answer to a simple question', *Psychological Bulletin*, Vol. 90, No. 1, pp. 89-101.

Totman, R. (1990), 'Mind, Stress and Health', Souvenir Press Ltd, London.

Tulving, E. (1983), *Elements of Episodic Memory*, Oxford University Press, Oxford.

Turk, D.C., Meichenbaum, D., and Genest, M. (1983), *Pain and Behavioral Medicine: A Cognitive-Behavioral Approach*, Erlbaum, Hillsdale, New Jersey.

Vaillant, G. (1977), *Adaptation to Life*, Little Brown, Boston.

Van de Ven, A.H., and Ferry, D.L. (1980), *Measuring and Assessing Organizations*, John Wiley and Sons, Chichester.

Van Maanen, J. (1979), 'The Fact of Fiction in Organizational Ethnography', in J. Van Maanen (ed.), *Qualitative Methodology*, Sage Publications, London.

Van Sell, M. Brief, A.P., and Schuler, R.S. (1981), 'Role conflict and role ambiguity: Integration of the literature and directions for future research', *Human Relations,* Vol. 34, No. 1, pp. 43-71.

Vingerhoets, A.J.J.M., and Marcelissen, F.H.G. (1988), 'Stress research: Its present status and issues for future developments', *Social Science and Medicine*, Vol. 26, pp. 279-291.

Vitaliano, P.P., Russo, J., Carr, J.E., Maiuro, R.D., and Becker, J. (1985), 'The Ways of Coping Checklist: Revision and psychometric properties', *Multivariate Behavioral Research*, Vol. 20, pp. 3-36.

Walford, G. (1994), 'Educational Choice, Control and Inequity', in Scott, D. (ed.), *Accountability and Control in Educational Settings*, Cassell, London.

Wall, T.D., and Clegg, C.W. (1981), 'A longitudinal study of group work redesign', *Journal of Occupational Behaviour*, Vol. 2, pp. 31-49.

Wardwell, W.I., Hyman, M., and Bahnson, C.B. (1964), 'Stress and coronary disease in three field studies', *Journal of Chronic Diseases*, Vol. 17, pp. 73-84.

Watson, D. (1988), 'Intraindividual and interindividual analyses of positive and negative affect: Relation to health complaints, perceived stress and daily activities', *Journal of Personality and Social Psychology*, Vol. 54, No. 6, pp. 1020-30.

Watson, D., and Clark, L.A. (1984), 'Negative Affectivity: The disposition to experience aversive emotional states', *Psychological Bulletin*, Vol. 96, No. 3, pp. 465-90.

Watson, D., Clark, L.A., and Tellegen, A. (1988), 'Development and validation of brief measures of Positive and Negative Affect: The PANAS Scales', *Journal of Personality and Social Psychology*, Vol. 54, pp. 1063-70.

Weber, R.P. (1985), *Basic Content Analysis*, Sage Publications, Beverly Hills.

Weiss, C.H. (1975), 'Interviewing in evaluation research', in Struening, E.L., and Gutentag, W. (eds.), *Handbook of Evaluation Research*, Sage, Beverly Hills.

White, R. (1974), 'Strategies of Adaptation: An Attempt at Systematic Description', in Coelho, G.V., Hamburg, D.A., and Adams, J.E. (eds.), *Coping and Adaptation*, Basic Books, New York.

Wicklund, R.A. (1979), 'The influence of self-awareness on human behavior', *American Scientist*, Vol. 67, No. 2, pp. 187-193.

Wilby, P., and Crequer, N. (1989), 'Guide to the Education Reform Act', *The Independent*.

Williams, J.M.G., Watts, F.N., McLeod, C., and Mathews, A. (1988), *Cognitive Psychology and Emotional Disorders*, Wiley, Chichester.

Williams, S.L., and Rappoport, A. (1983), 'Cognitive treatment in the natural environment or agorophobics', *Behavior Therapy*, Vol. 14, pp. 299-313.

Wolcott, H.F. (1973), *The Man in the Principal's Office*, Holt, Reinhart and Winston, New York.

Wolcott, H.F. (1990), *Writing Up Qualitative Research*, Sage Publications Ltd, London.

Woolfolk, R.L., and Richardson, F.C. (1978), *Stress, Sanity and Survival*, Nal Penguin Inc, New York.

Wright, P.L., and Taylor, D.S. (1994), *Improving Leadership Performance: Interpersonal Skills for Effective Leadership*, (2nd. ed.), Prentice Hall, Hertfordshire.